Like many of you, I have read a lot of daily devotionals over my lifetime, but this one hits differently. Jaquelyn Patterson-Schaefer, whom I know personally to be an incredible human being and joyful follower of Jesus Christ, brings something new to the table. Written in a casual voice that many will find refreshing, *Joyous Faith* not only provides carefully curated Scripture readings inspired by the ebb and flow of the calendar year, but she also delivers daily practical ways to respond to God's holy Word. You are encouraged to think of this book not just as a spiritual exercise to check off your list of healthy daily habits, but as a shared adventure through the Scriptures. Whether it's suggesting a prayer walk in response to John 5:1–9, planting a small garden to drive home the teaching of the good soil in Matthew 13:23, or Christmas caroling as a way to invite others to find the rest promised in Matthew 11:28–30, layperson and pastor alike will be inspired to not just read the Bible but to live it out in their daily lives with joy. Today I am grateful for … Jaquelyn Patterson-Schaefer and *Joyous Faith*.

—Rev. Alton J. Ruff

A BIBLE DEVOTIONAL

JAQUELYN PATTERSON-SCHAEFER

JOYOUS FAITH: A BIBLE DEVOTIONAL
Copyright © 2025 by Jaquelyn Patterson-Schaefer
Illustrations by Clara Curic

All rights reserved. Neither this publication nor any part of this publication may be reproduced or transmitted in any form or by any means, electronic or mechanical, including photocopying, recording or any information storage and retrieval system, without permission in writing from the author.

Scripture taken from the Holy Bible, NEW INTERNATIONAL VERSION®, NIV® Copyright © 1973, 1978, 1984, 2011 by Biblica, Inc.® Used by permission. All rights reserved worldwide.

Soft cover ISBN: 978-1-4866-2752-3
Hard cover ISBN: 978-1-4866-2754-7
eBook ISBN: 978-1-4866-2753-0

Word Alive Press
119 De Baets Street Winnipeg, MB R2J 3R9
www.wordalivepress.ca

Cataloguing in Publication information can be obtained from Library and Archives Canada.

Thank You

I want to thank God for His unwavering love, guidance, and grace. Without His presence in my life, none of this would be possible. His faithfulness has been my anchor, and it's through Him that I've been able to write and share these words.

To my amazing husband and family, thank you for your endless love, support, and belief in me. Your encouragement has been my foundation, and I couldn't have done this without you.

I also want to express my gratitude to my church family, whose love and fellowship have nourished my spirit and inspired me every day. Your kindness reminds me of the beauty of community.

Finding the Right Bible for You

First and foremost, the best Bible is an open Bible. There are many versions and styles, but when it comes to choosing a Bible, it's all about finding one that resonates with you and supports your spiritual journey. For some, this might mean having more than one Bible, whether you're diving deep into study, looking for an easy read, or seeking something more reflective. Here are a few versions to consider, each with its own unique qualities.

New International Version (NIV)
Popular for its clarity, the NIV is widely appreciated for its straightforward language, making it easy to understand without sacrificing accuracy.

English Standard Version (ESV)
My minister recently brought this version to my attention. For a balance between accuracy and readability, the ESV is a great choice. Known for its precise translation, it works well for both deep study and everyday reading, offering a solid foundation for understanding Scripture.

King James Version (KJV)
A more traditional version, this might be the Bible for you if you appreciate classic poetic language. The KJV is celebrated for its majestic and literary style, having been a staple for centuries.

New Living Translation (NLT)
Easy to understand, the NLT offers a dynamic and thought-for-thought translation, which can be particularly helpful for people reading the Bible for the first time, or those seeking a more conversational tone.

The Message (MSG)
If you're looking for a modern, easy-to-read translation that captures the heart of the original texts with contemporary language, *The Message* could be a good option for you. It's not a direct translation; instead, it rephrases the original texts in

a way that's more accessible and relatable, making it perfect for those who want to experience the Bible in a fresh, engaging way.

First Nations Version: An Indigenous Translation of the New Testament

Beautifully written, this Bible paints a picture with words. A friend of mine recently recommended this to me. This version seeks to present the New Testament in a way that offers a unique perspective while enriching the spiritual experience.

Readers also have a selection of Bible styles to choose from.

Women's Bibles

This Bible is tailored to address the unique spiritual needs and concerns of women, often including devotionals, study guides, and other resources geared toward a female audience.

Colouring Bibles

Say what? Yes, for adults—some Bibles offer sections for reflection and artistic expression.

Journalling Bibles

Love to jot down thoughts or get a little creative? Journalling Bibles come with wide margins perfect for notes, prayers, doodles, or artwork—making your time in the Word personal and inspiring! (I recently purchased a journaling Bible and I am enjoying it so much.)

Giant or Large-Print Bibles

Perfect for those who prefer larger text for easier reading, reducing eye strain and making those lengthy study sessions more comfortable. (Note: This does make for a larger Bible.)

Compact Bibles

Ideal for anyone on the go, a compact Bible is easy to carry, and it fits neatly into a bag or purse, ensuring you can take your spiritual journey with you wherever you go.

In your exploration of Bibles, consider what you value most in a translation—whether it's readability, accuracy, cultural relevance, or devotional aids.

Bible Features

When choosing a Bible, you might want to consider specific features that can enhance your reading experience. Please, don't feel overwhelmed—I only mention these to help guide your decision, not to add pressure. Take your time and choose what works best for you, as you will likely have this book throughout your life!

- Bible Format: The format (online, Kindle, paperback, or hardcover) of your Bible can impact your reading experience. A compact paperback or Kindle might be easier on your wrists if you have arthritis, while online Bibles offer the convenience of access anywhere. Hardcover editions provide a more traditional, tactile experience.
- Red Letter Edition: With the words of Jesus highlighted in red print, this feature allows readers to easily identify and focus on the teachings of Christ, adding an extra layer of significance to their study.
- Maps: These can be helpful for understanding the geographical context of the Scriptures.
- Binding: Some Bibles come with additional features like **lay-flat bindings** so that the Bible can be easily opened without closing, while others may have **flexible covers** that are more portable. **Sewn bindings** last longer than glued ones.
- Thematic or topical index: This groups Bible passages by themes like peace, love, and guidance. The Bible I received as a teen had this feature, and I still use my student Bible today—it's so helpful for quickly finding what I need, especially during tough times.
- **Notes and Commentary**: Explanations of verses and context.
- Bookmarks: Some Bibles offer **two or more ribbon bookmarks**, allowing you to mark different sections at once. This is helpful if you're following multiple readings, such as a devotional passage, your main study reading, or a prayer section.

Ultimately, the best Bible for you will be one that not only aligns with your translation preferences but also includes the features that matter most to you, supporting and enriching your spiritual journey. And I want to reiterate—the best Bible is the one you open.

Bible Reading Accessories

While choosing the right translation is key, there are a few accessories that can enhance your Bible reading and study experience. These are by no means necessary, but I find that having a notebook and highlighters on hand makes my study time more enjoyable. I love sitting with my Bible, making notes, and reflecting on what I've read, and I thought you might find these suggestions helpful too.

- Bible Highlighters: These specially designed highlighters are perfect for marking important verses and passages without bleeding through the pages. Available in a variety of colours, they allow you to "highlight" (pun intended) important passages and/or create a visually organized and personalized study system. (I have also used pencil crayons or erasable crayons for a similar effect.)
- Post-its: Sticky notes are incredibly useful for jotting down thoughts, questions, or insights as you read. They're available in fun colours, and some are clear. (If you don't want to mark up your Bible, you can place the clear sticky note over where you want to underline.) They can be easily moved around, and are handy for those who don't like to mark in their Bible.
- Bookmarks: A bookmark is a simple and practical tool to help you keep track of where you are in your reading. Not only are they functional, but they can also reflect your personal style or faith, with some featuring inspirational quotes. A bookmark can also help you create a straight line for underlining a passage or marking where you left off. I go through a lot of bookmarks because I love to read, and I often use special ones, like notes from my mom or a picture of my son. It's a sweet way to keep them close to my heart while I read.
- Journal: Keeping a journal alongside your Bible reading can provide a space for deeper reflection, prayer requests, and personal growth. Whether you prefer a lined notebook, a guided journal, or blank pages to allow for some artistic flair, this accessory can help you track your spiritual journey over time.
Tabs for the Books of the Bible: Tabs make it easier to navigate your Bible quickly, especially in study groups or personal reading, and they can be found in a variety of colours.

How to Use This Book

Welcome to this journey of joyous faith, where each day offers a chance to connect with God's Word in a meaningful way. Think of this as a shared adventure—we are in this together! I have aligned the Bible readings with the calendar year. If you start on January 1, begin with the readings for that day and continue through the year. If you join us later, such as on November 7, start with that day's reading, continue through December 31, and then begin again at January 1 to experience the full journey.

This book is a wonderful resource to use year after year. Since some holidays fall on different dates each year, I've included a holiday adjustment chart. This will allow you to easily find the specific holiday readings for each year. For example, since Lent occurs at different times each year, you can simply refer to the chart. Once Lent begins, you can skip ahead to the special readings for that season.

Each day offers a fun suggestion for expressing your faith, enjoying a lively activity, or deepening your spiritual journey. Feel free to embrace all, pick a few, or skip any—these ideas are here to add a joyful spark to your faith. Choose the ones that resonate with you and let them enhance your sense of joyous faith!

My hope is that as we traverse this year together, your heart will be filled with joy and gratitude, deepening your connection to God's story. Enjoy this journey, and may it bring you as much joy and inspiration as it has brought me.

Holiday Adjustment Chart

Holiday (Start date)	2026	2027	2028	2029	2030
Shrove Tuesday	FEB 16	FEB 23	FEB 28	FEB 13	FEB 25
Lent (Starts on Ash Wednesday)	FEB 18	FEB 10	FEB 14	MAR 6	FEB 26
Purim (Begins at Sundown)	FEB 25	MAR 16	MAR 5	FEB 24	MAR 15
World Day of Prayer	MAR 6	MAR 5	MAR 3	MAR 1	MAR 6
Passover (Pesach) (Begins at sundown and lasts for eight days)	MAR 31	APR 9	MAR 30	APR 22	APR 9
Mother's Day	MAY 10	MAY 9	MAY 14	MAY 13	MAY 12
Shavuot (Feast of Weeks lasts for two days)	MAY 17	MAY 26	MAY 16	JUN 3	MAY 22
Pentecost	MAY 24	MAY 23	MAY 28	MAY 20	JUN 9
Trinity Sunday	MAY 31	MAY 30	JUN 4	MAY 27	JUN 16
Father's Day	JUN 21	JUN 20	JUN 18	JUN 16	JUN 16
Rosh Hashanah (Begins at sundown and lasts for two days)	SEP 18	SEP 6	SEP 21	SEP 30	SEP 19
Yom Kippur (Begins at Sundown)	SEP 28	SEP 15	OCT 1	OCT 9	SEP 28
Sukkot (Feast of Tabernacles) (Begins at sundown and lasts for seven days)	OCT 4	SEP 21	SEP 25	OCT 13	OCT 9
Thanksgiving (Canada)	OCT 12	OCT 11	OCT 9	OCT 14	OCT 13
Shemini Atzeret/Simchat Torah	OCT 5	SEP 26	OCT 1	OCT 15	OCT 13
Thanksgiving (USA)	NOV 26	NOV 25	NOV 23	NOV 28	NOV 27
Hanukkah (Begins at Sundown and lasts for eight days)	DEC 25	DEC 7	DEC 12	DEC 22	DEC 21

* For the Jewish holidays, you will find a brief description of each long with a selected Bible reading to reflect on and celebrate the occasion.

Dates to Celebrate

EVERY DAY IS A GOOD DAY TO CELEBRATE OUR FAITH!

For your convenience, I have provided a list of Christian, Jewish, and mainstream holidays in the chart for quick reference. Many Christian celebrations are cherished by various denominations, each adding its unique perspective to the shared joy of faith. Each date has its own significance, allowing for deep reflection on faith, community, and the values these celebrations represent. I've done my best to list these in order, but some holidays don't occur on a set day, so those times have been noted. To find the exact days to celebrate in any given year, feel free to use your favourite search engine or the chart above.

Why include Jewish holidays? Because guess what—Jesus was Jewish, lol! On the Jewish holidays, I've noted their significance for Jesus and our Christian faith.

Why include mainstream holidays? These dates highlight moments when we might want to celebrate a little extra and give thanks for God's love and creation. For example, Earth Day is an opportunity to reflect on our gratitude for all of God's creation, and Thanksgiving (both Canadian and American) is a special time of gratitude. I am particularly grateful for my grandmother, and in the readings section, you'll find a special tribute to her, which I hope you'll appreciate when you get there.

So add these dates to your calendar, and add a few of your own. I hope that every day you can see His love surrounding us.

New Year's—January 1

The New Year offers a meaningful opportunity for Christians to reflect on God's faithfulness over the past year, renew their commitment to spiritual growth, and set new goals aligned with their faith. It's a time to express gratitude, seek God's guidance for the future, and embrace the hope and transformation that come with a new year.

Epiphany—January 6

Epiphany commemorates the visit of the Magi to the baby Jesus, symbolizing His manifestation to the Gentiles (non-Jewish). This celebration highlights Christ as a light for all people. It's a time to reflect on revelation, mission, and the universality of Christ's message.

Valentine's Day—February 14

Valentine's Day, named after Saint Valentine, is a celebration of love and affection. While its origins are in Christian martyrdom, it's now a secular holiday focused on romantic love. Christians may reflect on love through 1 Corinthians 13:4–7, which speaks of love's patience, kindness, and truth.

Shrove Tuesday

Shrove Tuesday, also known as Pancake Day, is the day before Ash Wednesday and marks the final day of feasting before the start of Lent. Traditionally, it's a day for using up rich, fatty foods like eggs, milk, and sugar, which were often given up during the Lenten fast. It's a joyful, light-hearted day to gather with loved ones, indulge a little, and prepare for the more solemn days of Lent.

Ash Wednesday—Forty-Six Days Before Easter

Ash Wednesday marks the start of Lent, a period of fasting, reflection, and repentance. The imposition of ashes serves as a reminder of human mortality and the need for reconciliation with God. It's a sombre day where Christians turn their hearts toward forgiveness.

Lent—Forty Days (Excluding Sundays) Leading up to Easter

Lent is a time of spiritual reflection, fasting, and prayer, recalling Jesus's forty days in the wilderness. Christians focus on repentance and spiritual discipline, often giving up certain luxuries to prepare for Easter and grow closer to God.

World Day of Prayer—The First Friday of March Each Year

The World Day of Prayer is a special occasion when people from all Christian denominations and diverse backgrounds join to pray for peace and justice. It's a heartfelt day dedicated to fostering unity and addressing important social and global issues through prayer and compassionate advocacy.

International Women's Day—March 8

This is a day to celebrate the achievements, contributions, and resilience of women around the world. As we mark this day, let's acknowledge the diverse roles women play in our lives and communities and commit to supporting gender equality and empowerment. Reflecting God's love and justice, may we work together to uplift and affirm the value and dignity of every woman.

Purim—Begins at Sundown on the Fourteenth Day of the Hebrew Month of Adar

Purim celebrates the story of Esther, in which we see God's saving power over Haman's plot to destroy the Jews (Esther 9:18–32). Although there's no direct New Testament reference to the story, Jesus would have known and celebrated this victory. Christians can see Purim as a reminder of God's protection in our lives and celebrate His faithful deliverance through all circumstances.

Pi Day—March 14

Today is a delightful nod to the mathematical constant π (pi), which represents the ratio of a circle's circumference to its diameter. It's a day to embrace all things circular, including yummy pies! For Christians, Pi Day can be a joyous occasion to celebrate the creativity and order God has woven into the universe. We can even use the theme of circles to remind ourselves of God's everlasting love—just like a circle has no beginning or end, His love for us is eternal. So let's whip up some pies, share them with others, and take a moment to thank God for the joy and sweetness in our lives!

Saint Patrick's Day—March 17

Saint Patrick's Day honours Saint Patrick, the patron saint of Ireland, who is credited with bringing Christianity to the Irish people in the fifth century. While it has become a largely secular celebration, it holds deep religious meaning for Catholics, especially in Ireland. The holiday is often associated with themes of missionary work, courage in faith, and spreading the gospel.

International Day of Happiness—March 20

This is a day to celebrate and promote the pursuit of happiness and well-being around the world. As we observe this day, let's reflect on the joy that comes from living in harmony with one another and embracing God's blessings.

Passover (Pesach)—Starts on the Fifteenth Day of the Hebrew Month of Nisan and Lasts for Seven or Eight Days, Depending on the Jewish Tradition

Passover, which commemorates God's deliverance of the Israelites from Egypt, was celebrated by Jesus during the Last Supper (Matthew 26:17–30). For Christians, Passover is a reflection of Jesus's role as the ultimate Passover Lamb. We celebrate His sacrifice, which brought us freedom from sin and gives us eternal life, and we use this time to renew our commitment to following Him.

Palm Sunday—Sunday Before Easter

Palm Sunday marks Jesus's entry into Jerusalem, greeted by crowds waving palm branches. It signifies the beginning of Holy Week, the final week before Easter, and invites reflection on Christ's humility and His journey to the cross.

Maundy Thursday—Thursday Before Easter

This day commemorates the Last Supper, when Jesus instituted the Eucharist and commanded His disciples to love one another. Foot-washing ceremonies in some traditions reflect Jesus's humility and service. It's a powerful reminder of fellowship, love, and sacrifice.

Good Friday—Friday Before Easter

Good Friday is the day Christians remember the crucifixion of Jesus. It's a solemn day of mourning and reflection on Christ's sacrifice for humanity. Many churches observe quiet services, focusing on the Passion narrative and the depth of God's love shown through Jesus's death.

Easter Sunday—First Sunday After the First Full Moon Following the Spring Equinox

Easter celebrates the resurrection of Jesus Christ, the cornerstone of Christian faith. It's a day of joy and hope, commemorating Christ's victory over sin and death. Churches around the world celebrate with festive services, proclaiming the salvation offered through Jesus.

Earth Day—April 22

This day provides a meaningful opportunity for Christians to reflect on our stewardship of God's creation. It's a day to honour the beauty of the world God has entrusted to us and to take action to care for the environment with gratitude and responsibility. By promoting environmental stewardship, we can better fulfill our call to love and protect the earth for future generations.

MOTHER'S DAY—SECOND SUNDAY IN MAY

This is a day to cherish and celebrate mothers, mother figures, and all those who nurture and care for us with unconditional love. Whether biological mothers, stepmothers, grandmothers, or other influential women, let's give thanks for their devotion and support. As we honour them, may we reflect God's grace and appreciate the many ways these remarkable individuals impact our lives with their compassion and care.

ASCENSION DAY—FORTY DAYS AFTER EASTER SUNDAY

Ascension Day remembers Jesus's return to heaven after His resurrection. It marks the completion of His earthly mission and the beginning of His reign at God's right hand. Christians reflect on the promise of His return and the gift of the Holy Spirit to guide and empower them.

INTERNATIONAL DAY OF FAMILIES—MAY 15

This is a day to celebrate and strengthen the bonds within families and communities. As we observe this day, let's cherish and support our loved ones, reflecting God's love and grace in our homes. May we nurture these relationships with kindness and understanding, honouring the essential role that family plays in our lives.

SHAVUOT (FEAST OF WEEKS)—SIXTH DAY OF SIVAN IN THE JEWISH CALENDAR

Shavuot celebrates the giving of the Torah and the first fruits of the harvest. Jesus would have honoured this holiday, which is connected to Pentecost (Leviticus 23:15–22), when the Holy Spirit was given to the early believers. For Christians, Shavuot is a wonderful time to celebrate the gift of the Holy Spirit and the new covenant in Christ, which empowers us to live out our faith.

PENTECOST—FIFTY DAYS AFTER EASTER

Pentecost commemorates the descent of the Holy Spirit on the apostles, empowering them to spread the gospel. It's often considered the birthday of the Church. Many Christians celebrate this day with joyful services, reflecting on the Spirit's power to guide and inspire their faith.

Trinity Sunday—Sunday After Pentecost

Trinity Sunday honours the mystery of the Holy Trinity—Father, Son, and Holy Spirit. This day emphasizes the unity and relationship within the Godhead. Christians meditate on the significance of the Trinity, which forms the foundation of their faith and worship.

World Environment Day—June 5

This is a day to raise awareness and take action for the protection of our planet. As we observe this day, let's honour God's creation by committing to sustainable practices and environmental stewardship, working together to safeguard the earth for future generations and nurture the beauty and vitality of the world around us.

World Ocean Day—June 8

This is a day to celebrate the beauty and importance of our oceans and to recognize our responsibility to protect and preserve them. As we observe this day, let's reflect on God's creation and commit to being good stewards of the environment, working together to care for the oceans and all life they support.

Father's Day—Third Sunday in June

This is a day to honour and appreciate fathers, father figures, and all those who take on the role of guiding, supporting, and loving us. Whether biological fathers, stepfathers, grandfathers, or mentors, let's express our gratitude for their sacrifices and strength. As we celebrate, may we reflect God's loving care and recognize the diverse ways these important figures shape and nurture our lives.

International Day of Friendship—July 30

This is a day to celebrate and strengthen the bonds of friendship across cultures and communities. Let's embrace this day with a spirit of love and unity, reflecting Christ's call to build meaningful relationships and support one another with kindness and understanding.

International Day of World's Indigenous Peoples—August 9

This is a day to honour and celebrate the rich cultures, traditions, and contributions of Indigenous peoples worldwide. Let's approach this day with respect and solidarity, embracing our Christian call to justice and supporting the rights and

DATES TO CELEBRATE

dignity of Indigenous communities as we work together to build a more inclusive and compassionate world.

INTERNATIONAL YOUTH DAY—AUGUST 12

This is a day to celebrate and uplift the energy, creativity, and potential of young people around the world. As we recognize their contributions and aspirations, let's support and guide them with love and wisdom, reflecting Christ's hope for their future and empowering them to make a positive impact in their communities.

WORLD HUMANITARIAN DAY—AUGUST 19

This is a day to honour and support those who selflessly work to alleviate suffering and bring aid to those in need. As we observe this day, let's be inspired by Christ's example of compassion and service, committing ourselves to acts of kindness and justice for the marginalized and vulnerable in our world.

INTERNATIONAL LITERACY DAY—SEPTEMBER 8

This is a day to celebrate and promote the gift of literacy, recognizing it as a vital tool for empowering individuals and communities. As we observe this day, let's be inspired by our Christian call to educate and uplift others, fostering opportunities for growth and understanding through the written word.

ROSH HASHANAH (JEWISH NEW YEAR)—TYPICALLY IN SEPTEMBER, ON THE FIRST TWO DAYS OF THE HEBREW MONTH OF TISHRI

Rosh Hashanah marks the beginning of the Jewish New Year, a time of reflection, and the joyful sound of the shofar calling the faithful to introspection. Jesus, being Jewish, would have observed this day of new beginnings. Christians can see it as a chance to reflect on their own faith journey, using this time to embrace God and ask Him for a clean slate in their walk with Christ. Rosh Hashanah reminds us of the day when the trumpet will sound again, announcing Jesus's return (1 Corinthians 15:52).

WORLD GRATITUDE DAY—SEPTEMBER 21

This is a day dedicated to recognizing and appreciating the blessings in our lives, making it a perfect opportunity to reflect on God's goodness together with family and friends. As Christians, we can embrace this day by expressing our gratitude to God for His countless gifts and grace.

YOM KIPPUR (DAY OF ATONEMENT)—TENTH DAY OF TISHRI IN THE JEWISH CALENDAR

Yom Kippur, the holiest day in Judaism, is all about repentance and atonement. Jesus would have joined in the solemn reflection and prayer, which focuses on seeking reconciliation with God, just as described in Leviticus 23:26–32. For Christians, this day can be a moment to reflect on Jesus's ultimate atonement for our sins, reminding us of the incredible grace we've received through His sacrifice.

WORLD MENTAL HEALTH DAY—OCTOBER 10

This is a day to reflect on and embrace the holistic care of everyone, recognizing the importance of mental well-being alongside spiritual and physical health. Let's come together in compassion and support, honouring God's call to love one another fully and to care for the whole person, nurturing minds and hearts with kindness and understanding.

ORANGE SHIRT DAY—SEPTEMBER 30

Orange Shirt Day is a meaningful chance to honour the children impacted by Canada's residential school system. It invites us to reflect on reconciliation, healing, and understanding, embodying the love Jesus teaches. By wearing orange, we show our support for Indigenous communities and commit to creating a future where every child is valued and embraced in unity and respect!

SUKKOT (FEAST OF TABERNACLES)—BEGINS ON THE FIFTEENTH DAY OF TISHRI AND LASTS FOR SEVEN DAYS

Sukkot is a joyous festival celebrating God's provision during the Israelites' journey in the wilderness (Leviticus 23:33–44), and Jesus would have celebrated it, as noted in John 7. This holiday reminds Christians to reflect on God's faithful provision in our lives, recognizing that everything we have comes from His hand, just as He provided for the Israelites in the desert.

SHEMINI ATZERET/SIMCHAT TORAH—THE TWENTY-SECOND DAY OF TISHRI

Shemini Atzeret and Simchat Torah celebrate the conclusion of Sukkot and the joy of completing the Torah reading cycle at the end of the Feast of Tabernacles. While not directly mentioned in the New Testament, Jesus would have taken part in this celebration of Scripture. For Christians, this is a wonderful opportunity to celebrate God's Word, appreciating its wisdom and allowing it to shape our lives with joy and purpose.

Thanksgiving (Canadian)—Second Monday in October

Thanksgiving in Canada is a time to give thanks for the harvest and the blessings of the year. It's also a time for families to gather, share meals, and reflect on gratitude.

Halloween—October 31

While Halloween has its roots in various traditions, the word "Halloween" comes from the Christian tradition: Hallows means "saints," so the word is short for "All Hallow's Eve," as this pumpkin-filled day falls on the night before All Saints' Day. Christians can use this day to reflect on themes of light overcoming darkness. Halloween is a fall holiday that provides a fun opportunity for families and communities to come together in celebration.

All Saints' Day—November 1

All Saints' Day honours all the saints, known and unknown, who have lived lives of holiness and devotion. It's a celebration of the communion of saints, reminding Christians of their connection to those who have gone before them. In some traditions, this day is also an opportunity to remember and celebrate deceased loved ones. Not all Christian denominations celebrate All Saints' Day.

Remembrance Day—November 11

Remembrance Day invites us to reflect on the bravery and sacrifices of those who served in the armed forces, showcasing a spirit of love and selflessness that resonates with our Christian values. It's a reminder to cherish our freedom and the peace we enjoy, encouraging us to spread kindness and gratitude in our communities. As we honour these heroes, we can also celebrate the hope for a world filled with harmony and understanding.

Thanksgiving (US)—Fourth Thursday in November

Thanksgiving in the US is a secular holiday where people gather to express gratitude for the blessings of the year, often centring on a shared meal. Many Christians use this day to thank God for His provisions and blessings. Churches may hold special services of thanksgiving.

Advent—The Four Sundays Before Christmas
Advent is a season of waiting and preparation for the coming of Christ. It reflects both the anticipation of Jesus's birth at Christmas and the expectation of His second coming. Christians use this time for reflection, prayer, and acts of charity as they prepare their hearts for the celebration of Christ's arrival.

International Day of Persons with Disabilities—December 3
International Day of Persons with Disabilities is a time to honour and uplift the inherent dignity and worth of every individual, recognizing and addressing the challenges faced by people with disabilities in a spirit of compassion and inclusivity.

Hanukkah (First Candle Lit)—Begins on the Twenty-Fifth Day of Kislev in the Jewish Calendar and Lasts for Eight Days
Hanukkah, the Festival of Lights, celebrates the rededication of the Temple and the miracle of the oil. Jesus observed this holiday, also known as the Feast of Dedication or the Festival of Lights (John 10:22), reminding Christians that He is the Light of the World. Hanukkah encourages us to reflect His light in our lives, celebrating God's miracles and His constant presence, even in challenging times.

Christmas—December 25
Christmas celebrates the birth of Jesus Christ, the Saviour of the world. It's a joyful celebration of the incarnation—God becoming human. Christians focus on themes of love, peace, and the hope brought into the world by Jesus. Many churches hold festive services, with candlelight and carols, to celebrate this miraculous event.

Twelve Days of Christmas—December 25–January 6
The Twelve Days of Christmas isn't just a festive song—they're actual days celebrated by many Christians, including Catholics, Anglicans, and some Orthodox traditions, beginning on Christmas Day and leading up to Epiphany, honouring the season with joy, reflection, and tradition.

1. December 25, Christmas Day: Celebrates the birth of Jesus Christ
2. December 26, St. Stephen's Day: Honours St. Stephen, the first Christian martyr.
3. December 27, St. John the Apostle's Day: Commemorates St. John, the beloved disciple of Jesus.
4. December 28, Feast of the Holy Innocents: Remembers the children killed by King Herod in his attempt to eliminate the newborn Jesus.
5. December 29, St. Thomas Becket's Day: Celebrates the martyrdom of Thomas Becket, the Archbishop of Canterbury.
6. December 30, Feast of the Holy Family: Honours the Holy Family of Jesus, Mary, and Joseph.
7. December 31, New Year's Eve: A time for reflection and anticipation of the coming year.
8. January 1, Feast of the Solemnity of Mary: Celebrates Mary, the Mother of God, and marks the beginning of the new year.
9. January 2, Feast of Saints Basil the Great and Gregory Nazianzen: Honours these important early Christian theologians.
10. January 3, Feast of the Most Holy Name of Jesus: Recognizes the significance of the name of Jesus.
11. January 4, Feast of Saint Elizabeth Ann Seton: Celebrates the life and work of the first American-born saint.
12. January 5, The Eve of Epiphany: Prepares for the Feast of the Epiphany, which celebrates the visit of the Magi to the infant Jesus. The Twelfth Night, or January 5, marks the end of the Christmas season and leads into Epiphany on January 6, which celebrates the revelation of Christ to the Gentiles through the visit of the Magi.

January 1
NEW YEAR'S DAY

MATTHEW 5:3–10, THE BEATITUDES

I love exploring the beauty of traditions, and on this eighth day of Christmas, we're reminded of the eight Beatitudes. In these blessings, Jesus speaks directly to those who are humble, meek, and longing for peace. He shows us that true happiness doesn't come from earthly wealth or power, but from living in harmony with God's love and compassion. As we reflect on these Beatitudes, we're called to carry Christ's light into the world, sharing hope, kindness, and peace with those around us. Let's carry this message of love and joy in our hearts as we step into the New Year, ready to bring a little more goodness to the world!

As you begin this New Year, you could start a "Blessings Jar." We like to write down an act of kindness, mercy, or joy we've experienced or shared throughout the year. Just like the Beatitudes, this simple act will remind you of how God's love works through you, filling your year with His peace and grace. On New Year's Eve, you can spend time reflecting on these blessings with family and friends.

Reflections ...

TODAY I AM GRATEFUL FOR ... _____

_____
_____
_____
_____

January 2
GALATIANS 5:22–23

THE FRUITS OF THE SPIRIT

Happy ninth day of Christmas! Today, we celebrate the nine fruits of the Spirit, which serve as a blessed reminder of the qualities we're called to embody as followers of Christ: love, joy, peace, forbearance, kindness, goodness, faithfulness, gentleness, and self-control. These aren't just qualities to admire—they're gifts we can nurture and grow in our own hearts. Imagine the transformation in your life and relationships as you plant the seeds of these virtues, allowing them to flourish and reflect God's love to those around you. What a beautiful way to carry His light into the world!

What better way to celebrate the ninth day of Christmas than to choose one of the nine fruits of the Spirit to focus on for the week. I love a good journaling activity! Keep a simple journal to track your progress and reflect on how you've embodied that fruit in your daily life. As you do, you'll draw closer to God and spread His love to those around you.

Reflections ...

TODAY I AM GRATEFUL FOR ... _____

_____
_____
_____
_____
_____
_____

Exodus 20

The Ten Commandments

In my head, I'm singing, "On the tenth day of Christmas" as I write—though, let's be honest, "Ten Commandments" doesn't quite have the same ring as "ten lords a-leaping!" Before Jesus came, God gave us the Ten Commandments to guide our lives and relationships. These timeless principles were designed to help us live with love, respect, and integrity. The commandments remind us to honour God and one another, offering a solid foundation for building strong, faithful relationships. How wonderful it is to reflect on these teachings as we embrace love and unity in our lives!

Let's use this as an opportunity to focus on strengthening relationships with family and friends. Write a note of appreciation or spend quality time with someone you cherish, showing them the love and respect they deserve. By doing this, you honour God's commandments and bring joy to those around you.

Reflections ...

Today I am grateful for ... _____

_____
_____
_____
_____
_____
_____

January 4
Matthew 28:16–20

The Great Commission

On the eleventh day of Christmas, we read in Matthew 28:16–20 about how Jesus gives His disciples the powerful call to go and make disciples of all nations, sharing the message of His love and hope. This is such a sweet reminder. Just as the apostles were called to spread Christ's love, we too are invited to share that love with those around us, through both our words and our actions.

For the eleventh day of Christmas, celebrate the eleven faithful apostles by performing an act of faith, service, or evangelism. It wouldn't hurt to volunteer at a local charity, serve your community, or even simply lend a helping hand to someone in need. We have an amazing program at our church called Love Your Neighbour, and it provides food and hot meals to those in our community. Even small acts can reflect the love and kindness that Christ called us to share, and they allow us to be a part of His mission of spreading hope and joy to the world.

Reflections ...

Today I am grateful for ... _____

_____
_____
_____
_____
_____
_____

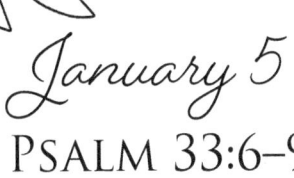

January 5
PSALM 33:6–9

On the twelfth day of Christmas, we arrive at the grand finale of this beautiful season, and what better way to end our journey than to be reminded that God's Word is powerful and true. He created the heavens and the earth with just a word, and His voice brings order to the chaos. The same Creator who spoke the world into being is present in our lives today, guiding us with His truth and love. How beautiful is that? This reading is a call to trust in His power, to let His Word shape us, and to stand in awe of His greatness.

As we round out the twelve days of Christmas, take a moment to memorize the twelve points of the Apostles' Creed? Each one highlights a key part of our faith, from God's creation to the life of Jesus and the work of the Holy Spirit. I remember my mom making me memorize it when I was younger, and it has been such an anchor of my faith ever since.

Reflections ...

TODAY I AM GRATEFUL FOR ... _____

_____
_____
_____
_____
_____

January 6
Epiphany

Matthew 2:1–12

I absolutely love Epiphany! In our home, it's the day we move our wise men into our manger scene. They've made their way steadily across our living room throughout the Christmas season to arrive today. My son used to love moving the figures each day of their journey. On Epiphany, we celebrate the moment when Christ's light was revealed to the Gentiles, as the Magi travelled from afar to worship Him. What a joyful reminder that Christ came for all people, showing us that God's love knows no boundaries.

One of my mom's dear friends always hosted an Epiphany (or Three Kings) dinner, and it became a cherished tradition. By hosting a King's Supper, you could incorporate star-themed décor, like star-shaped cookies, star ornaments, or candles to remind us of the guiding star that led the Magi to Christ. It's a beautiful way to celebrate the manifestation of Jesus to the world and to share His light with those around you!

Reflections ...

Today I am grateful for ... _____

_____
_____
_____
_____
_____
_____

January 7
MATTHEW 3:13–17

Now that we've wrapped up our holiday readings, we move into a different season. This is a time of new beginnings, when we turn our focus to the start of Jesus's public life, ministry, and the lessons He teaches us.

In Matthew 3, Jesus comes to the Jordan River to be baptized by John. Though He has no sin, He chooses to do this, setting an example of humility and obedience to God. This marks the start of a new chapter, not only in Jesus's life, but in the lives of all who follow Him. It reminds us that every new season—whether in the life of Christ or our own—is an opportunity to live with purpose, humility, and a heart of obedience to God.

Make time today to get some fresh air. Even if it's just a short walk. Take a deep breath and appreciate the beauty around you. I love walking our dog, Joy, in the morning; it helps me start the day with a grateful heart. Just as Jesus took time to connect with the Father, we too can find moments of peace in the simple act of stepping outside. How will you connect with God today?

Reflections ...

TODAY I AM GRATEFUL FOR ... _____

_____

_____

_____

_____

January 8
1 John 3:11–21

Today's passage invites us to renew our relationships with family, friends, or even strangers, fostering peace and unity as we step into the new year. It reminds us that love isn't just a feeling—it's a calling. We're asked to love one another as God loves us, and love isn't just about emotions—it's about our actions. It may not always be easy, but it is what we're called to do.

Do you take the time to tell those around you that you love them? Let's make a point of expressing just how much people mean to us. Whether through a quick text, a call, or even a handwritten note, those simple words can truly brighten someone's day. I am blessed to have parents who exemplified this. And just like God calls us to love one another, let's be intentional in sharing that love today!

Reflections ...

TODAY I AM GRATEFUL FOR ... _____

_____
_____
_____
_____
_____
_____

January 9
2 Corinthians 1:3–7

In 2 Corinthians 1:3–7, we're reminded that God is the ultimate source of comfort, offering us His love and peace not only in our moments of joy, but also in times of hardship. As we step into this new year, we can embrace the knowledge that God's comfort is always available, and we're called to share that same love and comfort with others. This new beginning reminds us that as we receive His peace, we're invited to spread that peace and kindness wherever we go, offering hope to those around us. And how cool is that?

Is today the perfect time to try something new? Maybe consider starting a book club with friends or church members. At our church, we have a wonderful, uplifting book club filled with amazing, supportive women. It's such a joy to grow together, deepen our understanding of Scripture, and share in meaningful conversations that help us all thrive in our faith. Could a book club be just the thing you've been waiting for?

Reflections ...

TODAY I AM GRATEFUL FOR ... _____

_____
_____
_____
_____
_____

January 10
1 JOHN 4:7–10

In today's passage, we're reminded that love is a gift from God, and we're called to share that love with everyone around us. His love forms the foundation of all we do, and as we reflect that love in our lives, we spread His light to others. His love also renews us, bringing us fresh strength and hope each day. It's a precious truth that love is a gift that comes directly from God. How will you share this today?

Send a note of appreciation to someone who truly deserves it—perhaps your church secretary, janitor, or someone else who works behind the scenes. A thoughtful message can brighten someone's day and remind them of how much they are valued. I find that even a simple thank you can make a world of difference by showing appreciation for the work they do.

Reflections ...

TODAY I AM GRATEFUL FOR ... _____

_____
_____
_____
_____
_____
_____
_____

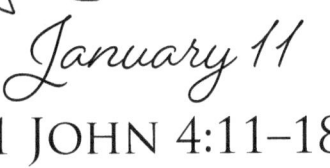

1 John 4:11–18

Isn't it such a comfort to know that God's perfect love casts out all fear? His love strengthens and renews us every day. When we rest in His love, we are freed from the anxieties and worries that try to take hold of us. His love is a safe place where we find peace and confidence, knowing that nothing can separate us from His care. As we embrace His love, we're empowered to step forward with courage and trust, knowing He is always with us, guiding and protecting us.

Today let's create something that reflects God's love in your life. Bring out your creative side and paint a Bible verse on a canvas, make a prayer journal for a friend, or write out your favourite verses to display in your home. What would fill your bucket and help you connect with God's Word?

Reflections ...

Today I am grateful for ... _____

_____
_____
_____
_____
_____

January 12
1 John 4:19–5:4

It's such a beautiful truth that we are able to love because God first loved us. His love is the source of everything good in our lives, and when we reflect on His love, it naturally overflows into how we love others. By recognizing the depth of His love for us, we're reminded to love generously, just as He has loved us—unconditionally and endlessly.

Gather your family together and begin a simple family devotional time in the evenings. You can read a Bible story together, talk about its message, and close with a prayer. It's a wonderful way to grow in love as a family and to remind each other of God's great love for you.

Reflections ...

TODAY I AM GRATEFUL FOR ... _____

_____
_____
_____
_____
_____
_____

January 13
PROVERBS 6:6–11

This reading reminds me of Doris Day's cheerful version of "High Hopes"—it's about believing that with determination, we can achieve great things! Just as the ant diligently works and prepares for the future, we're called to be wise and intentional in our actions. This passage encourages us to stay focused, even when things seem tough, knowing that hard work and faith will bring us through.

Commit to praying for specific people or issues that are in your heart. You could also partner with a friend or family member and agree to pray for each other's concerns throughout the month. This shared commitment will not only strengthen your prayer life but also bring you closer together in faith and love. And if you need a smile today, take a listen to "High Hopes." It is sure to brighten your day!

Reflections ...

TODAY I AM GRATEFUL FOR ... _____

_____

_____

_____

_____

_____

January 14
JOHN 3:22–30

Today's reading reminds us that everything we have, including our gifts and insights, are blessings from God. Just as John the Baptist recognized that his role was part of a larger plan, we too are invited to trust in God's timing and provision for our lives. Baptism reminds us that God cleanses us and making us new in Christ. It's a precious truth that we should humbly accept what God gives us, knowing that He equips us for exactly what we need in each season of our lives.

My mom keeps a spiritual journal, writing down insights from Scripture, prayers, and moving phrases. She's pretty awesome like that! You can also record moments of joy, struggle, and growth, or what you're learning about yourself and your faith. I talk about journaling a fair amount, but I enjoy different types of journaling and sometimes feel drawn to one style over another—expressing myself this way really helps me process my thoughts and feelings. Maybe ask yourself if journaling could help you reflect on your own spiritual journey.

Reflections ...

TODAY I AM GRATEFUL FOR ... _____

January 15
JOHN 5:1–9

In this passage, we see Jesus healing the man by the pool of Bethesda, offering him a new beginning. We often see January as a time of new beginnings, and I love how this story aligns beautifully with that theme. When I read this story, I am struck by how even when others overlooked this man, Jesus saw his true self—his heart, his struggles, his pain—and responded with compassion, offering healing and a new chapter in His life. Jesus meets us where we are, welcoming us just as we are, and bringing healing to our hearts. It's a powerful reminder that just as Jesus healed the man at the pool, He meets us in our weaknesses and offering us strength, starting a new chapter in our lives.

As we reflect on this passage and the fresh starts we're called to in the new year, consider taking a prayer walk, if the weather allows. Use this time to pray for the world, your community, and your loved ones. I have a spiritual playlist that I enjoy listening to while running—it helps me reflect and stay connected with God. I pray that this walk could be a time of healing for you, allowing God's peace to fill your heart and renew your spirit as you step forward into this new season.

Reflections ...

TODAY I AM GRATEFUL FOR ... _____

_____

_____

_____

January 16
John 5:10–18

In this passage, we see the tension between tradition and the freedom that Jesus brings. The religious leaders were so focused on the rules that they missed the miracle happening right before their eyes—the healing of the man at the pool. It's like when a butterfly struggles to break free from its cocoon—though the struggle is difficult, it's also part of the transformation. Jesus shows us that following Him isn't about rigid rules, but about the freedom and grace He offers, which renew and transform us from the inside out. And how cool is that?

Consider how even in the midst of struggles and new beginnings, we can find freedom in Jesus. One great way to explore this further is through Bible studies. As I write, my mom and I are finishing up a Bible study on Galatians at our church, and every study brings new insights and perspectives that make the Bible come alive. Whether you join a study at church or with a small group of friends, these moments together can deepen your understanding of Scripture and help you grow in faith and community.

Reflections ...

Today I am grateful for ... _____

_____
_____
_____
_____

January 17
JOHN 5:19–29

In this reading, Jesus speaks of the deep connection He shares with the Father, showing us that He does nothing apart from God's will. It's a beautiful reminder that Jesus's work reflects God's heart, and that through Him, we're invited to participate in the same love and purpose. Jesus offers us a chance to be born anew, just as He calls the dead to life, inviting us to follow Him in faith and obedience, trusting in His perfect will.

A great song that connects with this passage is "I Can Only Imagine" by MercyMe (one of my favourite bands). While not directly from the text, it beautifully captures the awe and reverence of being in God's presence, much like the power and authority Jesus speaks of in John 5:19–29. This song invites reflection on the gift of eternal life and the beauty of being in harmony with God. If you haven't heard it, take a listen (you can thank me later).

Reflections ...

TODAY I AM GRATEFUL FOR ... _____

_____
_____
_____
_____
_____

January 18
JOHN 5:30–47

This passage beautifully highlights Jesus's divine authority and the powerful testimony that affirms His identity as the Son of God. He points to the Scriptures, the testimony of John the Baptist, and His own works as clear signs of who He is. Jesus reminds us that our faith is anchored in the truth of who He is, inviting us to respond with open hearts, ready to receive the abundant life He offers. We're encouraged that embracing Jesus opens the door to our hearts, where His truth transforms and brings a new beginning.

What do you love about winter? Whether it's skiing, snowshoeing, or simply enjoying the stillness of freshly fallen snow, winter brings its own special beauty. Even if you're not a fan of the cold, take a moment to appreciate the season's quiet moments. The crisp air and peaceful surroundings are little reminders of God's constant presence, offering us comfort amid change. I pray that these small joys renew your spirit, just as God renews our hearts each day.

Reflections ...

TODAY I AM GRATEFUL FOR ... _____

_____

_____

_____

_____

_____

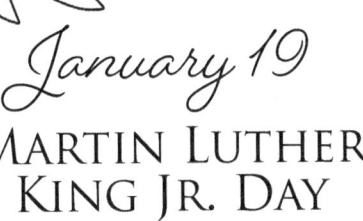

January 19
MARTIN LUTHER KING JR. DAY

PSALM 23:1–4

Psalm 23 reminds us that God is our Shepherd, guiding us with love and care, leading us to rest and peace even during life's struggles. As we walk through the valleys of life, we need not fear, for God is with us, offering comfort and protection. His presence is a constant reminder that no matter what we face, we are never alone.

On this day, we honour the life, legacy, and work of Dr. Martin Luther King Jr. He was a deeply religious man whose faith in God was central to his message of equality, justice, and peace. Have you heard his famous "I Have a Dream" speech? What an inspiring message this Baptist minister left us with.

Reflections ...

TODAY I AM GRATEFUL FOR ... _____

_____
_____
_____
_____
_____
_____
_____

January 20
LAMENTATIONS 3:22–23

I love the promise we find in this verse! God's love and compassion are never-ending, always fresh, and new each day. No matter what challenges we face, His faithfulness remains steady, and we can take comfort in knowing that every morning brings a new opportunity to experience His grace. When I lost my grandmother, it rocked me to my core, but God was there, always loving me, guiding me, surrounding me with peace and the knowledge that she was in a better place.

When our loved ones are gone, it's hard to work through the grief. Finding Bible verses that resonate with you, and journaling, can help. Do what you need to do to grieve. And God is right there with us every step of the way. God knows what's in your heart, but sometimes we need a moment to process it ourselves. For me, journaling can be a way to work through the emotions. If you are struggling, I pray this helps you grieve, and as you write and process your emotions, now that God is right there with you. He loves you—rough edges and all.

Reflections ...

TODAY I AM GRATEFUL FOR ...

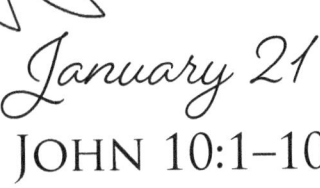

John 10:1–10

In this passage, Jesus lovingly calls Himself the Good Shepherd, offering us His guidance, protection, and care. He knows each of us by name and invites us to follow Him to a life of abundance, peace, and joy. It's a comforting reminder that, amid life's chaos, Jesus is there, guiding us with love and offering us a path full of grace and hope. His voice is the one we can trust above all others, leading us to where we truly belong.

Write a letter to yourself, to be opened at the end of the year. Share your hopes, prayers, and goals for your spiritual growth in the coming months. You could even create a vision board focused on your faith journey, reflecting on areas where you want to grow. I love a good vision board! This is a beautiful way to intentionally follow the Good Shepherd's call and make space for His guidance and love throughout the year!

Reflections ...

Today I am grateful for ... _____

_____
_____
_____
_____
_____

January 22
ROMANS 12:1-2

Paul calls us to offer ourselves to God as living sacrifices, holy and pleasing to Him, transforming us from the inside out. This reading assures us that when we give ourselves fully to God, He doesn't just change our actions, but He renews our hearts and minds, guiding us toward His perfect will. Each day offers a new opportunity to be transformed, and through His grace, we are made new.

As I'm writing this, I'm listening to Carrie Underwood's version of the hymn "I Surrender." How perfect is that? As you pray today, reflect on your heart's surrender to God. Ask Him to transform your mind and spirit, helping you align with His will for your life. You can journal your thoughts or simply sit quietly in prayer: "Father, Humbly I offer myself to you." Trust that as you offer yourself to Him, He will renew and guide you.

Reflections ...

TODAY I AM GRATEFUL FOR ... _____

_____
_____
_____
_____
_____
_____

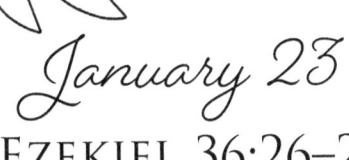

January 23
Ezekiel 36:26–27

Have you ever longed for a transformation in your heart? In this passage, God promises to give us a new heart and a new spirit, signifying His deep desire for us to live in alignment with His will. This is a beautiful truth: God works from the inside out, transforming our hearts so we can reflect His love and grace in all that we do.

Another way to connect with God's message is by making a list of movies or documentaries with a biblical message that you'd like to watch this year. (I love The Chosen series). Whether they help you dive deeper into your faith, inspire transformation, or share beautiful testimonies of God's work, these films can be a great tool to guide your spiritual journey. Don't forget the popcorn!

Reflections ...

TODAY I AM GRATEFUL FOR ... _____

_____
_____
_____
_____
_____

January 24
MARK 5:1–20

Jesus shows us His incredible power by healing a man who had been tormented for so long. It's a reminder that no matter how deep our struggles, Jesus has the power to transform and restore. He reaches out to the broken, offering healing and hope. As we reflect on His love and grace, we're reminded that nothing is too big for Him to handle.

Does winter have you down? Why not start planning a spring getaway? Think of it as a time for a reset and relaxation. I love checking out new churches when we travel. There is so much we can learn from one another. Where will the Spirit guide you?

Reflections ...

TODAY I AM GRATEFUL FOR ... _____

_____
_____
_____
_____
_____
_____

Feast of the Conversion of St. Paul

MARK 16:15–18

Have you ever heard of the Feast of the Conversion of St. Paul? Many in the Catholic and Orthodox traditions celebrate this day, reflecting on the powerful transformation Paul experienced when he encountered Christ. His conversion reminds us of the incredible ways God can change our hearts. Jesus calls us to go out into the world and share His message with others. What a powerful reminder that our faith isn't just for ourselves—it's meant to be shared with those around us. Jesus invites us to step beyond our comfort zones, spread His love, and bring hope to the world, just as He sent His disciples to do.

Are you happy with the direction your spiritual journey is going in? Consider journaling about the ways God has transformed you, or sharing your testimony with a friend or family member. Just as Paul's conversion was a turning point in his life, could your story be an encouragement to others on their faith journeys?

Reflections ...

TODAY I AM GRATEFUL FOR ... _____

_____
_____
_____
_____
_____

January 26
REVELATION 21:5–7

Have you ever thought about how complete and all-encompassing God's love truly is? His promise of renewal touches everything—creation, our hearts, and all of humanity. What a comforting reminder that God's work of restoration isn't a far-off hope; it's happening now, both in our lives and in the world around us. Through His grace, He's transforming us, our relationships, and all of creation, bringing us closer to His perfect peace.

Make time to reflect on an area of your life or a relationship where you long to see God's hand. Write it down and pray, asking God to bring His transformation and healing. When I write in my spiritual journal, I like to light a candle to symbolize Christ's light at work.

Reflections ...

TODAY I AM GRATEFUL FOR ... _____

_____
_____
_____
_____
_____
_____

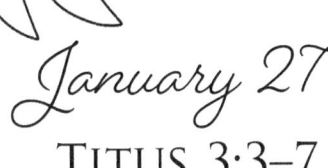

January 27
TITUS 3:3–7

Have you ever taken a moment to reflect on the depth of God's grace toward you? Today's passage reminds us that it's not our own actions, but God's great love and mercy that cleanse and renew us. His grace is like a refreshing wave that washes over us, freeing us from all that holds us back. How does it feel to rest in the knowledge that His kindness and love are the true source of our salvation, and they are ever-present, always ready to restore us?

Considering God's renewing grace, spend some time cleansing and refreshing your living space. Whether it's tidying up or deep cleaning, could you use this time as a physical reminder of the spiritual renewal God offers? If so, why not invite His peace and love to fill your home, just as He fills our hearts with His grace.

Reflections ...

TODAY I AM GRATEFUL FOR ... _____

_____
_____
_____
_____
_____

January 28
LUKE 1:1–4

Luke's writing shows a deep commitment to sharing the truth of God's love, ensuring that others can clearly understand His teachings and be reborn. Our faith is best shared through thoughtful action—whether by telling stories, singing, or living out God's love. How can we honour God by sharing His truth? And who do we know who needs to hear it?

How do you show your love for God? For me, music is a way I express my love and connection with Him. It brings my heart closer to His. Today, try to feel God's love through music. Sing a song that brings you peace, or listen to a song that inspires you. Let music draw you nearer to God today!

Reflections ...

TODAY I AM GRATEFUL FOR ... _____

_____
_____
_____
_____
_____
_____

January 29
ISAIAH 40:28–31

Isaiah 40:28–31 is a reading brimming with God's comfort and power. It starts with reassuring words that soothe our souls and then transitions into a vivid depiction of God's majesty and the strength He offers. Doesn't this passage just invite you to marvel at God's greatness and find solace in His unending support and promises?

I love to let my family know how much I love them. I can be a bit of a goofball at times, but I love them! Maybe you could bake a cake or prepare a special treat for your family—just to celebrate one another. What can you do today to share moments of connection and joy with those closest to you?

Reflections ...

TODAY I AM GRATEFUL FOR ... _____

_____
_____
_____
_____
_____
_____

January 30
MARK 3:13–19

Jesus called His disciples to follow Him, offering them a new beginning and a new purpose. He didn't choose them because they were perfect, but because He saw their potential. That moment marked a new beginning for them, one of transformation and mission. Jesus saw the unique value in each of them and called them to something greater—just as He calls each of us each and every day. The world can be chaotic and loud. Pray to Him and be sure to listen.

Think of someone you've been meaning to reconnect with—maybe an old friend, a family member, or even someone you've lost touch with. Take a moment to make a list of people you'd like to reach out to. Can you set a goal to contact one of them this week, whether by phone, text, or even a handwritten note?

Reflections...

TODAY I AM GRATEFUL FOR ... _____

_____
_____
_____
_____
_____
_____

January 31
2 Corinthians 5:14–17

Paul reminds us that the love of Christ has the power to transform us. His love doesn't just change us for the moment—it makes us into new creations, free from the past, empowered to live with purpose and hope. As we experience this transformation, we're invited to live out His love in our relationships and actions, reflecting the grace He has shown us.

Today, try to respond with grace in tense moments. If someone cuts you off in traffic, instead of getting frustrated, think that maybe they're rushing to help someone or have an urgent need. It's a simple reminder to choose kindness and patience, just as God shows us His grace every day. Can you take those little moments to reflect His love and peace in our daily lives?

Reflections ...

TODAY I AM GRATEFUL FOR ... _____

February 1
JEREMIAH 1:4–10

In Jeremiah 1:4–10, we hear God's gentle and loving words to Jeremiah, reminding him that even before he was born, God knew him and had a wonderful plan for his life. What a comforting thought—God has a special calling for each of us, designed with love and care. Even on days when we feel unsure or less than perfect, we can trust that God sees our true worth, knows us intimately, and has a beautiful purpose for us, filled with hope and grace.

Make time to reflect on His personal calling for you. Spend some time in prayer, asking God to reveal His loving purpose for you, and celebrate the gifts He has given you. We can all be struck by "imposter syndrome." I can't even count the number of times I've felt unequal to the task of writing this book, but I pray you will let your heart be filled with hope and excitement for the journey ahead!

Reflections ...

TODAY I AM GRATEFUL FOR ... _____

_____
_____
_____
_____
_____

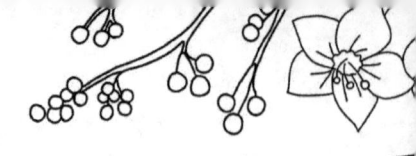

February 2
ISAIAH 41:8–10

Have you ever felt weighed down by life's challenges, only to find that God's strength is there to lift you up? In these verses, God reminds us that He is always by our side, offering unwavering comfort and strength. He tells us not to fear, because He is with us, upholding us with His righteous hand. How cool is it that God gives us the hope and courage to face any situation, knowing that His love and presence will never leave us?

Think about a time when you felt God's strength and hope carry you through a tough moment. I was recently going through a hard time, and a neighbour came by and stopped to speak with me—I mean really speak with me. Maybe you can help a neighbour or check in on a friend who needs encouragement. How can you use these simple acts of kindness to remind others of God's love and the hope He offers us all?

Reflections ...

TODAY I AM GRATEFUL FOR ... _____

_____
_____
_____
_____
_____

February 3
Psalm 40:1–11

Today's reading gently reminds us of God's deep and unwavering faithfulness. The psalmist shares that in our waiting, God lovingly lifts us from the depths, placing a new song of hope and joy in our hearts. Even when we feel overwhelmed, we can rest in the assurance that God is always present, meeting us where we are with His boundless love and grace. His timing is perfect, and His care for us is constant, never leaving us to walk through life's challenges alone.

Think about the times God has rescued you, I know He has picked me up off the ground more than once—and thank goodness He did. I love Anne Wilson's song "Strong." It reminds us of God's unwavering faithfulness and strength. I tried singing this song once at church, and the words struck me so beautifully that they rocked me to my core. Does music move you that way too? Where it just humbles you?

Reflections ...

TODAY I AM GRATEFUL FOR ... _____

_____
_____
_____
_____
_____

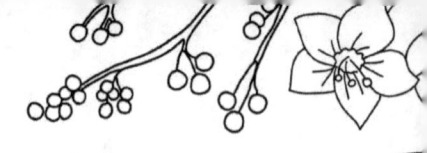

February 4
Psalm 126

In Psalm 126, we see how God brings restoration and joy, even after seasons of hardship. The psalmist speaks of God's faithfulness in turning sorrow into laughter and mourning into gladness. No matter the challenges we face, God's love has the power to restore and renew, bringing hope and peace where there once was despair. We can feel His faithful hand lifting us up, filling our hearts with joy once again.

Make time to give thanks for the good things God has done in your life, no matter how big or small. It just takes a moment to send a text or make a quick call to encourage someone, reminding them of God's goodness. Currently, I have a friend going through cancer treatments, and I try to send her a joke a day just to make her smile and let her know I care. Maybe you can brighten someone's day with a simple act of kindness too.

Reflections ...

TODAY I AM GRATEFUL FOR ... _____

_____
_____
_____
_____
_____

February 5
ISAIAH 40:28–31

Isaiah 40:28–31 reminds us of God's eternal strength and unfailing care. In times when we feel weary or overwhelmed, God promises to renew our strength. He gently assures us that even when we're exhausted, He will lift us up and carry us, just as He does with the weak and weary. His love and grace never fail, and through Him, we're empowered to rise above life's challenges with renewed hope.

Sometimes we need to pause and reflect on God's inexhaustible strength. Some of my favourite ways to connect with God are through quiet prayer, taking a walk in nature, listening to Christian music, or reading. Whatever way feels right for you, can you allow yourself to slow down and embrace His peace today, trusting that He will renew your strength, just as He promises in Isaiah?

Reflections ...

TODAY I AM GRATEFUL FOR ... _____

_____
_____
_____
_____
_____

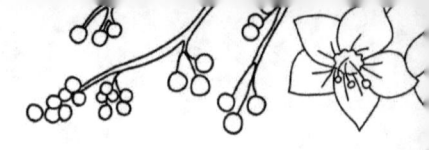

February 6
PSALM 138

While reflecting on Psalm 138, we're reminded of God's incredible faithfulness and the power of His loving promises. The psalmist expresses deep gratitude for God's unwavering love, knowing that He listens to our hearts and answers our prayers with kindness. Even in challenging moments, God's greatness and goodness shine through, filling our hearts with hope and confidence that He is always with us. (Cue song "Our God Is an Awesome God"!)

I've found that living with a heart full of gratitude brings so much joy, and I really try to make it a daily habit. One of my favourite things to do is write down three things I'm thankful for each day—it's a simple little practice, but it always helps me focus on the positive, no matter what's going on. That's why I put it in my book! Take a few minutes to think of three things you're grateful for and see how it brightens your day. You might be surprised at how much joy it can bring!

Reflections ...

TODAY I AM GRATEFUL FOR ... _____

_____
_____
_____
_____
_____
_____

February 7
ISAIAH 49:1–6

Through today's reading, we're reminded of God's call on our lives to serve others. He has uniquely chosen and equipped each of us to be a light to those around us, sharing His love and grace in tangible ways. Whether it's through our actions or words, God invites us to bless others and bring His hope into their lives.

How is God calling you to serve others. This week, look for an opportunity to bless someone—whether through an act of service, a kind word, or simply by listening to them. I mean, truly taking the time and listening to them. I've been working on this myself. It fosters deeper connections and, in turn, a more joyful heart. Happy listening!

Reflections ...

TODAY I AM GRATEFUL FOR ... _____

_____
_____
_____
_____
_____
_____

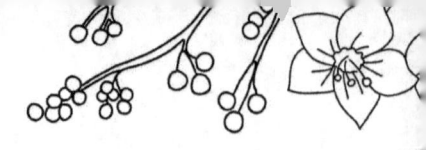

February 8
2 CORINTHIANS 4:1–6

Today's reading reminds us of the incredible treasure of the gospel we are called to embrace deep into our hearts. Paul encourages us to remain faithful in sharing God's love, even in hard times, because the light of Christ shines through our weaknesses. God's grace and power are at work in us, and He calls us to carry this treasure not for our own glory, but to reflect His goodness and truth to the world.

Reflect on the treasure of the gospel that you carry in your heart. How does God's light shine through you? You know those people who have made a difference in your life. (For me, one of my Sunday school teachers just came to mind.) What if today, you were that light for someone?

Reflections ...

TODAY I AM GRATEFUL FOR ... _____

_____
_____
_____
_____
_____
_____

February 9
PSALM 51:1–13

David pours out his heart to God, asking for forgiveness. It's a powerful reminder that no matter how far we may feel we've strayed, God's love and mercy are always ready to restore us. When we invite God into our hearts, He not only cleanses us but also fills us with a renewed sense of hope and joy.

What does having a *Joyous Faith* mean to you? Whether it's feeling God's love within your heart or spreading that love through acts of kindness, let your spirit be filled with joy and gratitude. Set a positive intention for the day—maybe by volunteering or even just offering a smile to someone who needs it. Embrace God's light and let it shine brightly through your actions!

Reflections ...

TODAY I AM GRATEFUL FOR ... _____

_____
_____
_____
_____
_____
_____

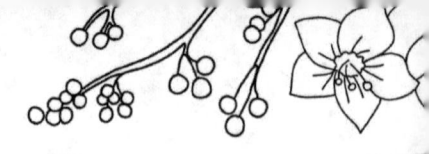

February 10
Romans 5:12–21

Paul beautifully contrasts the impact of Adam's sin with the grace we receive through Jesus Christ. While sin entered through one man, grace entered through Christ, and His gift of salvation is greater than all our mistakes. God's grace is more than enough to cover our shortcomings, and through Christ, we are made new. The hope we have in Christ allows us to live with love, joy, and a renewed spirit each day.

It's time to start spreading some love! How about baking Valentine's Day cookies for your neighbours? It's a simple, sweet gesture that can bring so much joy and serve as a reminder of the grace and kindness we've received from Christ. Watch their faces light up when you drop them off—it's a small way to reflect the love He has shown us.

Reflections ...

TODAY I AM GRATEFUL FOR ... _____

_____
_____
_____
_____
_____
_____
_____

1 Corinthians 9:24–27

Paul encourages us to run the race of life with purpose and discipline, much like an athlete preparing for a big event. Just as athletes stay focused and give their best, we too are called to live with intention, growing in faith and love as we walk with Christ. The journey may not always be easy, but with God guiding us, every step we take strengthens us for the race ahead. Embracing that hope in Christ allows us to stay focused on the finish line, knowing that every effort is worth it.

Let's put this into action today! Think of one area in your life where you can train and focus with the same discipline as an athlete. Maybe it's setting aside time for prayer (that's me!), serving others, or working on a specific spiritual goal. Start small, but remember—every step is a victory! Just like in a race, progress may take time, but with God's strength, you'll keep moving forward toward that ultimate prize. You've got this! No … we've got this!

Reflections …

TODAY I AM GRATEFUL FOR … _____

_____
_____
_____
_____
_____

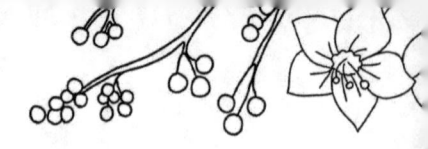

February 12
Psalm 121

Have you ever felt like you needed a reminder that God is always there to protect and guide you? This beautiful psalm offers just that—a message of hope and trust in God's unwavering care. It speaks of God as a constant helper who won't let His people stumble, offering us encouragement that He is always watching over us. No matter where life takes us, we can rest in the assurance that God's protection is ever-present, and His love never fails. Pretty cool, eh?

How about making today a fun, memorable time with family? Plan a cookoff night and split into teams to see who can create the best pizza or dessert—our family pizza-making challenge was a hoot! Could this be a fun new way to connect, share some laughter, and celebrate the simple blessings of life?

Reflections ...

Today I am grateful for ... _____

_____
_____
_____
_____
_____

February 13
Psalm 1

Psalm 1 contrasts the ways of the righteous and the wicked, urging us to delight in God's Word and follow His guidance. Like a tree planted by streams of water, the righteous grow and bear fruit, rooted in God's love and truth. The reading also reminds us that when we live according to God's ways, our lives become reflections of His goodness and love, and we begin to share that love with others in the most meaningful ways. Let the hope that lives in this psalm enter your heart.

On the eve of Valentine's Day, focus on an act of love that reflects God's unconditional love for us. What unexpected kindness can you show someone today?

Reflections ...

TODAY I AM GRATEFUL FOR ... _____

_____
_____
_____
_____
_____
_____

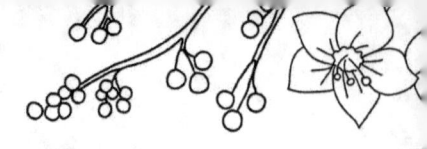

February 14
VALENTINE'S DAY

JOHN 15:9–17

Happy Valentine's Day! Today's reading is a wonderful love letter that shows us just how deep and limitless Jesus's love is for us. He invites us to love one another just as He has loved us—it's the kind of love that's selfless, sacrificial, and unbreakable—the kind that brings people together. It's a love that transforms us, lifting us up and filling our hearts to overflow with joy and kindness. What a gift it is to share this love with the world!

Celebrate Valentine's Day by expressing love to others. Whether it's spending quality time together, writing a heartfelt note, or simply offering a kind word, be a reminder of the love in our call to love one another. I love to wear pink or red—it's a fun way to spread cheer to those around you!

Reflections ...

TODAY I AM GRATEFUL FOR ... _____

_____
_____
_____
_____
_____
_____

February 15
GENESIS 17:1–7, 15–16

God's covenant with Abraham is such a thoughtful indication of how much He cares for us! Just as He promised Abraham that He would be his God and bless him with many descendants, God extends that same invitation to each of us. His love is constant, and He calls us into a personal relationship in which we can trust in His promises. Embracing this hope is a reminder that no matter what challenges we face, God's faithfulness remains steady, and His promises are sure. Just like He renewed His covenant with Abraham, how awesome is it that we can also take this opportunity to refresh our hearts!

When you talk to God in prayer, consider how faithful He's been in your life and thank Him for His never-ending love. I know, I know, but I'll say it again—I love journaling. And my prayer journals help me. Prayer journaling is often my quiet time to gather my thoughts. It's a peaceful time alone—just me, my coffee, and God. Looking back through my journals, I can see how God answers my prayers—and more often than not, it was in a totally surprising way. But whether you journal your thoughts or just spend some peaceful time with Him, let today be a moment to renew your walk with God.

Reflections ...

TODAY I AM GRATEFUL FOR ... _____

_____

_____

_____

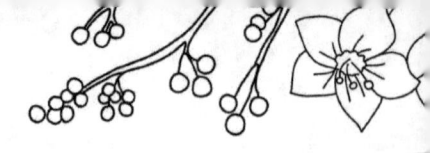

February 16
Genesis 18:1–15

Throughout this reading, we see the beautiful story of God's incredible promise to Abraham and Sarah—a promise that, in the midst of doubt, they would have a child. It's such a reminder that with God, nothing is impossible! Even when it feels like we're waiting for something big, God's faithfulness is always there, and His timing is perfect. Just as He brought laughter and joy to Sarah in a way she never expected, He can fill our lives with joy and hope, even in the most surprising ways.

After Valentine's Day, plan regular "date nights" with your special someone or friend? It doesn't have to be anything fancy—maybe a cozy dinner, a walk, or a movie night. Setting aside time for these simple moments of connection can really strengthen relationships and fill your heart with joy. It's a way to nurture those bonds and celebrate the love you share, day after day!

Reflections ...

TODAY I AM GRATEFUL FOR ... _____

_____
_____
_____
_____
_____
_____
_____

February 17
Ezekiel 17:22–24

God promises to take something small and humble, like a branch, and make it grow into something strong and fruitful. Even when we feel small or insignificant, God has the power to lift us up and use us for His glorious purposes. His faithfulness is constant, and He can transform our lives, just like a tiny sprout growing into a mighty tree.

Feeling inspired? Get creative and organize a fun talent show with your family, friends, or church group? It's a wonderful way to celebrate the unique gifts and talents God has given each of us. Whether you sing, dance, or share something special like a beautiful quilt you made, it's a perfect opportunity to encourage one another and see how God is at work in our lives!

Reflections ...

TODAY I AM GRATEFUL FOR ... _____

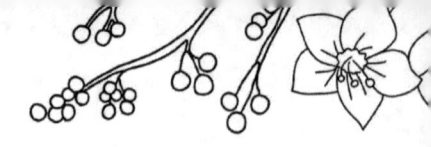

February 18
LEVITICUS 23:33–43

Leviticus 23:33–43 is a beautiful passage that celebrates the Feast of Tabernacles, a time for the Israelites to remember God's faithfulness in their journey and to rejoice in His provision. Isn't it amazing that God designed this celebration as a time to rest, to give thanks, and to be together?

This month, introduce yourself to someone new at church? Whether they're a visitor or someone you haven't connected with yet, take a moment to say "hello" and share a smile. You can embrace the joy of making someone feel seen, and you might even end up making a new friend, or finding a new coffee partner!

Reflections ...

TODAY I AM GRATEFUL FOR ... _____

_____
_____
_____
_____
_____
_____
_____

February 19
EXODUS 34:29–35

Isn't it incredible to imagine Moses coming down from Mount Sinai, his face literally glowing from being in God's presence? This beautiful moment reminds us that when we spend time with the Lord—through prayer, worship, or simply being still before Him—His light begins to shine through us, too. It's like MercyMe's "I Can Only Imagine"—just picturing being that close to His glory stirs the soul with hope! God doesn't just want us to observe His light; He invites us to *carry* it, becoming living reflections of His love in a world that so desperately needs it.

Let's be intentional about echoing God's light—do one kind thing for someone you don't know. Buy a stranger a coffee, hold the door with a big smile, or offer a sincere compliment. These small sparks of kindness are how we share His radiance, just like Moses, and brighten someone else's day with God's love! You've got this—go shine!

Reflections ...

TODAY I AM GRATEFUL FOR ... _____

_____

_____

_____

_____

_____

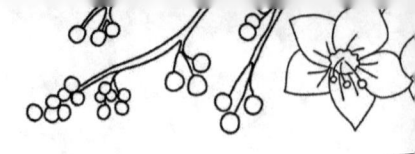

February 20
LUKE 9:18–27

When Jesus asks, "Who do you say I am?" it's not just a question for His disciples—it's a tender, hope-filled invitation for each of us to reflect on who He is in our lives. In this moment, we see Jesus drawing us into deeper relationship, encouraging us to anchor our identity and future in Him. How comforting it is to know that our hope is in the One who knows us by name and walks with us every step of the way!

Find a quiet moment to answer Jesus's question for yourself: "Who do you say I am?" Write it down, sing it, whisper it in prayer—whatever feels true to your heart. Let this be a gentle reset, reminding you of the solid hope you have in Christ, and watch how that hope begins to shape your day!

Reflections...

TODAY I AM GRATEFUL FOR ... _____

_____
_____
_____
_____
_____
_____

February 21
Deuteronomy 26:1–11

In Deuteronomy, God lovingly invites the Israelites to bring their first fruits—not out of obligation, but as a joyful response to His faithful care. It's a moment of remembering, of pausing to say, "Thank You, Lord, for all You've done." And what a hopeful reminder for us, too: God has walked with us through every season, and His goodness continues to pour out, even when we don't see the full harvest yet. May we offer our hearts with gratitude, trusting in His continued provision and love.

Celebrate God's goodness and the joy of community by hosting a little DIY night with friends! Bring out some paints, markers, or card stock—anything colourful and creative. Put on some music, laugh, share stories, and enjoy being together. Could this be a new way to strengthen bonds, nurture joy, and mirror the vibrant hope we carry in Christ?

Reflections ...

TODAY I AM GRATEFUL FOR ... _____

_____
_____
_____
_____
_____

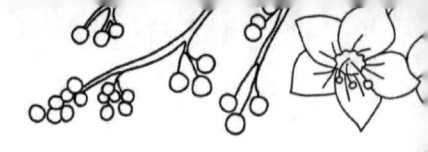

February 22
Ezekiel 34:11–12

The book of Ezekiel is one of the major prophetic books in the Old Testament, written by the prophet Ezekiel during the Babylonian exile. Ezekiel 34:11–12 is a comforting promise from God. He says, *"I myself will search for my sheep and look after them"* (v.11). Isn't that just the kindest, most hope-filled reminder of his undying love for us? Our Shepherd doesn't leave us wandering; He seeks us out with tenderness and care. Isn't it inspiring to know that no matter how scattered we may feel, He's always close, gently gathering us back into His embrace?

Let your heart be lightened with some good, soul-refreshing laughter. Consider planning a cozy movie night with friends or family, and choose a feel-good comedy that invites everyone to share in the joy. I find that joy is a beautiful expression of hope, and laughter has a tender way of reminding us that we're never alone.

Reflections ...

TODAY I AM GRATEFUL FOR ... _____

_____
_____
_____
_____
_____
_____

February 23
LUKE 15:1–10

Isn't it amazing to know that God rejoices over each one of us? In this passage, Jesus shares that heaven celebrates when even one person who was lost is found. It's a gentle reminder that we are deeply known, lovingly pursued, and never too far from grace. God's heart is full of hope for us—even in our wanderings—and His joy is in welcoming us home again and again.

Create a little bit of light for those tougher days. Start a list of your favourite Bible verses—ones that lift your spirit, remind you of God's promises, and bring you peace. Keep it somewhere you can return to often, like a journal, your phone, or taped on your mirror. Let these words be your gentle reminders that you are loved.

Reflections ...

TODAY I AM GRATEFUL FOR ... _____

_____
_____
_____
_____
_____
_____

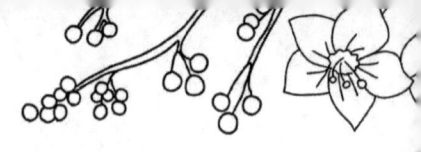

February 24
John 12:20–23

In these verses, we see a beautiful turning point—when Jesus hears that people from outside the Jewish community want to see Him. It's a moment full of meaning and quiet anticipation. Jesus knows that His journey to the cross will soon begin, but even in this, we see the seeds of hope being planted. Even in seasons of waiting or uncertainty, God is at work, bringing hope to life in ways we may not yet see.

Plant a small seed this week—it's February, so I'm speaking figuratively, of course. Maybe it's writing down one goal you'd like to grow toward, or something you'd like to achieve. You can have it. Put it somewhere you'll see it and be reminded that even the smallest beginnings can bloom with God's love and grace. beautifully it grows.

Reflections ...

TODAY I AM GRATEFUL FOR ... _____

_____
_____
_____
_____
_____
_____

February 25
GENESIS 28:10–22

Jacob's dream is such a tender and awe-inspiring reminder that God is always with us—no matter where we are or what we're going through. Through this reading, we glimpse a sacred connection between heaven and earth, a reassurance that God's promises and presence are never out of reach. What inspires you from this passage? Is it the knowledge that He walks beside us? Is it His faithfulness and love?

For a special family activity, plan a "screen-free" evening together. Set aside the distractions of technology and truly engage with one another—play a board game (I love game nights!), share a meal, or simply talk. I find that this kind of intentional time not only deepens your connections but gently echoes God's invitation to slow down and be present—in His love and with one another. What does family time mean to you?

Reflections ...

TODAY I AM GRATEFUL FOR ... _____

_____
_____
_____
_____
_____
_____

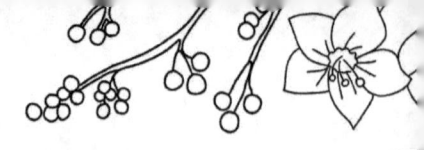

February 26
HEBREWS 9:11–14

Jesus's sacrifice is a powerful reminder of His love for us. By offering His own blood, He entered the heavenly sanctuary to purify our hearts, not just outwardly but deeply within. Through His act of love, we're drawn closer to God and given the hope of transformation and redemption. This passage calls us to deliberate over the incredible grace God has shown us, a grace that is always available, no matter our past or present struggles. We are always enough for Him. Take a moment to read that again. We are always enough for Him. Often we do things too quickly in our everyday lives, but I want you to really reflect on that. You are enough.

Check out the song "All My Hope" by Crowder. This song fills my heart with the truth of where our hope truly lies. Let the lyrics encourage you to place your trust in God's unshakeable love and grace. As you listen, consider the hope that Jesus offers us, and allow that truth to bring peace and joy to your heart.

Reflections ...

TODAY I AM GRATEFUL FOR ... _____

_____
_____
_____
_____
_____

February 27
Psalm 117

Psalm 117 is like a sacred whisper, and acknowledgement that God's love is for all people, everywhere. And how profound is that? It's the shortest chapter in the Bible, but its message is powerful: God's faithfulness reaches across the earth, and His love extends to all nations. This reminder of God's universal love brings hope and joy, knowing that His grace is available to every person, everywhere. We are all part of His family, and His mercy is unending.

Create a "thankful jar" for your family. Fill it with little notes of gratitude, each highlighting something special you appreciate about a family member during the day. Every evening, you can take turns pulling out a note to celebrate each other and recognize the blessings that God has placed in your family.

Reflections ...

Today I am grateful for ... _____

_____
_____
_____
_____
_____

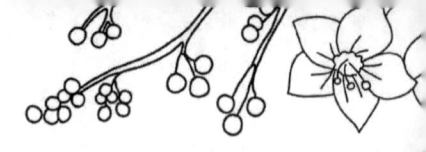

February 28
Genesis 15:1–12, 17–18

God makes a beautiful and faithful covenant with Abram, promising him descendants as numerous as the stars. This reminder of God's unwavering faithfulness is something we can embrace deep within our hearts as we read His promises and the ways He continues to guide and bless us. And just as God made a covenant with Abram, we're invited into a deep relationship with Him ourselves.

As a display of God's kindness, surprise someone with their favourite snack or treat today. Whether it's baking something or picking up their favourite coffee or dessert. How can you show someone today that you care?

Reflections ...

TODAY I AM GRATEFUL FOR ... _____

_____
_____
_____
_____
_____
_____
_____

March 1
JOEL 2:12–13

The book of Joel is truly fascinating! Joel is one of the twelve minor prophets in the Old Testament, but don't let the term "minor" fool you—its message is incredibly powerful. Joel 2:12–13 invites us into a season of deep reflection and repentance, reminding us of God's limitless mercy and faithfulness. Have you asked God into your heart today? His grace is readily available to refresh, guide, and transform you.

Make some time to explore the twelve minor prophets (Hosea through Malachi). Often referred to collectively as "the twelve" in Jewish tradition, each of these books is filled with important messages of judgement, hope, repentance, and restoration. Great things often come in small packages. Dive into one or two of these books and the powerful truths they hold. Though these writings are shorter, what unexpected lessons have you learned?

Reflections ...

TODAY I AM GRATEFUL FOR ... _____

_____
_____
_____
_____
_____
_____
_____

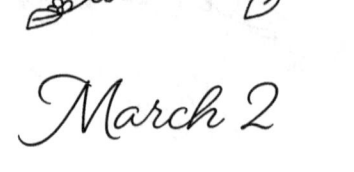

March 2
Genesis 1:26–31

As we enter this season, Genesis 1:26–31 invites us to remember God's beautiful design in creating humanity in His own image. He entrusted us with the responsibility to care for and steward the earth. Not only does He call us to consider our role as caretakers of creation but also challenges us to renew our commitment to protecting and nurturing the world around us. Have you considered how you reflect His love, goodness, and care?

Let's embrace this season by taking small, intentional steps to care for God's creation! Whether it's planting a garden, reducing waste, trying a plant-based meal (yes, come to the dark side lol), or supporting eco-friendly businesses, our choices matter. Can you take a moment to meditate on how you can live more mindfully in harmony with the world? God has entrusted us to look after this world we live in. How can you renew your commitment to being a loving steward of God's creation?

Reflections ...

TODAY I AM GRATEFUL FOR ... _____

_____

_____

_____

_____

_____

_____

March 3
2 PETER 2:1–10

Peter, one of the twelve apostles, was named Simon before Jesus gave him the name "Peter," meaning "rock." This name symbolized the foundational role he would play in building the Church. Like Peter, we too are called to grow in grace and integrity. As a follower of Christ, how do your actions echo goodness, knowledge, and self-control?

I love camping. You can take a quiet moment and just gaze at the stars. Tonight, look up, and let the vast beauty of God's creation remind you of His greatness and love. Spend a few moments in prayer or quiet contemplation. Can you feel His peace fill your heart and renew your spirit?

Reflections ...

TODAY I AM GRATEFUL FOR ... _____

_____
_____
_____
_____
_____
_____

March 4
2 Peter 2:11–22

Peter reminds us to stay anchored in God's truth, especially during times of temptation or confusion. Could this month be the perfect time to take this to heart—a time to pause, deliberate, and hold or return to God's path with renewed purpose and hope? Through repentance and steady trust in God's guidance, we can open ourselves to His transforming love and grace.

Let's live this out with a small but meaningful act. This week, surprise your minister or a church leader with their favourite coffee or a kind note. (I always get our youth leaders' coffee order.) It's such a sweet way to say, "Thank you." Don't you find that when we lift each other up on our faith journeys, it makes us feel closer to God?

Reflections ...

TODAY I AM GRATEFUL FOR … _____

_____
_____
_____
_____
_____
_____
_____

March 5

Jude 1–25

Isn't it amazing that the book of Jude, though only twenty-five verses long, carries such a powerful and hope-filled message? Jude, the brother of James, encourages us to stand strong in our faith, even when the world pulls us in different directions. It's a bold little letter that reminds us we're held by God's love, called to live with purpose, and invited to display His grace every day. That kind of hope doesn't just stay in our hearts—it overflows and renews our soul.

Let's pass that hope along. Think of someone who's brought joy or encouragement into your life (say your favourite new author—wink, wink, nudge, nudge). Then send them a note, a text, or give them a call. It doesn't have to be fancy—just sincere. I like to sign these "From a friend." I like to keep them guessing, lol. You never know how much a simple "thank you" can brighten someone's day!

Reflections ...

TODAY I AM GRATEFUL FOR ... _____

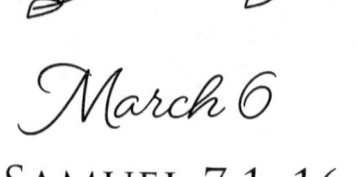

March 6
2 SAMUEL 7:1–16

In the book of Samuel, we read how God makes a heartfelt promise to David—not just for his lifetime, but for generations to come. It's a reminder of God's incredible faithfulness and His desire to be in lasting relationship with His people. This promise encourages us to trust in the bigger picture of God's loving plan, even when we can't see it all just yet. Can you see how His kindness invites us to respond with grateful hearts and open hands?

Head outside and enjoy the last of the winter season—maybe it's spring skiing, a chilly nature walk, or simply soaking up the fresh air before the warmth rolls in. As you enjoy God's creation, spend a few moments in quiet gratitude, as His faithfulness follows us through every season—both in nature and in your life.

Reflections...

TODAY I AM GRATEFUL FOR ... _____

_____
_____
_____
_____
_____
_____
_____

March 7

JAMES 4:11–17

James reminds us how important it is to speak kindly, live humbly, and trust God with our plans. This passage invites us to step back and ask if we're living with grace toward others and letting God shape our future. Real change begins in our hearts, and sometimes that means repenting of pride or unkindness and letting God lead us with a fresh perspective. What an amazing assurance that each day is a new chance to start again, in step with His love.

Bring the fresh energy of spring into your home by decorating with bright colours and cheerful touches! Add a vase of flowers, a pastel tablecloth, or even a new candle to brighten your space. As you refresh your home, let it be a gentle reminder to refresh your spirit too. You could say a simple prayer: "Dear heavenly Father, please fill this home with your love and grace, and help all who live here to surrender their cares and worries to you.

Reflections ...

TODAY I AM GRATEFUL FOR ...

March 8

INTERNATIONAL WOMEN'S DAY

RUTH 1:16–17

Ruth's words to Naomi come straight from the heart. Her deep loyalty and love show us what it means to walk alongside someone in faith, even through uncertainty. Ruth didn't just stay—she embraced a new beginning, trusting that God would meet her in the unknown. When you reflect on Ruth's story, what resonates with you?

In celebration of International Women's Day, take time to honour a woman in your life who has inspired you with her kindness, strength, or faith—just like Ruth. Send her a thoughtful note, drop off a treat, or simply call and tell her how much she means to you. These small gestures can be powerful and mirror the beautiful loyalty and generosity Ruth so powerfully lived out.

Reflections ...

TODAY I AM GRATEFUL FOR ... _____

_____
_____
_____
_____
_____
_____
_____

March 9
MATTHEW 7:24–27

This is another of my favourite readings (the wise and foolish builders). I distinctly remember learning this passage in Sunday school. The wise builder builds his house on the rock, and when the storms come, it stands firm. But the foolish builder builds his house on the sand, and when the storms come, it falls with a great crash. This passage reminds us of the importance of building our lives on a firm foundation—God's Word. Just like a house built on rock can withstand storms, don't you find that when we root ourselves in faith and the teachings of Christ, we can face life's challenges with confidence and stability?

Celebrate the sweetness of March by enjoying some maple syrup—whether it's drizzled over pancakes or enjoyed on a spoon! If you're able, visit a local maple syrup hut to see the process firsthand and appreciate the beauty of this seasonal treat. As you indulge in the sweetness, take a moment to give thanks for God's steady and abundant love that nourishes us every day.

Reflections ...

TODAY I AM GRATEFUL FOR … _____

_____

_____

_____

_____

March 10
International Day of Awesomeness

Revelation 3:15–20

Revelation 3:15–20 reminds us that God doesn't want us to live halfway—He desires our whole hearts. He gently calls us to turn back when we've drifted, to open the door when we've shut Him out, and to let His love renew us from the inside out. This passage is such a beautiful invitation to repentance—not with shame, but with hope. He's not waiting with disappointment, but with open arms and the promise of a blank page. How does it feel to know that every moment is a new chance to choose Him again?

It's the International Day of Awesomeness, and what better way to celebrate than embracing the awesome truth that God is still working in you! Take a few minutes to consider where He might be inviting you to start fresh—then write down one small, grace-filled step you can take. Bonus joy points: tell someone else something awesome you see in them. God's goodness is contagious—let's share it generously today!

Reflections ...

Today I am grateful for ... _____

_____
_____
_____
_____
_____

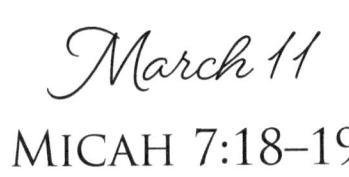

March 11

MICAH 7:18–19

What an incredible comfort it is to know that God delights in showing mercy. These verses paint such a hopeful picture—our sins, no matter how big or small, are swept away into the depths of the sea, gone for good. God doesn't hold our mistakes over us; instead, He welcomes us back with open arms, ready to renew our hearts and restore our joy. His forgiveness invites us to walk forward with fresh hope, knowing we are deeply loved and completely forgiven.

Brighten someone's day with a heartfelt note of encouragement. I love leaving heartfelt notes for people to find! Think of a friend or family member who could use a reminder of how much God loves them. How can you let them know that they're never alone, and that God is always there to bring love, renewal, and peace?

Reflections ...

TODAY I AM GRATEFUL FOR ... _____

_____

_____

_____

_____

_____

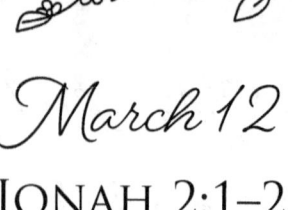

March 12
Jonah 2:1-2

Have you ever had one of those "belly of the fish" moments—where you feel stuck, overwhelmed, or unsure of the way forward? Jonah's prayer reminds us that even from the deepest places, God hears us. It's a beautiful picture: when we cry out in honesty, God meets us with compassion and grace. No moment is too messy or too far gone for His love to reach. When we turn to Him, we open the door to restoration and fresh beginnings.

Treat yourself to something uplifting! Head out to a local concert or community play—something creative and joy-filled that reminds you of God's goodness. Let it renew your spirit and maybe even inspire a prayer of gratitude for how far God has carried you. A little joy goes a long way!

Reflections ...

TODAY I AM GRATEFUL FOR ... _____

_____
_____
_____
_____
_____
_____
_____

NATIONAL GOOD SAMARITAN DAY

JAMES 1:19–27

James reminds us of the importance of being quick to listen, slow to speak, and slow to anger. It's such a beautiful call to act with integrity and compassion, which aligns perfectly with the spirit of National Good Samaritan Day. James encourages us to not only hear the Word but to live it out through action. Our faith is truly visible when we show kindness and compassion, just like the Good Samaritan, to those around us. Every small act of love and service makes a big difference in showing God's heart to the world. If you're up for another good reading today, check out the Good Samaritan parable (Luke 10:25–37).

As we celebrate National Good Samaritan Day, let's embrace the spirit of kindness and service by performing a random act of kindness. Whether it's helping a neighbour or donating to someone in need, every small act can make a big difference. Let's spread love and make the world a brighter place, one thoughtful act at a time!

Reflections ...

TODAY I AM GRATEFUL FOR ... _____

_____
_____
_____
_____

March 14
Pi Day (3.14)

2 Kings 5:1–14

Today we read about Naaman, a powerful commander who initially struggles to follow God's simple instructions, thinking they're beneath him. But when he humbles himself and obeys, he is healed. God's ways are often unexpected, and when we trust and follow His guidance, even when it doesn't make sense, He brings about incredible transformation in our lives. Sometimes, the simplest steps of obedience lead to the most profound changes, just as they did for Naaman.

Today we celebrate Pi Day (3.14). Pi is the amazing mathematical constant that helps us measure circles and reminds us how math shows up in the most unexpected places—from the swirl of galaxies to the rings of a tree trunk and even in the shape of a pie! But beyond the numbers, Pi Day is a fun reminder of the beauty and order in God's creation. Whether it's the precise laws of math or the patterns we see in nature, everything reflects the brilliance of His design. So today as we enjoy a slice of pie (or two). Can take a moment to marvel at the Creator behind it all?

Reflections ...

TODAY I AM GRATEFUL FOR ... _____
_____
_____
_____
_____

March 15

PROVERBS 1:1–7

This passage in Proverbs is like a gentle nudge inviting us to seek wisdom from the Lord. It reminds us that true wisdom begins with a healthy respect for God and His teachings. When we align our hearts and actions with His guidance, we live in a way that honours Him. Just like a wise person builds their life on the foundation of God's wisdom, we too are called to build our lives with His truth as our guide.

If gardening is your thing, today might be the perfect day to order or start your seeds indoors. Just like planting seeds and nurturing them to grow, we can cultivate wisdom in our lives by seeking God's guidance daily. This year, we're planting extra vegetables to share with the local food bank. What seeds can you sow of kindness and generosity, both in our gardens and in our hearts?

Reflections ...

TODAY I AM GRATEFUL FOR ... _____

_____

_____

_____

_____

_____

March 16
1 Peter 2:11–25

Peter encourages us to live honourably, even in the face of suffering, and to follow the example of Christ, who endured hardship with grace and humility. This reading reminds us that we're called to live as strangers and pilgrims in this world, seeking to show God's love and light, even when it's difficult. Christ's example of patience, humility, and love calls us to serve others and to bear witness to how His goodness renews our lives.

I love creating playlists, especially when they fill me with inspiration and draw me closer to God. That's why I have a few different Christian playlists—some that focus on joy, others more moving, and some that just bring a smile to my face. Make some time to listen to music that brings you peace and connects your heart with God's presence—who knows, maybe you'll be inspired to create a new playlist or two!

Reflections ...

TODAY I AM GRATEFUL FOR ... _____

_____
_____
_____
_____
_____
_____

March 17

St. Patrick's Day

JAMES 1:2–4

What makes this passage particularly interesting is the idea of joy during hardship. James is teaching us that trials aren't just obstacles to endure, but they're also tools that shape our character, deepen our faith, and lead us to spiritual maturity. The more we persevere through difficulties, the more we grow in endurance and, ultimately, in completeness and spiritual strength. This teaching challenges us to shift our perspective—rather than seeing tough times as setbacks, can you see them as a chance to grow closer to God and renew your faith?

For St. Patrick's Day, wear green and enjoy a family supper together! We like to make a lentil shepherd's pie and Irish soda bread. As you gather around the table, talk about the importance of standing firm in your beliefs. This is a fun way to celebrate a holiday and your faith!

Reflections ...

TODAY I AM GRATEFUL FOR ... _____

_____
_____
_____
_____
_____
_____

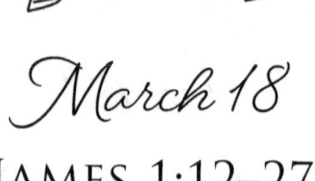

March 18
James 1:12–27

Through this passage, James encourages us to stay strong in life's trials, reminding us that perseverance leads to maturity. He also speaks about the importance of being doers of the Word, not just hearers, urging us to live out our faith in practical ways. True faith is reflected in how we treat others, care for those in need, and live with integrity and love in our daily actions.

As the weather starts to warm up, it's a perfect time to tackle spring cleaning. Start by going through your closet and donating items you no longer need. It's a simple yet meaningful way to declutter your space and share with others. Let your actions echo the generosity and love God calls us to live out every day.

Reflections ...

TODAY I AM GRATEFUL FOR ... _____

_____
_____
_____
_____
_____
_____
_____

MARK 3:31–35

Jesus shares that true family isn't just about physical ties, but about living in alignment with God's will. He reminds us that when we embrace God's love and walk in His ways, we become part of a new, spiritual family. This passage invites us to experience grace—knowing that we belong to something far greater, bound by love and purpose that transcends anything we could imagine.

As the snow melts and we start seeing signs of spring, take some time to clean out your car. Clear away the winter clutter and refresh it for the warmer months ahead. I like to crank up the sound on some Christian rock music—it makes spring cleaning so much more enjoyable!

Reflections ...

TODAY I AM GRATEFUL FOR ... _____

_____
_____
_____
_____
_____

March 20

INTERNATIONAL DAY OF HAPPINESS

ISAIAH 43:18–19

Today's reading speaks to the incredible hope God offers, urging us to forget the past and embrace the new things He is doing. This reading is like a friendly nudge to our hearts—that God is always at work, bringing forth new beginnings and opportunities for growth. And wouldn't today be the perfect time to meditate on God's promise of transformation and newness?

Happy International Day of Happiness! What better way to celebrate than soaking up some sunshine, starting something new, or simply enjoying the fresh feel of spring! It's the perfect reminder that God is always at work, bringing refreshment and joy into our lives—inside and out!

Reflections ...

TODAY I AM GRATEFUL FOR ... _____

_____
_____
_____
_____
_____
_____

March 21

MATTHEW 9:9–13

Did you know that the Gospel of Matthew was written by Matthew—a tax collector before he became one of Jesus's disciples? In those times, tax collectors were often despised for being corrupt, but Jesus saw beyond Matthew's past and called him to follow Him. Matthew 9:9–13 is a powerful reminder that all are welcome to God's grace. Just as Jesus called Matthew to follow Him, He calls each of us to embrace the opportunity for refreshment and transformation through His love.

Why not plan a potluck brunch with friends? It's a simple way to connect, share a meal, and celebrate the love we experience through Jesus. As you gather, could you share how God is renewing your heart and life, and share the joy of His grace with those you care about?

Reflections ...

TODAY I AM GRATEFUL FOR ... _____

_____

_____

_____

_____

_____

March 22
Psalm 46:1-3

What a comforting and powerful psalm! Psalm 46:1–3 reminds us that *"God is our refuge and strength, an ever-present help in trouble."* Even when life feels chaotic or uncertain, God remains steady and close. These verses offer such a heartwarming reminder that we're never alone—and that in His presence, we can find the courage to begin again. When we lean into His strength, we're renewed from the inside out, ready to face whatever comes next with faith and peace.

Celebrate that sense of renewal with something joyful! Plan a fun night out with friends or family—maybe it's bowling, laser tag, or grabbing a favourite treat together. Laughter, connection, and simple fun are beautiful ways to experience God's goodness and recharge your spirit along the way.

Reflections ...

TODAY I AM GRATEFUL FOR ... _____

_____
_____
_____
_____
_____
_____
_____

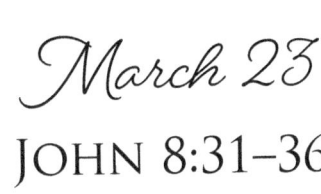

March 23

John 8:31–36

Jesus reminds us in today's passage that when we hold fast to His teachings, we will know the truth—and the truth will set us free. In Christ, we're no longer bound by past mistakes, fear, or doubt. Instead, we're invited into a life of freedom, joy, and purpose. Living in His truth brings a deep, lasting kind of freedom that transforms our hearts and renews our spirit each day.

Let's celebrate that freedom with something fun—how about a thrift store challenge? If there's one thing I absolutely love, it's treasure hunting at thrift stores! Grab a friend and challenge each other to find the funniest, cutest, or most out-there outfit. You'll laugh, bond, and maybe even find a new favourite piece—all while enjoying a light-hearted reminder that joy and freedom go hand in hand.

Reflections ...

TODAY I AM GRATEFUL FOR ... _____

_____
_____
_____
_____
_____

March 24
Hebrews 12:1–3

Hebrews 12:1–3 offers such a meaningful message that we're not alone in our faith journey—we're surrounded by a *"great cloud of witnesses,"* and we're invited to run our race with perseverance, keeping our eyes on Jesus. When life feels heavy or overwhelming, this passage encourages us to lean into His strength and let go of the things that weigh us down. Ask yourself if Jesus, who endured so much for our sake, walks alongside us every step of the way? Where do we want our steps to take us?

As we embrace the call of spring, I love to celebrate God's goodness, decorating my home with fresh, vibrant colours or some cheerful flowers. This simple little refresh can be such a joyful symbol of the new beginnings God brings into our lives—especially in this season of growth and hope. Can your space mirror the lightness and beauty He's placing in your heart?

Reflections ...

TODAY I AM GRATEFUL FOR ... _____

_____
_____
_____
_____
_____
_____

PHILIPPIANS 4:11–13

Today's reading is such an encouraging reminder that contentment isn't about having everything go perfectly—it's about trusting in Christ no matter the circumstances. Paul shares that he has learned to be content, whether in plenty or in need, because his strength comes from Christ. That kind of heart renewal—where peace replaces striving—is such a gift, and it invites us to lean into God's grace, knowing He is enough for every season.

Nothing says spring like baking up something sweet and seasonal. How about a carrot cake or lemon bars to share with friends or neighbours? Let your kitchen be a place of joy and generosity, and as you bake, thank God for the change He brings to our hearts and homes. Bonus points if you sneak a little treat for yourself too—you've earned it!

Reflections ...

TODAY I AM GRATEFUL FOR ... _____

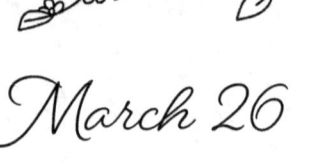

March 26
Luke 17:11–19

This beautiful passage tells the story of ten lepers who were healed by Jesus, but only one returned to give thanks—and he was a Samaritan, someone seen as an outsider. His gratitude opened the door to even deeper healing, not just physically but spiritually. This moment reminds us that renewal often begins with a thankful heart. Don't you find that when we pause to acknowledge what God has done for us, we experience His grace in a fuller, richer way?

To embrace this message, consider starting a prayer circle with friends or family. You can take turns leading each week, with themes like healing, forgiveness, or hope—whatever is on your hearts. I find that this is a beautiful way to grow together in faith, support one another, and celebrate the blessings God brings into your lives, big and small.

Reflections …

TODAY I AM GRATEFUL FOR … _____

_____
_____
_____
_____
_____
_____
_____

March 27
Isaiah 2:1–5

Isaiah shares a beautiful vision of peace with us, where nations come together to walk in the light of the Lord. It's a reminder that God's ultimate plan for us is one of unity, learning, and transformation. As we follow His ways, we're invited to leave behind old patterns and step into a life shaped by His peace and purpose. How hopeful is that?

Embrace that spirit of togetherness with a fun cooking night! Have you ever made sushi? We love making vegetarian sushi—it's surprisingly easy and such a fun way to get creative in the kitchen. Invite some friends or family to join in, roll up your sleeves, and enjoy a night of laughter, delicious food, and connection.

Reflections ...

TODAY I AM GRATEFUL FOR ... _____

_____
_____
_____
_____
_____
_____

March 28

JEREMIAH 33:14–16

Jeremiah 33:14–16 reminds us of God's promise to bring restoration and righteousness through His faithful love. Even in times of waiting or uncertainty, we are assured that God's plans are always unfolding—He is a God who keeps His promises and brings hope to His people. This passage is like a warm embrace from heaven. Isn't that a beautiful encouragement to hold close to our hearts?

Think of someone you haven't spoken to in a while—maybe an old friend or a family member. This week make it a priority to give them a call, even if it's just to say, "I love you" and catch up. Your voice might be the little spark of joy they need today, a reminder of God's love and the power of connection.

Reflections ...

TODAY I AM GRATEFUL FOR ... _____

_____
_____
_____
_____
_____
_____

March 29
2 Peter 1:1–11

Through 2 Peter we are asked to diligently pursue a life of virtue and godliness, to grow in our faith and knowledge of Jesus Christ. Peter emphasizes the importance of adding qualities such as goodness, knowledge, self-control, and love to our lives, so we may bear fruit in our walk with God. By doing so, we can confidently experience the promises God has given us and grow stronger in our faith.

Have you ever arranged a fun car run with friends? My parents love doing this. Plan a scenic route that allows you to enjoy each other's company, share stories, and speak of how you seek God's direction in your life. Can you take this time to talk about how you can grow in faith and encourage one another to live more intentionally for Christ?

Reflections ...

TODAY I AM GRATEFUL FOR ... _____

_____
_____
_____
_____
_____

March 30
James 5:1–6

James reminds us here that it's not about what we have, but *how* we live with what we've been given. This passage gently nudges us to look into our hearts. Are we using our time, gifts, and resources in a way that honours God and uplifts others? This season is a beautiful opportunity to turn away from anything that holds us back and to lean into a life of generosity, grace, and compassion.

Spring cleaning time—garage edition! As you swap out skis and snowshoes for gardening tools and bikes, take it as a little spiritual reset too. Let the clearing of clutter be a reminder to release anything in your heart that no longer serves God's purpose, and make space for the new and good things He's growing in you this season.

Reflections ...

TODAY I AM GRATEFUL FOR ... _____

_____
_____
_____
_____
_____
_____
_____

ZECHARIAH 1:3–6

Zechariah shares a heartfelt call from God: *"Return to me … and I will return to you."* What a beautiful promise! These words remind us that no matter how far we've wandered, God always invites us back with open arms. Turning our hearts toward Him brings restoration, not just for us personally, but for our families, communities, and beyond.

Pray for those in government—locally, nationally, and globally. Ask God to guide their hearts with wisdom, justice, and compassion. As you do, can this be a gentle reminder that we're all called to be part of God's work in the world—starting with prayer and love for others?

Reflections …

TODAY I AM GRATEFUL FOR … _____

_____
_____
_____
_____
_____
_____

April 1
April Fools' Day

JOHN 11:25–26

John 11:25–26 reminds us that Jesus is the resurrection and the life. Even in the face of death, He offers us eternal life and hope. Just as He brought Lazarus out of the tomb, He brings us out of our struggles, offering a second chance. This reading echoes in my heart that old hymn "Blessed Assurance," as our hope is never in vain, and we can find strength in His promises, no matter what we face.

On April Fools', we like to celebrate with a backwards dinner. Like the surprise of Lazarus walking out of the tomb, surprise your family with a savory shepherd's pie that looks like a cupcake, or make brownies that look like burger patties. It's a fun, creative way to bring laughter and joy to others, while also being thankful for the creative and joyful spirit that God gives us. Spread a little kindness with a surprise that brings a smile!

Reflections ...

TODAY I AM GRATEFUL FOR ... _____

_____
_____
_____
_____
_____
_____

Isaiah 65:17–25

Our reading today speaks of a beautiful new creation, where God promises to restore the world and bring peace, joy, and abundance to all who trust in Him. It's a wonderful reminder that the true treasures of life are found in God's eternal promises, not in the temporary things of this world. The imagery of a renewed earth invites us to look forward with hope, knowing that God is making all things new. What a comforting thought that, no matter the circumstances, His plan is full of love and restoration!

Take your Bible outside and enjoy a peaceful moment in nature. You might need to bundle up before you find a quiet spot, free from distractions, and read the Scriptures while surrounded by the beauty of God's creation. Let this time be an opportunity to shift focus from material wealth to the lasting treasures of God's Word. It's the perfect way to reconnect with what truly matters—His love, peace, and promise of renewal!

Reflections ...

TODAY I AM GRATEFUL FOR ... _____

_____

_____

_____

_____

_____

April 3
JOHN 14:1–6

This reading is such a beautiful and comforting reminder from Jesus that He is the way, the truth, and the life. In this passage, He reassures us that we have nothing to fear, for He has already prepared a place for us. This incredible promise brings peace to our hearts, knowing that we are never alone on our journey. As we follow Him, He leads us toward hope, love, and eternal life. What a gift to rest in the knowledge that Jesus is always guiding us with His love.

In the spirit of new beginnings and the changing seasons, I enjoy getting outside. With the budding trees and the birds singing, spring is a beautiful time to get out there and enjoy! This simple act will not only help you appreciate the beauty of God's creation but also serve as a reminder of the life and hope we have in Christ!

Reflections ...

TODAY I AM GRATEFUL FOR ... _____

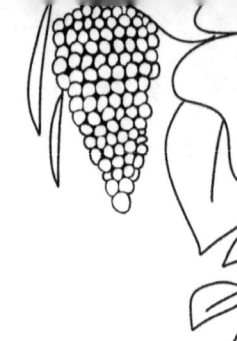

Luke 23:27–43

Today's reading offers us a powerful glimpse into Jesus's final moments on the cross, when He extends mercy and love even in His suffering. He assures the criminal beside Him that today he will be with Him in paradise, reminding us of the depth of His grace. Jesus's sacrifice is a reminder that no matter what we've done, we can find forgiveness and redemption in Him. This passage challenges us to live with the same grace and compassion, embracing the hope and love He offers to all. Will you accept the challenge?

To embrace the joy and love that Easter brings, I like to host a family coffee or hot chocolate bar, and our favourite toppings include whipped cream and grated chocolate—and don't forget those peppermint sticks. It's a sweet way to enjoy time together, celebrate the season, and remember the warmth of God's love that surrounds us. Plus, it's a fun activity for everyone to get creative and enjoy!

Reflections ...

TODAY I AM GRATEFUL FOR ... _____

_____
_____
_____
_____
_____

April 5
ROMANS 8:18–25

In today's reading, Paul reminds us that while we face challenges now, they are nothing compared to the glory that awaits us. Just as creation eagerly waits for spring, we too long for the redemption God promises. It's an inspiring message that Paul gives us—to hold on to hope, trusting that God is always at work, even in the waiting.

Celebrate the season with an early spring bonfire! Spring and fall are great times to power down those phones and power up the family time! Okay, any time is good for family time, but spending time with loved ones around the fire, wrapped up in cozy blankets and enjoying some classic s'mores is a great way to enjoy the season. It's a perfect way to embrace the warmth of togetherness and the joy of the season while remembering the love and light that Jesus brings into our lives.

Reflections ...

TODAY I AM GRATEFUL FOR ... _____

_____
_____
_____
_____
_____

April 6
1 Corinthians 15:3–4

Paul reminds us of the heart of the gospel: that Christ died for our sins, was buried, and rose again on the third day, just as Scripture foretold. This passage encapsulates the hope we have in the resurrection, the cornerstone of our faith. It's a sacred truth that because of Jesus's sacrifice and victory over death, we are invited to walk in newness of life, embracing the hope He offers us.

As the seasons shift, leaning into the coziness with a family pajama party is one of my favourite things to do. Pick a night, grab your fluffiest PJs (I like to order matching ones), make some snacks, and snuggle in for fun. God delights in our joy and togetherness—what a sweet way to celebrate His good gifts!

Reflections ...

TODAY I AM GRATEFUL FOR ... _____

_____
_____
_____
_____
_____
_____
_____

April 7
LUKE 24:13–35

In this passage, two disciples are walking along the road to Emmaus, discussing the events surrounding Jesus's death, when Jesus joins them, but they don't immediately recognize Him. Sometimes, like the disciples, we may not immediately recognize Jesus in our daily lives, but He's always walking alongside us, guiding us toward hope and understanding.

I love supporting the buy local movement. Not only does it feel good to support our local businesses, but it's also a fun way to connect with your community and support a local business. So why not call up a girlfriend and spend the day exploring some nearby shops? Oh, and maybe visit your favourite coffee joint while you're at it. As you enjoy time together, remember that God's presence is in the everyday moments, and even small acts can be a way to experience His love and joy. He's walking right there with you. Can you welcome Him in?

Reflections ...

TODAY I AM GRATEFUL FOR ... _____

_____
_____
_____
_____
_____

John 20:19–23
(Jesus Appears to the Disciples)

In today's reading, we see Jesus coming to His disciples, offering peace and commissioning them to carry His message to the world. The disciples, once fearful, are filled with the Holy Spirit, empowered to spread the good news. This moment reminds us that just as Jesus gave His disciples the gift of the Spirit, we too are called to live out our faith boldly and with the peace that only He can provide.

Have you heard "Holy Spirit" by Francesca Battistelli? She is one of my favourite singers. (And I know it's not the month for it, but if you haven't checked out her Christmas album, it's awesome!) Listening to this song beautifully echoes the invitation for the Holy Spirit to move within us, empowering us to live as Jesus did—full of peace, love, and purpose. How is the the Holy Spirit moving in your own life? Is He encouraging you to embrace God's calling and share His love with others? And seriously, check out her Christmas album, lol!

Reflections ...

Today I am grateful for ... _____

_____
_____
_____
_____
_____

April 9
John 21:1–14

As we read through John 21, we see the disciples after Jesus's resurrection, still grappling with the shock and wonder of it all. When they encounter Him on the shore, He provides them with a miraculous catch of fish, reminding them of His care and faithfulness. Just as He showed Himself to His disciples, He continues to make His presence known in our lives, inviting us to experience His peace and provision. Will you accept the invitation?

Creating a memory garden can be a meaningful way to reflect on God's love, or those whom we've lost. You can plan the garden now for planting in the warmer weather. What flowers, plants, or symbolic items (maybe a prayer bench or a rock—for me, it's a red cardinal for my grandmother) could you use to represent hope and life? If you live in an apartment, you could add a potted plant to your balcony. This simple yet powerful activity allows for personal introspection while honouring the resilience and memory of others.

Reflections ...

TODAY I AM GRATEFUL FOR ... _____

_____

_____

_____

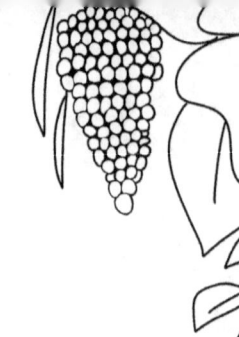

April 10
ACTS 1:9–11

As Jesus ascended to heaven in Acts 1:9–11, His disciples were filled with awe and wonder. The angels' message—*"This same Jesus, who has been taken from you into heaven, will come back in the same way you have seen him go …"*(v. 11b)—reminds us that Christ's work on earth is not finished—He will return in glory. Does this promise fill you with hope, joy, and the assurance that Jesus reigns from heaven while we wait for His triumphant return?

I really like how serving others can make an impact in your community. We love to volunteer—whether through your church (we have a hoot volunteering with our community suppers), a local charity (like the Special Olympics—what a great charity with amazing athletes), or in support of a neighbour—is a tangible way to live out God's call. As you embrace the opportunity to serve, I pray that you are filled with joy and excitement, knowing that Jesus is right there with you every step of the way.

Reflections ...

TODAY I AM GRATEFUL FOR ... _____

_____
_____
_____
_____

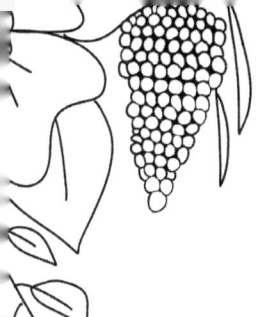

April 11
MARK 16:9–20

After Jesus's resurrection, He appeared to His disciples, showing them His power over death. He then ascended to heaven, commissioning His followers to go into the world and spread His message. This passage reminds us that we are called to carry on the work of sharing God's love and hope with others. As we embrace the call to be His witnesses, we can remember that we don't do it alone—Jesus is with us every step of the way!

Building on this reading, why not make some time to help a neighbour with errands? I have to give my dad props on this one. Whether it's picking up groceries, offering a ride, or just lending a hand, these small acts of service show the love of Christ to others in tangible ways. Serving others is a powerful reminder that we are called to share Jesus's love and hope wherever we go. Oh, and don't let my dad know that he inspired this writing today, as I don't want him to get a big head!

Reflections ...

TODAY I AM GRATEFUL FOR ... _____

_____
_____
_____
_____

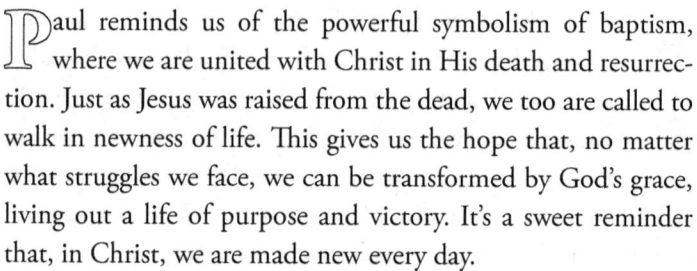

April 12
Romans 6:3–11

Paul reminds us of the powerful symbolism of baptism, where we are united with Christ in His death and resurrection. Just as Jesus was raised from the dead, we too are called to walk in newness of life. This gives us the hope that, no matter what struggles we face, we can be transformed by God's grace, living out a life of purpose and victory. It's a sweet reminder that, in Christ, we are made new every day.

I am working on praying out loud in a group setting. It doesn't come naturally to me—it's like suddenly I get stage fright. Praying one-on-one? Bring it on! But I always seem to stumble when it comes to praying in a group. Is it just me? But whatever you are working on in your prayer game, know that God loves us and He is our biggest cheerleader. So let's be faithful in praying for those around us and trusting in God's transformative power!

Reflections ...

TODAY I AM GRATEFUL FOR ... _____

_____
_____
_____
_____
_____

April 13
Exodus 12:1–14

In today's reading, God gives the Israelites instructions for the first Passover, a pivotal moment in their history. The blood of the lamb, placed on the doorposts, would protect them from the final plague, marking them as God's people. This act of obedience and God's deliverance became a powerful symbol of His protection and faithfulness. It reminds us that, just like the Israelites, we are covered by the blood of the Lamb—Jesus Christ—and are called to remember His sacrifice and the freedom He brings into our lives.

As the seasons change, I love to take some time to recharge and enjoy God's creation? Plan a weekend getaway to a nearby park or a cozy retreat spot. Would you try hiking, relaxing by a lake, or simply enjoying the beauty of nature? How could you refresh your spirit and concentrate on the freedom and protection God provides?

Reflections ...

TODAY I AM GRATEFUL FOR ... _____

_____

_____

_____

_____

JOYOUS FAITH

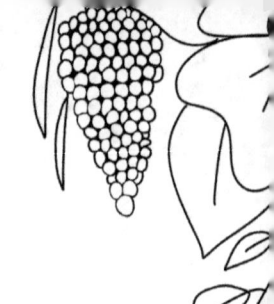

EZEKIEL 37:1–14

In Ezekiel 37:1–14, God demonstrates His awe-inspiring ability to bring life into the most hopeless and desolate situations. He takes dry bones, symbolizing despair and death, and breathes new life into them, creating a vast army. This passage reminds us that no matter how impossible our circumstances may appear, God has the power to restore, revive, and transform what seems beyond hope. His power is ever-present, offering us the chance to experience His miraculous work in our lives.

With the arrival of spring, it's fun to get creative and make a spring wreath? One of my girlfriends taught me the art of wreath-making, and it's best not to overthink it. Gather some fake flowers and ribbons to craft your very own vibrant creation. As you create, think of the renewal God offers, just like the flowers and beauty that come back to life each year. It's a simple and joyful way to celebrate the season of new beginnings!

Reflections ...

TODAY I AM GRATEFUL FOR ... _____

_____
_____
_____
_____
_____

April 15
Luke 24:36–49

In today's passage, Jesus appears to His disciples, offering them peace and reminding them of the mission ahead. His presence brings joy and clarity, and He empowers us to share the good news with others. Just as the disciples were sent to spread the message, we too are called to bring hope and love to those around us.

At our church, we have a wonderful coffee hour after service—a time to connect, share, and build community. If you enjoy this time of fellowship, why not consider volunteering to host a coffee hour at your church? And though we're blessed to have a strong coffee hour program at our church, they always need volunteers! It's a simple way to bring people together, offer hospitality, and create a welcoming space where God's love can be shared.

Reflections ...

TODAY I AM GRATEFUL FOR ... _____

_____

_____

_____

_____

_____

April 16
John 1:14–18

In this passage, we're reminded that Jesus, the Word made flesh, came to dwell among us, bringing grace and truth. His presence brings light into the darkness and fills us with the fullness of God's love. Just as we savour sweet, refreshing moments in life, like enjoying seasonal fruits, we can embrace the refreshing presence of Christ in our hearts, bringing us joy, peace, and nourishment for our spirits.

While I cherish the newness of spring, I like to break up my spring cleaning into different tasks. If you are a spring cleaner too, you can take this time to thank God for all the blessings He has given you. It's a wonderful way to start fresh and invite God's presence into every corner of your life! Oh, and I find a little TobyMac makes the cleaning go a lot faster!

Reflections ...

TODAY I AM GRATEFUL FOR ... _____

_____
_____
_____
_____
_____
_____
_____

April 17
1 THESSALONIANS 4:13–18

In today's reading, Paul offers comfort and hope, reminding us that even in the face of loss, we have the promise of eternal life in Christ. He encourages us to live with the joyful expectation that one day we'll be reunited with loved ones, and that the Lord will return to bring us home. This beautiful truth fills us with peace and hope, reminding us to live each day with purpose and anticipation of the glory to come.

Speaking of encouragement and purpose, I have a confession to make: I love lists. Creating a spring bucket list is a perfect way to intentionally focus on activities and goals that will help you grow. Using coloured pens, I jot down things I'd like to accomplish, like watching a sunset, trying a new spring recipe, or taking a peaceful walk in nature each weekend. Having this all laid out keeps me on track and ensures that I prioritize those things that make me feel more connected to Jesus—and it looks pretty too! Let this season of renewal remind you to stay connected to the True Vine as you bear the fruit of joy and growth!

Reflections ...

TODAY I AM GRATEFUL FOR ... _____

_____

_____

_____

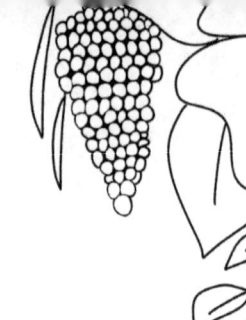

April 18
ACTS 17:24–28

Today we read about Paul speaking to the people of Athens, reminding them that God is the Creator of the world and everything in it. He emphasizes that God doesn't dwell in human-made temples but is present everywhere, and we, His creation, live and move through Him. This passage speaks to the profound connection between God and the world He made, calling us to recognize that all of creation mirrors His glory and invites us to seek Him. What connections do you see?

Spring is the perfect time for a make-over, and your digital life is no exception! I recently made this a priority for myself, and I am so happy I did. Take a breath and then take stock and declutter your phone, or unsubscribe from those newsletters that are cluttering up your inbox. Set a goal to create more space for joy and connection in your world, and make room for the things that truly inspire you.

Reflections ...

TODAY I AM GRATEFUL FOR ... _____

_____
_____
_____
_____
_____

April 19
1 Corinthians 15:12–22

Paul, in his wisdom, powerfully reminds us of the living hope we have through the resurrection of the dead in Jesus Christ. The resurrection isn't just a distant promise for the future; it is a present reality that empowers us with victory over death and the assurance of eternal life. As we read these verses, we're called to live boldly with hope, knowing that our faith is anchored in the triumph Christ has already secured on our behalf.

To celebrate this incredible gift, it's fun to brighten someone's day by sharing a resource that has inspired you? Whether it's a book, sermon, reading, or a meaningful quotation, it's a beautiful way to spread the joy and hope of the resurrection. Often my friends share a quick note over Facebook Messenger. This often starts a good conversation about some aspect of our faith journey, and usually a few smiles to boot!

Reflections ...

TODAY I AM GRATEFUL FOR ... _____

_____
_____
_____
_____
_____

COLOSSIANS 3:1–4

In Colossians, Paul encourages us to set our hearts and minds on things above, where Christ is, rather than being focused on earthly things. As we embrace the newness of life in Christ, we're reminded to seek what is eternal and live in the joy of God's presence. This passage invites us to lift our hearts to God, not just in thought, but in action, as we endeavour to echo His love through every part of our lives.

Taking care of our body is important, too. I love classes that mix God's message with fitness or fun. Whether you're stretching, dancing, or just enjoying the rhythm of the movement, it's a wonderful way to honour God by looking after your body while keeping your mind focused on the joy He offers!

Reflections ...

TODAY I AM GRATEFUL FOR ... _____

_____
_____
_____
_____
_____
_____
_____

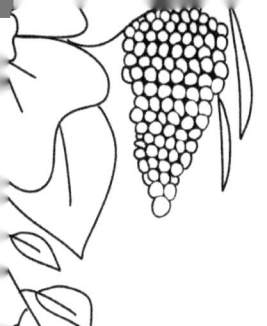

April 21
LUKE 16:1–15

Jesus often used parables to teach big spiritual truths in relatable, everyday ways—and Luke 16 is no exception. This unique passage invites us to think deeply about how we use what we've been given. While it can feel like a tricky story at first, it ultimately reminds us that God values faithful hearts, generous spirits, and wise stewardship. How do you feel Luke, a physician and close companion of Paul, highlights Jesus's teachings about compassion, justice, and integrity—especially when it comes to how we care for others and handle what's entrusted to us?

Let's turn today into a joyful celebration! Choose a quirky national day—maybe it's National Ice Cream Day, Pizza Day, or even Wear Your Favourite Colour Day—and go all in! Invite friends or family to join in, whether in person or virtually, and share some laughs and sweet treats. Aren't these light-hearted moments beautiful ways to live out Christ's joy and love in community?

Reflections ...

TODAY I AM GRATEFUL FOR ... _____

_____

_____

_____

April 22
Earth Day

1 John 2:1–17

John's words are like a warm hug of encouragement. He reminds us that even when we stumble, Jesus is our advocate and guide. In this passage, we're called to live in the light by following God's commands, especially the command to love. What's so beautiful is the reminder that love isn't just a feeling—it's how we live, treat others, and care for what God has made.

I love to celebrate—as in, let me loose and I would throw a party every day of the year! And celebrating Earth Day is a good one. By caring for God's creation, you can bring your community together! If your church has adopted a road (like ours has!), gather a group to do a spring clean-up. It's a joyful, hands-on way to display God's love and stewardship while enjoying the beauty of nature and the fellowship of others. Don't forget to laugh, snap a group photo, and maybe even finish with a warm cup of coffee or cocoa!

Reflections ...

TODAY I AM GRATEFUL FOR ... _____

_____
_____
_____
_____
_____

April 23

1 THESSALONIANS 1:1–5

Paul's opening words in 1 Thessalonians are filled with warmth, gratitude, and encouragement. He reminds the believers that their faith, love, and hope are not just noticed—but deeply cherished. Isn't it heartening to know that our efforts to live out our faith can inspire and encourage others?

Isn't this a gorgeous time of year? Getting outside for a springtime stroll might seem like a small thing, but as Paul has shown us, the smallest acts can have the biggest impact. These gentle hints of spring are reminders of God's renewal all around us.

Reflections ...

TODAY I AM GRATEFUL FOR ... _____

_____
_____
_____
_____
_____
_____
_____

April 24
PSALM 118

God's unwavering goodness and faithfulness are constants in our lives, no matter the circumstances. In times of joy and difficulty, we're reminded that the Lord is our refuge and strength, providing us with hope and peace. His love encourages us to celebrate life with gratitude and trust, knowing that He is always with us.

One of my favourite verses from Psalm 118 is, "This is the day that the Lord has made; let us rejoice and be glad in it" (Psalm 118:24, ESV), reminding us to find joy in each day and appreciate God's creation. "This is the Day" is one of my favourite songs from my childhood. What's one of your favourite childhood songs?

Reflections ...

TODAY I AM GRATEFUL FOR ... _____

_____
_____
_____
_____
_____
_____

April 25
ACTS 13:30–37

How beautiful is this truth: *"But God raised Him from the dead."* In Acts 13:30–37, Paul reminds us of the unshakable hope we have in the resurrection of Jesus. This passage is a celebration of God's power over death and His faithfulness to fulfill every promise. As we journey through Easter and Lent, it's the perfect time to reflect on the life that comes through Christ—life, freedom, and joy that no grave can hold back!

I was lucky to have gone to a great church camp during my summers. They still have the most beautiful outdoor chapel down by the lake. Paul always seems to hit home for me, and the sign at the entrance to the camp says "Welcome Home." We attend their Family Camp, and now is the time to book those spots. Whether it's a church camp or just a camp camp, I hope you too can find time as the warmer weather approaches to soak in not only the sun but also the Word of God.

Reflections ...

TODAY I AM GRATEFUL FOR … _____

_____
_____
_____
_____
_____

April 26
Ezekiel 37:1–14

What an incredible image—dry bones coming to life! In Ezekiel 37:1–14, God shows us His power to restore and renew, even in the most hopeless situations. This passage reminds us that no matter how dry or weary our hearts may feel, God can breathe life into us. His Spirit brings healing, revival, and hope, turning what once seemed lost into something beautifully alive again. Now *that's* worth celebrating this season!

I am blessed to have many friends who love to hike, and taking a prayer walk with a friend is a great way to experience God's presence in nature. Begin with a short prayer, then walk and discuss God's love and guidance as you enjoy the beauty of the world around you. It's a peaceful way to connect with Him and each other while soaking up the wonders He's created!

Reflections ...

TODAY I AM GRATEFUL FOR ... _____

April 27
Matthew 28:1–10

Matthew 28:1–10 tells the beautiful story of the moment when the women discovered that Jesus had been resurrected—an event that changed the world forever! Just as the angels declared, *"He is not here; he has risen,"* we are reminded that in Christ, death has been defeated, and hope is renewed. What feelings does the resurrection stir in you? His resurrection brings joy, peace, and the promise of eternal life, and this hope is something we can carry with us each day, shining brightly in the way we live and love.

I'm lucky in that my work colleagues are pretty close. They are quick to offer a helping hand with a task, give words of encouragement, or surprise someone with a small treat. When you do this, you share Christ's love and kindness in the workplace. Let your actions be a simple reminder of God's love for all!

Reflections ...

TODAY I AM GRATEFUL FOR ... _____

_____
_____
_____
_____
_____

REVELATION 21:1–5

Revelation 21:1–5 brings a beautiful promise from God, reminding us that one day, He will make all things new. In this passage, we see a vision of a world without pain, tears, or suffering, where God's presence is our comfort and joy forever. This hope for restoration can give us peace in our hearts, knowing that no matter what challenges we face, God is always working toward something better for us.

When was the last time you took a moment to relax and recharge? I need to prioritize this myself. Well, how about we both plan a family movie night? Just like a warm reminder of the comfort and grace God offers us, put on one of your favourite films (likely a super hero movie for me), snuggle up with a blanket, and let the joy and peace of the evening refresh your spirit. And don't forget the popcorn—sometimes, it's the simple things that are the biggest blessings!

Reflections ...

TODAY I AM GRATEFUL FOR ... _____

_____
_____
_____
_____

April 29
LUKE 24:1–12

In Luke 24:1–12, we read the incredible story of the women discovering that Jesus has risen from the dead. Their hearts were filled with awe and joy, and their lives were forever changed by the miraculous event. Jesus's resurrection brings hope and renewal to us all—just as spring brings new beginnings.

Who's up for trying a new spring recipe? I really enjoy cooking with fresh, seasonal ingredients like strawberries, peaches, or rhubarb, and whip up a delicious treat. Sharing it with a friend or family member can be a small yet meaningful way to show them God's love and generosity, just as the women joyfully shared the good news of Jesus's resurrection.

Reflections ...

TODAY I AM GRATEFUL FOR ... _____

_____
_____
_____
_____
_____
_____

JOYOUS FAITH

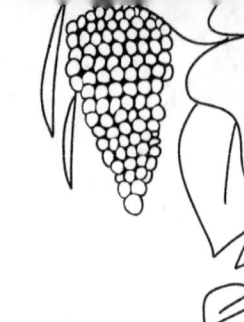

LUKE 24:44–53

In Luke 24:44–53, we read Jesus's final words to His disciples, reminding them of the Scriptures and the mission He was entrusting to them. His resurrection opens our minds to the truth of God's plan, and through the Holy Spirit, we're empowered to share His love and grace with the world. Jesus's words fill us with joy and purpose as we walk in His truth, knowing that we are part of His grand plan.

Taking care of yourself and the body God gave you honours that gift. A pedicure is a simple way to refresh and recharge, allowing you to pause and enjoy a moment of peace in His presence. I am plagued by ticklish feet syndrome; however, my mother swears that a pedicure can be relaxing. Maybe pamper yourself and take a moment to thank God for His love and care in every area of your life.

Reflections ...

TODAY I AM GRATEFUL FOR ... _____

_____
_____
_____
_____
_____
_____

May 1
ACTS 19:11–20

In this powerful reading, we see God's miracles unfold through Paul, showcasing His incredible strength and the profound impact of true faith. However, it also serves as a warning against the misuse of Jesus's name, reminding us of the importance of authenticity in our relationship with God. Let's consider how we honour His power in our lives and ensure that our faith is genuine, rooted in love and respect for His divine authority. This call to authenticity encourages us to live out our faith in meaningful ways so others can witness the transformative power of God in us.

With Mother's Day approaching, I am often reminded of the many wonderful women in my life. Sending them a card or note is a thoughtful way to celebrate the important women who have shaped you and to share God's love through your words. Whether it's a simple note or a heartfelt letter, your words can bring joy and encouragement!

Reflections ...

TODAY I AM GRATEFUL FOR ... _____

_____
_____
_____
_____
_____

May 2
1 PETER 4:1–11

First Peter 4:1–11 teaches us that living with love and serving others is a core part of our calling as followers of Christ. Peter encourages us to use our gifts to help and encourage one another, demonstrating kindness and generosity through every action. Whether it's through hospitality, prayer, or just loving those around us, we're reminded to display God's grace in everything we do, especially in times of challenge.

To put this into practice, why not offer to cut your neighbour's lawn? Now, our neighbour's lawn is perfect; however, everyone gets busy, and this can be a simple way to show kindness and serve those around you. Acts of service like this help build a sense of community and allow us to share God's love in tangible ways. Your small act of love could make a big impact!

Reflections ...

TODAY I AM GRATEFUL FOR ... _____

_____
_____
_____
_____
_____
_____

May 3
1 Peter 2:4–10

As believers, we're called to be living stones, carefully built into a spiritual house by God's amazing grace. Jesus is the cornerstone, the foundation that holds everything together, and through Him, we are a chosen people, set apart to proclaim His greatness. What a gift to know that we are deeply loved and have a purpose in His plan. Can you share that gift with someone today?

To celebrate the beauty of family traditions and the bonds that hold us together, it's fun to gather your loved ones for a cooking lesson. Before my son went off to university, I decided it was time to teach him a few family staples—some cherished family recipes that have been passed down through the generations, and I shared the stories behind each dish. For us, spending time in the kitchen is a time to connect and unwind.

Reflections ...

TODAY I AM GRATEFUL FOR ... _____

_____
_____
_____
_____
_____

May 4
2 Timothy 2:1–10

Second Timothy 2:1–10 provides a powerful reminder that the journey of faith requires both spiritual and physical strength. Paul encourages Timothy to be strong in grace and to endure hardship like a soldier of Christ. This passage challenges us to cultivate both our inner faith and the outer strength needed to fulfill God's calling.

Being outdoors allows me to unwind. There are some great spiritual podcasts I have lined up to enjoy while walking outside. Have you ever considered how you can build spiritual and physical endurance, strengthening your relationship with God and preparing yourself to serve Him even more? Consider it your moment to nurture both body and soul!

Reflections ...

TODAY I AM GRATEFUL FOR ... _____

_____
_____
_____
_____
_____

May 5
JAMES 2:1–13

James 2:1–13 challenges us to show no favouritism, reminding us that God calls us to love and treat everyone equally, regardless of their status or appearance. This passage highlights the importance of kindness, mercy, and compassion in our interactions with others, echoing the love God shows us. Consider how this passage calls us to embrace others with grace, offering hospitality and acceptance to all, as we seek to live out our faith in practical, loving ways.

I love herbal teas. In fact, I have a whole drawer in our kitchen organized with hibiscus and chamomile teas. But that's just the tip of the iceberg. It's nice to take a moment to sip and reflect on how you can be more inclusive and show kindness to everyone you encounter. Just like exploring new flavours, let your actions show the love and mercy God extends to us all—one cup of kindness at a time!

Reflections ...

TODAY I AM GRATEFUL FOR ... _____

May 6
Matthew 5:14–16

We are invited to be *"the salt of the earth"* and *"the light of the world"*—powerful metaphors that describe our role in making a positive impact. Just as salt enhances flavour, and light dispels darkness, we're called to be a source of positive influence, spreading God's love and truth in our daily lives. How can you embody these qualities in your interactions with others so that you can make a difference by living out your faith with authenticity, joy, and grace?

Have you made time to get to know your minister better? Whether it's through a coffee chat or simply a kind conversation, you can encourage them in their role and be reminded of how God uses the people around us to bless and strengthen our faith. It's a beautiful way to live out the love and grace God shows us each day!

Reflections ...

TODAY I AM GRATEFUL FOR ...

May 7
LUKE 5:1–11

Today's reading invites us to step into the moment when Jesus called His disciples to leave everything behind and follow Him. It's a powerful reminder that Jesus sees us right where we are and calls us into something bigger and more beautiful than we could ever imagine. Just as He called the disciples to trust Him and step out in faith, how are you embracing the call and adventure of following Him?

This week, take a moment to remind someone of their worth in Christ. A simple, thoughtful word or a small act of kindness can go a long way in showing others that they are chosen and precious to God. You are part of His beautiful work—spread His love, and let others feel His grace and joy through you!

Reflections ...

TODAY I AM GRATEFUL FOR ... _____

_____
_____
_____
_____
_____
_____

May 8
Hebrews 10:19–25

What an inspiring reminder that we are invited into the presence of God with confidence and boldness because of the incredible grace of Jesus! We no longer need to approach God with fear or hesitation, but with hearts full of gratitude, knowing that we have His love and support. And, as the verse encourages, we're meant to encourage and spur each other on in faith, love, and good deeds. Ask yourself how you will encourage others this week.

Spring planting season is drawing closer. I'm filled with the excitement of adding new raised vegetable beds to our lawn. Let's consider how the process mirrors God's work in us. Just as we plant seeds and care for them, trusting they'll grow into something beautiful, we can trust that God is cultivating something beautiful in our lives as well. I love how spending time in the garden reminds me that God is near.

Reflections ...

TODAY I AM GRATEFUL FOR ... _____

_____
_____
_____
_____
_____

May 9
PHILIPPIANS 2:1–4

In today's verses, Paul lovingly calls us to embrace unity and humility within our community of faith. This passage teaches that our relationships with one another should be marked by kindness and selflessness, echoing the heart of Christ. As we reflect on these beautiful values, let's consider how we can actively support and uplift each other, fostering a spirit of togetherness that displays God's love in our lives.

As Mother's Day approaches, I like to order flowers or a corsage for my mom and mother-in-law, or someone who's had a special influence on my life. Simple acts of love echo the care and comfort Jesus offers us. Can you take a moment to brighten someone's day? It just might remind them of God's love and peace.

Reflections ...

TODAY I AM GRATEFUL FOR ... _____

_____
_____
_____
_____
_____
_____

May 10
1 Corinthians 13:4–7

Love is truly the foundation of everything we do. In this passage, we're reminded that love is patient, kind, and unselfish. It doesn't boast or envy, but rather uplifts and encourages. When we choose to love, we display God's love and create a space where others feel valued and cared for. This love is the heart of our relationships, and through it, we can bring light and hope to the world around us.

One of the simplest things that brings me happiness is grabbing some sidewalk chalk to leave a cheerful, encouraging message for my neighbours to see. Whether it's a simple "You are loved!" or a verse that brings hope, this small act can brighten someone's day. It's a fun and creative way to share love and positivity with those around you.

Reflections ...

TODAY I AM GRATEFUL FOR ... _____

_____
_____
_____
_____
_____
_____

May 11
1 Thessalonians 1:1–10

First Thessalonians 1:1–10 is a beautiful opening to Paul's letter to the Church in Thessalonica, offering a heartfelt reflection on their faith and perseverance. Paul highlights their work of faith, labour of love, and steadfastness of hope in Jesus Christ. This not only demonstrates the deep impact of the Thessalonian believers' faith, but also serves as a model for how we can live out our own faith—actively, lovingly, and with steadfast hope, even in times of struggle.

"I Will Follow" by Chris Tomlin is a wonderful song that resonates with the themes of living out our faith and following Christ, just as the Thessalonians did. It can serve as a great musical example of this passage, reminding us to continue in our walk with God, inspired by faith, love, and hope. If you haven't heard it, I encourage you to check it out.

Reflections ...

TODAY I AM GRATEFUL FOR ... _____

_____
_____
_____
_____
_____
_____

May 12
1 Thessalonians 2:1–12

In today's reading, Paul shares his approach to sharing the gospel, which was filled with love, care, and tenderness—like the love a mother shows for her children. He nurtured the Thessalonians, encouraging them with patience and kindness. This passage reminds us that as we share our faith, we're also called to build loving, supportive relationships that help others grow in their own journeys, just as Paul did for the early church.

Recently one of my girlfriends gave birth, and it brought back so many memories. Today is the perfect day to reach out to a new mother who might need some encouragement or support. A simple message, a phone call, or offering a helping hand can mean the world to someone navigating the beautiful but challenging journey of motherhood. It might be just what she needs, and it's a beautiful way to echo the love and nurturing spirit of Christ in someone's life.

Reflections ...

TODAY I AM GRATEFUL FOR ... _____

_____
_____
_____
_____

May 13
1 Thessalonians 2:13–20

First Thessalonians 2:13–20 offers a powerful reminder of the importance of perseverance and faith, especially in times of difficulty. Paul expresses profound gratitude for the Thessalonians' acceptance of God's Word, despite facing opposition. This passage calls us to hold fast to the truth of the gospel, just as the Thessalonian church did, and to support one another in our journeys of faith. The love and care Paul showed for this community displayed the beauty of living in harmony, united in truth and purpose. And isn't that what we're all called to do?

Reach out to someone in your church community with a kind word or a prayer. Maybe there's someone who's been quietly struggling or simply needs a reminder of God's love and strength. Just like Paul's letter to the Thessalonians, your simple act of encouragement can lift their spirits and help strengthen the bond of faith between you. Let's build each other up with love and prayer.

Reflections ...

TODAY I AM GRATEFUL FOR ... _____

_____
_____
_____
_____

May 14
1 Thessalonians 4:1–12

In 1 Thessalonians 4:1–12, Paul calls us to live lives that honour God by focusing on loving one another and mirroring our faith in every action. Paul reminds us that our daily interactions—the way we treat others—are a powerful testimony to the world of God's love and grace. When we live with holiness and integrity, we not only grow closer to God, but we also invite His peace and joy into our hearts. It's humbling to know that our choices, big or small, can show God's love and bring us into deeper communion with Him.

Make time to intentionally show love to someone in your life. Whether it's through a kind word, a thoughtful gesture, or simply lending a hand, make it a point to display God's love in your actions. Let this be a reminder that we are called to live out our faith every day—through love, kindness, and integrity. You never know how your small act can make a big difference in someone's life!

Reflections ...

TODAY I AM GRATEFUL FOR ... _____

_____
_____
_____
_____
_____

May 15
JOHN 15:26–27

Jesus tells us in today's reading that the Holy Spirit will testify about Him, helping us bear witness to the truth. This reminds us of the power of remembering and sharing the stories of the past—both in faith and history. How has your past shaped who you are? Our past can be heavy, but you can lay down your burdens and move forward with the Holy Spirit.

Please tell me that I'm not the only one who loves to visit a museum or historical site. Could understanding your past help you appreciate God's faithfulness throughout history and inspires you to share His story with others? And it's fun too!

Reflections ...

TODAY I AM GRATEFUL FOR ... _____

_____
_____
_____
_____
_____
_____

May 16
John 16:5–15

Today's passage reminds us of the incredible gift of the Holy Spirit, our Helper, who guides us into all truth and helps us remember Jesus's teachings. The Spirit works within us, empowering us to live out God's love and wisdom. It's comforting to know that we're never alone in our journey—God's Spirit is always there—leading, comforting, and encouraging us every step of the way.

This week, take a moment to send a heartfelt thank you note to someone who has helped or inspired you. Whether it's a friend, family member, or mentor, expressing your gratitude not only brightens their day but also mirrors the encouragement and love we receive from the Holy Spirit.

Reflections ...

TODAY I AM GRATEFUL FOR ... _____

_____
_____
_____
_____
_____
_____

May 17
ACTS 1:15–17, 21–26

In this pivotal moment, the disciples, led by Peter, face the important task of replacing Judas. Their commitment to God's plan and the importance of community in fulfilling Scripture shine through as they gather to make this decision. Choosing Matthias after prayer and seeking divine guidance teaches us about the power of relying on God in our choices. And as they await the Holy Spirit at Pentecost, their unity and faithfulness serve as an inspiring example for us today.

To cultivate a sense of peace and purpose each day, consider establishing a consistent morning routine. This simple practice can set a positive tone for the day ahead. You might start with a moment of prayer, followed by activities that nourish your body and spirit, like enjoying a healthy breakfast or taking a few minutes to read Scripture. Just as the disciples relied on prayer, could this routine be a time to centre yourself and invite God's guidance into your daily life?

Reflections ...

TODAY I AM GRATEFUL FOR ... _____

_____
_____
_____
_____
_____

May 18
Hebrews 1:1–14

What an awe-inspiring reminder this passage offers! Hebrews begins by lifting our hearts and eyes to Jesus, declaring Him not only as the Son of God but as the radiance of God's glory and the exact representation of His being. It's beautifully humbling to know that the same Jesus who holds all things together also lovingly holds *us*—walking with us, guiding us, and shining His light into our lives. Through Him, we see the fullness of God's love, power, and purpose.

Let this majestic picture of Christ inspire you to soak in the wonder of creation. Start planning some hikes or outdoor adventures—maybe even pick up a guidebook with local trails. We've added "hike the full Bruce Trail" to our bucket list. How about you? Now's the perfect time to get outside, breathe in that fresh air, and contemplate the beauty and majesty of the One who created it all!

Reflections ...

TODAY I AM GRATEFUL FOR ... _____

_____
_____
_____
_____
_____

May 19
HEBREWS 2:1–18

Isn't it amazing to know that Jesus chose to step into our humanity—not from a distance, but right into the heart of our experience? These verses remind us that Jesus became like us so that He could fully understand us, walk with us through our pain, and ultimately free us from fear and sin. He is not a distant Saviour, but a compassionate and present one. What a comfort to know we're never alone—He's always near, offering hope, help, and grace.

There are few things I love more than catching up with friends over a cup of coffee. As you chat, share how your faith has shaped or comforted you—you never know how your story might speak to someone else's heart. It doesn't have to be formal—just honest, kind, and real. God works powerfully through simple conversations, and this could be just the encouragement someone needs!

Reflections ...

TODAY I AM GRATEFUL FOR ... _____

_____

_____

_____

_____

May 20
Hebrews 3:7–19

Hebrews 3:7–19 encourages us to be mindful of our hearts and to remain open to God's voice. The Israelites' experience in the wilderness serves as a warning against hardening our hearts when faced with challenges or doubts. God invites us to listen to Him with a soft heart, trusting that He is leading us toward peace and hope.

A lovely way to put this verse into action is by doing something special for someone you care about. Truly listen to them, find out what they love, and surprise them with something thoughtful. Whether it's a small gift, a kind word, or just a moment of your time, this act of love will brighten their day and show them how much they mean to you.

Reflections ...

TODAY I AM GRATEFUL FOR ... _____

_____
_____
_____
_____
_____
_____

May 21
Hebrews 4:1–16

Today we can approach God with confidence, knowing He offers us grace and mercy in our times of need. It encourages us to rest in His promises and trust that He understands us fully, offering perfect help and comfort. Jesus, our great High Priest, invites us to bring our struggles to Him, knowing that He deeply cares for us and will give us peace.

To show appreciation for your minister and all they do, consider surprising them with a kind word or thoughtful gesture. A simple note expressing your gratitude or a warm conversation can mean the world to them. By taking this small step, you not only uplift your minister, but you foster a supportive and loving community. Let's remind our leaders that their hard work and dedication truly make a difference in our lives and in the life of the church!

Reflections ...

TODAY I AM GRATEFUL FOR ... _____

_____
_____
_____
_____
_____

May 22
HEBREWS 5:1–14

Have you ever wondered what it truly means to grow in faith? This passage highlights that Jesus understands our struggles. Just like how we grow in wisdom and knowledge over time, we are called to deepen our understanding of God, learning from Jesus's example of obedience and compassion. Spiritual growth takes patience, and as we trust in Him, we are continually shaped and refined.

This week, set aside time to learn about something that truly interests you. Whether it's reading a new book (I love biblically-based fiction), exploring a topic online, or even taking a class, allow your curiosity to drive you toward deeper understanding. By seeking wisdom in the areas that spark your interest, you could grow closer to the heart of God, who delights in our desire to learn and grow.

Reflections ...

TODAY I AM GRATEFUL FOR ... _____

_____
_____
_____
_____
_____
_____

May 23
Hebrews 6:1–20

There's such a comforting beauty in this passage. God's promises are described as an anchor for the soul. That image reminds us that no matter how uncertain or stormy life may feel, God's love holds us steady. He is faithful, unchanging, and deeply invested in our journey. This kind of hope isn't wishful thinking—it's a confident trust in the One who never breaks His promises. And doesn't that fill your heart with peace?

Crank up some uplifting Christian music today. Whether you're driving, cleaning, or just need a little mood boost, tuning into your favourite Christian rock or worship playlist can be a fun and faith-filled way to connect with God's hope. Let the lyrics fill your heart with joy and remind you of the firm foundation you have in Him!

Reflections ...

TODAY I AM GRATEFUL FOR ... _____

_____
_____
_____
_____
_____

May 24
Hebrews 7:1–28

Hebrews 7 highlights the greatness of Jesus, someone who stands in perfect relationship with God on our behalf. Unlike the priests of the Old Testament, who needed to offer sacrifices over and over, Jesus's sacrifice is eternal, giving us a way to confidently approach God. When did you last thank Him for His righteousness and grace, which are the foundation of our salvation, allowing us to rest in His unending love and mercy?

Confession time: I am a random-acts-of-kindness junkie—dropping off some cookies at the local firehall, or muffins at the works department. These simple gestures show appreciation for those who serve. And the looks on their faces—priceless! It's a beautiful way to share God's love and bring a little joy to others!

Reflections ...

TODAY I AM GRATEFUL FOR ... _____

May 25
ACTS 2:1-21

What an incredible scene—wind rushing in, tongues of fire, and voices lifted in every language! This moment isn't just dramatic—it's deeply personal. It reminds us that the Holy Spirit is alive and active, filling each of us with boldness, guidance, and purpose. Just like the disciples, we're invited to step into the world with confidence, knowing that God's Spirit is with us, equipping us to share love, truth, and hope in powerful ways. Isn't it amazing to think that you are part of that story too?

Add a little joy to your garden this week by placing a bird bath outside! You could even grab a bird-watching book or app and see how many different species visit. It's a peaceful and playful way to connect with God's creation—and a lovely reminder of the beauty and life His Spirit brings!

Reflections ...

TODAY I AM GRATEFUL FOR ... _____

_____
_____
_____
_____
_____

May 26
JOHN 14:15–21

Through our reading today, Jesus promises to send the Holy Spirit to be with us, guiding and comforting us as we live out our calling to love and serve others. He assures us that if we love Him and follow His commands, we will experience His presence and peace. How amazing is this deep connection we have with God. He continuously nurtures and strengthens us through the Holy Spirit. But what does He ask from us in return?

To connect with nature and this calling, consider setting up a bird feeder in your yard or balcony. A family down the road from us has placed the cutest bird feeder/craft project in their front tree. Watching the different bird species that visit can bring a sense of peace and connection to God's creation, reminding you of His presence in all things. It's a simple yet meaningful way to nurture both your spirit and your surroundings!

Reflections ...

TODAY I AM GRATEFUL FOR ... _____

_____
_____
_____
_____
_____

May 27
2 Corinthians 4:7–10

Paul reminds us that though we may face difficulties, we carry the priceless treasure of God's light and grace within us. Our struggles do not define us; rather, it's the power of God working through our weaknesses that shines most brightly. Just as clay jars are delicate yet carry valuable contents, we too may feel worn, but we hold within us the love and strength of Christ, which sustains us through all things.

As we get into the rhythm of May, take time to thank those who work at the church—whether it's the janitor, the minister, or anyone who serves behind the scenes. These individuals often go unnoticed, yet they play an essential role in keeping the church running smoothly. Is there a way you can recognize and uplift those who carry the work of the church with grace and dedication?

Reflections ...

TODAY I AM GRATEFUL FOR ... _____

_____
_____
_____
_____
_____

May 28
JAMES 2:14–26

Faith is more than just words—it's something we live out through our actions, big or small. James reminds us that genuine faith shows up in the ways we care for others, love generously, and bring hope into everyday life. It's not always about grand gestures—often, it's the little things done with love that reveal a heart aligned with God's grace. Isn't it amazing how our everyday choices can become expressions of faith?

Refresh your front step or door with a cheerful new doormat! After a long winter, it's the perfect time to give your entrance a little pick-me-up. Choose one with a message like "God Bless" or "Bless This Home"—something that brings a smile to your face and welcomes others with a gentle reminder of God's love.

Reflections ...

TODAY I AM GRATEFUL FOR ... _____

_____
_____
_____
_____
_____

May 29
ROMANS 1:1-7

This reading is a blessed reminder of the grace we've received in Christ and the calling to share that grace with others. Paul speaks of being set apart for God's purpose, and we, too, are called to live out our faith with intention, spreading the message of Jesus's love. How will you embrace your identity and shine His light in the world?

Make time to consider your unique calling in Christ. How can you share His love with those around you? Whether through a simple act of kindness or an encouraging word, remember that you're part of something bigger. Let your actions today reflect the love and grace God has shown you!

Reflections ...

TODAY I AM GRATEFUL FOR ... _____

_____
_____
_____
_____
_____
_____

May 30
1 Corinthians 12:1–13

In today's reading, Paul beautifully highlights the diversity of spiritual gifts and their vital role in building up the Church. Each of us has been uniquely blessed with gifts that contribute to the unity and growth of our faith community. This passage reminds us that every gift, no matter how small, plays a significant part in God's work. Let's celebrate our individual contributions and embrace the wonderful ways we can support one another in love and service.

Take a moment today to pray for peace, both within yourself and in the world around you. Pray for peace in your relationships, your community, and the world, asking God to fill your heart with His calming presence. Let His peace guide your actions and bring healing to those who need it most.

Reflections ...

TODAY I AM GRATEFUL FOR ... _____

_____
_____
_____
_____
_____
_____

May 31
2 Corinthians 13:14

Today we celebrate the profound mystery of God as Father, Son, and Holy Spirit. Paul's blessing reminds us of the grace of Jesus, the love of God, and the fellowship of the Holy Spirit, inviting us into a deep and eternal relationship. This beautiful unity of the Trinity reflects how we, too, are called to live in unity and love with one another.

Contemplate the unity and love of the Trinity in your own life. You might pray a simple prayer of gratitude. Praying can seem intimidating, but you can start small: "God, help me live with a grateful heart. Guide me through my day." As you pray, consider how you can invite more of this divine unity and love into your daily life and relationships.

Reflections ...

Today I am grateful for ... _____

_____
_____
_____
_____
_____
_____

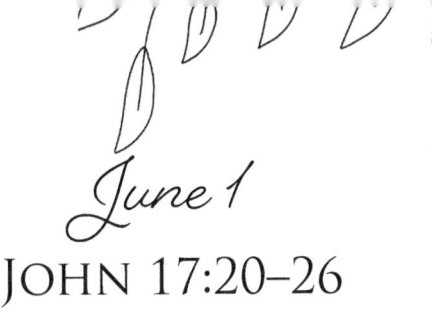

June 1
JOHN 17:20–26

Jesus prays for unity among His followers, asking that we may all be one, just as He and the Father are one. He desires for us to experience the same love and fellowship that He shares with the Father, echoing that unity in our relationships with one another. We're called to work together in love and harmony. How can you share the good news today?

Who loves moving for a good cause? I do! Participating in or organizing a charity walk or run to support a cause close to your heart combines physical activity with community service is a fantastic way to give back and make a difference. On my bucket list is organizing a fun walk with our church. How can you help to celebrate, connect with others, and work together as a community to impact the world around us?

Reflections ...

TODAY I AM GRATEFUL FOR ... _____

_____
_____
_____
_____
_____

June 2
1 Peter 1:1–9

Peter reminds us that even during trials, our faith is more precious than gold, and it's through our hope in Christ that we find true joy and peace. This passage calls us to live with integrity, hold tight to our salvation, and trust in Jesus. It challenges us to consider how we live out our faith, including our responsibility to care for God's creation.

As I am writing this, I'm getting ready for a women's weekend with our church. Retreats like these allow me to focus on my connection to God, and also help foster those meaningful relationships within the church family. If you haven't gone on a retreat before, you might want to look into it. There is such a variety of retreats available. Or create your own retreat! Invite friends to stay overnight. (Each friend can come prepped with their favourite Bible verse.)

Reflections ...

TODAY I AM GRATEFUL FOR ... _____

_____
_____
_____
_____
_____
_____

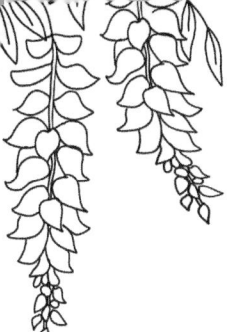

June 3
ROMANS 8:18, 26–27

Paul reminds us that our present sufferings are nothing compared to the glory that awaits us. The Holy Spirit plays a vital role in our lives, offering hope and encouragement as we navigate life's challenges. This passage assures us that even in moments of uncertainty, the Spirit intercedes for us, guiding our prayers and lifting our burdens. As we await Christ's return, we can trust in knowing that God is working all things together for our good, filling our hearts with a profound sense of hope.

Gather your family or friends and some colourful sidewalk chalk to create beautiful murals or drawings in your driveway. As you draw, consider writing messages of God's love and promises, perhaps incorporating verses or uplifting phrases that inspire you. This activity not only allows for artistic expression but also serves as a vibrant witness to your neighbours and passers-by, spreading joy and reminders of God's goodness in the world. Let your chalk art be a testament to the hope and encouragement you find in the Spirit!

Reflections ...

TODAY I AM GRATEFUL FOR ... _____

_____
_____
_____

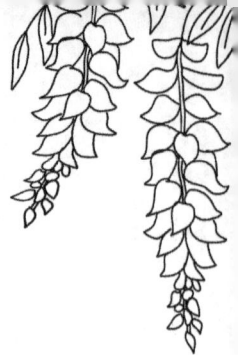

June 4
ACTS 19:1–10

In this beautiful passage, we witness Paul's incredible ministry in Ephesus, where the gospel takes root and transforms lives in profound ways. It's a powerful reminder of how God's message can bring about change not just in individuals but in entire communities—we just need faith and trust in God. Let's consider how we too can share the joy and hope of the gospel with those around us, creating ripples of positivity in our neighbourhoods. Just as the early church flourished through love and faith, we can be vessels of God's love today!

To celebrate this spirit of openness and connection, why not gather your loved ones for a walk under the moonlight? This is on my bucket list as well! A peaceful walk at night offers a beautiful opportunity to connect with each other in a meaningful way. It's a simple, yet profound, way to enjoy God's creation. Don't you think?

Reflections ...

TODAY I AM GRATEFUL FOR ... _____

_____
_____
_____
_____
_____

June 5
WORLD ENVIRONMENT DAY

PSALM 33:12–22

Psalm 33:12–22 reminds us that we are blessed when we trust in the Lord, who is faithful and full of love. His eyes are on those whose hope is in Him, and His promises are steadfast. We can take great joy knowing that God is always watching over us and working on our behalf, no matter the circumstances.

For World Environment Day, take time to contemplate how we, as stewards of God's creation, can care for the earth. Whether it's planting a garden, reducing waste, or simply taking a moment to appreciate nature, every action that honours the planet is a way to honour God. Would you consider organizing or joining an environmental initiative?

Reflections ...

TODAY I AM GRATEFUL FOR ... _____

_____
_____
_____
_____
_____
_____
_____

June 6
1 Peter 3:13–22

Peter encourages us to maintain hope and faith even in the face of suffering, reminding us that Christ, who suffered for us, provides the ultimate example of perseverance and trust in God. This passage challenges us to live boldly for Christ, with a heart full of love and a clear conscience, trusting that God will always guide and protect us, even through trials.

To help maintain your faith during difficult times, consider cultivating habits that draw you closer to God. I recently read a great book, *Pray Bold* by Joel Osteen, which encourages believers to pray with confidence and trust in God's power. Setting aside daily time for prayer can help you centre yourself in God's promises, drawing strength from His Word.

Reflections ...

TODAY I AM GRATEFUL FOR ... _____

_____
_____
_____
_____
_____
_____
_____

June 7
NEHEMIAH 8:1–12

This passage paints a beautiful scene—God's people, gathered as one, eagerly listening to His Word and finding both conviction and joy in its truth. Their tears turn into celebration as Ezra reminds them, *"The joy of the Lord is your strength."* It's a powerful reminder that God's Word doesn't just challenge us—it uplifts, renews, and fills us with a joy that's rooted deep in His presence and promises.

Make time to centre yourself in prayer, focusing on gratitude. Find a quiet space to think of the blessings in your life, acknowledging God's love and faithfulness. As you pray, express your thanks for the people around you, the experiences that have shaped you, and the simple joys that fill your days. This intentional act of gratitude not only deepens your connection with God but also brings fresh strength and joy to your heart—just like the people of Nehemiah's day.

Reflections ...

TODAY I AM GRATEFUL FOR ... _____

_____
_____
_____
_____

June 8
WORLD OCEAN DAY

MATTHEW 6:25–34

On World Ocean Day, we're reminded of God's beautiful creation and our responsibility to care for it. In Matthew 6:25–34, Jesus teaches us not to worry about the material needs of life, reassuring us that God cares for us deeply, just as He cares for the birds of the air and the flowers of the field. By trusting in God's provision, we can live with a mindset focused on His kingdom, rather than on earthly anxieties.

By helping to protect the environment, you not only contribute to the health of our oceans, but also live out a spirit of stewardship and trust in God's provision for all His creation. To honour both the day and this teaching, you could organize a local beach or park cleanup. Our church would be all over this, I'm sure. And it's a tangible way to care for God's creation and make a difference in your community.

Reflections ...

TODAY I AM GRATEFUL FOR ... _____

_____
_____
_____
_____
_____
_____

1 Peter 5:6–10

Peter reminds us of the importance of humility and trust in God's loving care, especially during challenging times. He assures us that God is not distant or indifferent to our struggles but is actively strengthening and restoring us. This encourages us to surrender our anxieties, knowing that God is always at work in our lives, perfecting, establishing, and settling us, no matter what we face.

Set an intention for the week. By intentionally living out your faith, you can remain grounded in God's strength and experience His peace throughout the week. How can you align your daily choices with your love for God, whether it's through prioritizing time for prayer, or being mindful of how you serve others?

Reflections ...

TODAY I AM GRATEFUL FOR ... _____

_____

_____

_____

_____

_____

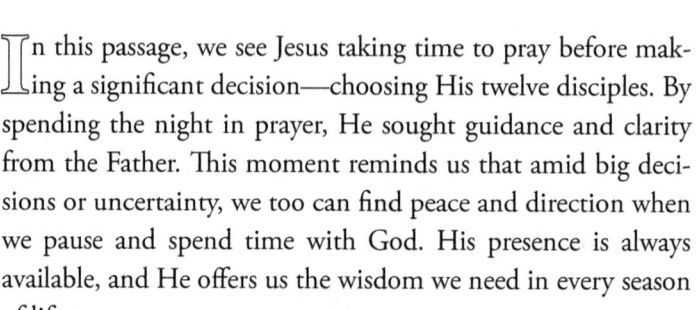

June 10
LUKE 6:12–16

In this passage, we see Jesus taking time to pray before making a significant decision—choosing His twelve disciples. By spending the night in prayer, He sought guidance and clarity from the Father. This moment reminds us that amid big decisions or uncertainty, we too can find peace and direction when we pause and spend time with God. His presence is always available, and He offers us the wisdom we need in every season of life.

Have you ever asked ask your family what their favourite ways to connect are? Maybe it's playing board games, cooking together, or sharing a walk. When we did this, the results were delightful! Try to incorporate more of those activities into your routine. It's a beautiful way to deepen your relationships and intentionally grow closer to each other while enjoying God's presence in your home!

Reflections ...

TODAY I AM GRATEFUL FOR ... _____

_____
_____
_____
_____
_____

June 11
GENESIS 12:1–4

God called Abraham to step out in faith, leaving behind the familiar to embrace the unknown. This act of obedience reminds us to strip away distractions and focus on what truly matters—our relationship with God. Just as Abraham trusted God's guidance, we're invited to trust Him in our spiritual journey.

Care for yourself, both physically and spiritually. Whether it's going for a walk, enjoying a nourishing meal, or simply resting, remember that looking after your body is an important part of your spiritual journey. As you take time to care for yourself, let it be a reminder that God cares for you deeply and wants you to feel refreshed and renewed in every way!

Reflections ...

TODAY I AM GRATEFUL FOR ... _____

_____
_____
_____
_____
_____
_____

June 12
2 Peter 1:12–21

Living faithfully and growing in the knowledge of Jesus Christ calls us to be intentional with the gifts God has entrusted to us. We're reminded to live with purpose, using our unique talents to serve others and mirror His love in tangible ways. As we seek to grow in godliness, it's important to recognize the ways in which our gifts can make a positive impact in our communities.

Why not organize a "gift-sharing" event with your family or church community? This is an opportunity for everyone to come together and share their individual talents—whether it's cooking (I would love some help), singing, crafting (I do have that wood project I could use a hand with), or any other skill. It's a wonderful way to connect with one another and demonstrate the love of Christ through your collective abilities.

Reflections ...

TODAY I AM GRATEFUL FOR ... _____

_____
_____
_____
_____
_____
_____

June 13
ESTHER 4:12–16

In this passage, Queen Esther faces a life-threatening situation but courageously chooses to act on behalf of her people, trusting God's timing and guidance. Her faith and bravery serve as a powerful example of standing up for justice, even when it's difficult or risky. This reading ties beautifully into the importance of courage, obedience, and trusting God's plan, especially when we're called to make difficult decisions or take bold actions for His glory.

Why not start planning a DIY family Olympics? I'm in! We did something similar with my husband's family, and it was such a blast! You can create simple games like sack races, bubble gum blowing competitions, three-legged races, or even a backyard obstacle course to get everyone moving, laughing, and enjoying each other's company—while also creating memories that show God's joy and love!

Reflections ...

TODAY I AM GRATEFUL FOR ... _____

_____
_____
_____
_____

June 14
2 Samuel 7:18–29

In today's passage, King David humbly responds to God's promises with a prayer of deep gratitude. He recognizes that everything he has, including his kingdom, is a gift from God. David's prayer is a reminder of God's unwavering faithfulness and how He blesses, sustains, and provides for us in ways we might not always expect. It's a call to pause and remember the ways God has been faithful in our own lives, even in the small, everyday moments.

June is a wonderful time for yard sales! Whether you're cleaning out your own home or hunting for great deals, it's a fun way to spend an afternoon. Plus, it's a chance to be good stewards of our environment by reusing items that are still perfectly good instead of sending them to the dump. It's a simple way to make a positive impact on both your home and the planet. Happy treasure hunting!

Reflections ...

TODAY I AM GRATEFUL FOR ... _____

_____
_____
_____
_____
_____

June 15
COLOSSIANS 1:13–20

Today, Paul reminds us of the incredible work Christ has done for us, delivering us from darkness and bringing us into the kingdom of light. This passage calls us to meditate on Christ's supremacy and the profound impact He has in our lives, not just spiritually, but physically as well. When we recognize Christ's greatness, we're inspired to live our lives in ways that honour Him, including caring for the bodies He has entrusted to us.

Looking for a challenge? You could take a step toward healthier living by giving up sugar for a month? This is a great way to take care of your body and feel more energized, both physically and spiritually. Our family is pretty adept at taking on wellness challenges. They can be a fun way to strengthen both your body and your faith as you honour God with your health!

Reflections ...

TODAY I AM GRATEFUL FOR ... _____

_____
_____
_____
_____

June 16
ACTS 9:1–19

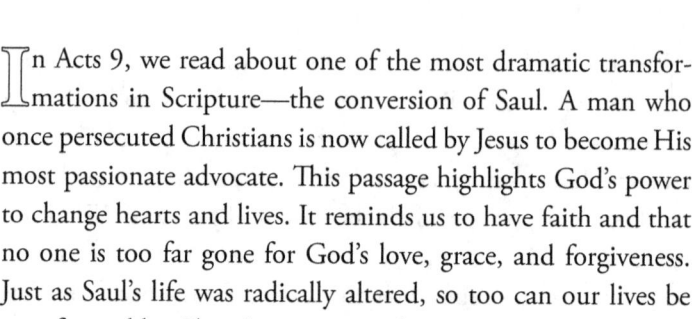

In Acts 9, we read about one of the most dramatic transformations in Scripture—the conversion of Saul. A man who once persecuted Christians is now called by Jesus to become His most passionate advocate. This passage highlights God's power to change hearts and lives. It reminds us to have faith and that no one is too far gone for God's love, grace, and forgiveness. Just as Saul's life was radically altered, so too can our lives be transformed by Christ's presence and power.

My great aunt was a missionary in India, and her dedication had a profound impact on so many lives, including mine. Take a moment today to pray for missionaries—both those you know personally and those spreading God's Word across the world. Ask God to bless and protect them as they serve, and to continue using them to bring His light to others, just as Saul's transformation turned him into one of the most powerful messengers of Christ's love.

Reflections ...

TODAY I AM GRATEFUL FOR ... _____

_____
_____
_____
_____

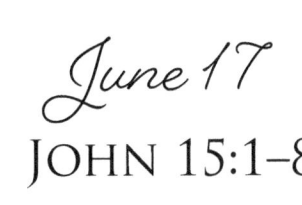

June 17
JOHN 15:1–8

In John 15:1–8, Jesus paints a beautiful picture of our relationship with Him—He is the vine, and we are the branches. Our ability to bear fruit depends on staying connected to Him and drawing strength from His life-giving presence. This passage invites us to look at how closely we are remaining to Jesus and how our lives can bear fruit for His kingdom. Just as a branch thrives when connected to the vine, we too flourish in Christ, living with purpose and fulfilling His plan for us.

I am a note-taker. So yes, that's me in the pews with my notebook, jotting down scripture and notes, and often drawing a funny face and handing it to my dad. But joking aside, there is often a passage that intrigues me during the service, and I like to take note to study it later. Am I the only one who does this? Taking time to explore God's Word helps me remain rooted in Him.

Reflections ...

TODAY I AM GRATEFUL FOR ... _____

_____
_____
_____
_____
_____

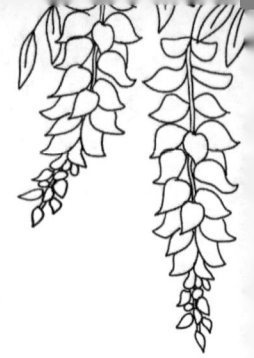

June 18
ACTS 3:12–19

The reading today invites us to consider the powerful invitation of repentance through Jesus. Peter calls the people to turn away from their wrongdoings and embrace God's forgiveness, a message that invites us to reflect on our own lives. Just as the people in this passage were called to change their hearts, we too are invited to let the Holy Spirit transform us, aligning our lives more closely with God's will.

As the school year comes to a close, let's take a moment to pray for our teachers and students, asking for a safe and joyful summer. You can send an anonymous note of encouragement to a teacher you know. I find that a simple message of appreciation can brighten their day and remind them of the profound impact they have on shaping young lives.

Reflections ...

TODAY I AM GRATEFUL FOR ... _____

_____
_____
_____
_____
_____
_____
_____

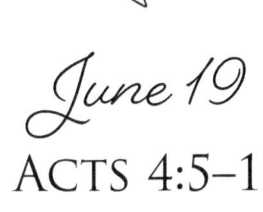

June 19
ACTS 4:5–12

Consider this reading as Peter boldly proclaims that salvation comes only through Jesus Christ, the cornerstone of our faith. Just like the early believers, we're invited to stand firm in our faith, trusting in the power of Jesus to guide and strengthen us. This verse encourages us to find confidence in His salvation and peace in His presence.

To embrace this peace, I like to practise mindfulness or meditation. Find a quiet space, focus on your breath, and let the love and strength of Jesus fill your heart. It's a gentle way to connect with His peace, and it can bring you a little calm and comfort throughout your day.

Reflections ...

TODAY I AM GRATEFUL FOR ... _____

_____
_____
_____
_____
_____
_____
_____

June 20
MATTHEW 13:23

In Matthew 13:23 of the abundant growth that comes when we nurture our faith. Just as the seed sown in good soil brings forth a fruitful harvest, when we let God's Word take root in our hearts, it transforms us and bears much fruit in our lives. This season, as nature blooms around us, let it serve as a reminder of the spiritual growth we can experience when we trust in God's love.

To celebrate this season of growth and abundance, consider planting something this summer—whether it's a flower, herb, or vegetable garden. As you care for it, contemplate how you can cultivate spiritual growth in your own life, nourishing your relationship with God and bearing fruit through your actions and faith. It's a simple yet powerful way to engage with the beauty of the season while nurturing your soul.

Reflections ...

TODAY I AM GRATEFUL FOR ... _____

_____
_____
_____
_____
_____
_____
_____

June 21
NATIONAL INDIGENOUS PEOPLES DAY

MARK 3:31–35

Jesus redefines the concept of family, expanding it beyond biological ties to include those who do the will of God. He emphasizes that spiritual bonds and obedience to God's will create a deeper connection than earthly relationships. We are challenged to consider the ways we connect with others through faith and love, and how we live as a part of God's family, called to live in unity and purpose.

I encourage you to read this passage from the New Testament Indigenous Bible, available online, and compare it to the version in your current Bible? I really enjoy how this scripture is expressed in this Bible. Reading the text in this version may deepen your understanding of both the text and the rich spiritual heritage of Indigenous peoples. This is a meaningful way to connect with the Word of God and honour the cultural history of those who have long honoured the Creator.

Reflections ...

TODAY I AM GRATEFUL FOR ... _____

_____
_____
_____
_____

June 22
PSALM 23:1–6

Psalm 23:1–6 beautifully reminds us that the Lord is our Shepherd, guiding us with loving care through both peaceful and challenging times. His presence provides comfort, peace, and protection, helping us walk through life with confidence and trust. We need to have faith and hold on to Him—He is always with us, leading us beside still waters and restoring our souls.

As you've probably guessed by now, I enjoy planning church events, For me, it has that element of loving kindness to it. Church events can help those needing a smile or some encouragement. If your church does not currently host a strawberry social, I strongly encourage you to try to start one. It's a delightful way to bring people together and create a sense of community. Our social team had a hoot organizing this event, and you could even make some homemade jam, symbolizing how, just like the berries, our words can be sweet and nourishing to others when shared with care and love.

Reflections ...

TODAY I AM GRATEFUL FOR ... _____

_____

_____

_____

June 23
James 3:13–18

This passage invites us to consider what true wisdom looks like in the eyes of God. It's not about cleverness or status but about living with humility, kindness, and peace. The wisdom from above is gentle, merciful, and sincere, and when we live it out, it brings a beautiful harvest of righteousness and harmony into our lives and communities. Isn't it comforting to know that God's wisdom helps us build a life rooted in grace?

To connect with this theme of wisdom, take a bike ride around your neighbourhood. As you pedal through familiar streets or new paths, notice the beauty around you and let it stir up gratitude. How can you bring more gentleness, patience, and kindness into your daily encounters? It's a refreshing way to clear your mind and let God's peaceful wisdom sink into your heart!

Reflections ...

TODAY I AM GRATEFUL FOR ... _____

_____
_____
_____
_____
_____

June 24
EPHESIANS 2:1–10

OK, this reading is one of my favourites too—it's such a powerful reminder of just how amazing God's grace is. Paul beautifully reminds us that we were once spiritually lost, but through Christ, we are made alive and restored—not because of anything we did, but because of His unshakable love. It's humbling and hopeful all at once, knowing that we are God's handiwork, created for a life filled with purpose, goodness, and grace.

If you're a dog person like me (our pup Joy lives up to her name every single day), consider volunteering at a local animal shelter. It's such a fun and fulfilling way to share love and kindness—plus, who doesn't need a little tail-wagging happiness? Bringing joy to God's creatures is a beautiful way to echo His goodness and bring a smile to your face.

Reflections ...

TODAY I AM GRATEFUL FOR ... _____

_____
_____
_____
_____
_____

June 25
JOHN 3:1–8

In this powerful encounter, Jesus gently explains to Nicodemus that being "born again" means experiencing a spiritual renewal through the Holy Spirit. It's such a hopeful image—like a fresh breeze sweeping through our hearts, making room for grace, growth, and transformation. Just as the wind moves in ways we can't always see, the Spirit works within us to renew us from the inside out, guiding us toward a life full of love, purpose, and God's presence.

Celebrate this season by trying your hand at a maple syrup–infused recipe—maybe some maple-glazed roasted veggies or fluffy maple muffins! It's a sweet and simple way to get creative in the kitchen and share something lovely with others. A home filled with warm, maple-scented goodness is a small but joyful way to embrace God's renewing love!

Reflections ...

TODAY I AM GRATEFUL FOR ... _____

_____
_____
_____
_____
_____

June 26
Romans 8:1–17

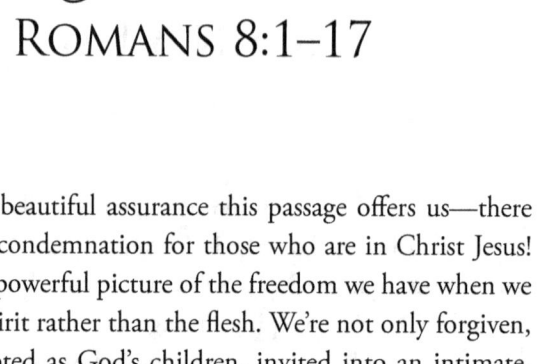

What a beautiful assurance this passage offers us—there is no condemnation for those who are in Christ Jesus! Paul paints a powerful picture of the freedom we have when we live by the Spirit rather than the flesh. We're not only forgiven, but also adopted as God's children, invited into an intimate, grace-filled relationship with Him. This life in the Spirit brings peace, strength, and purpose, reminding us that we belong fully and completely to a God who loves us beyond measure.

Crazy idea, but what if you hosted a gratitude dinner this week? Gather a few friends or family members and share a simple meal together. Don't forget to invite me! Before eating, invite everyone to name one thing they're thankful for. It's such a meaningful way to celebrate God's goodness, deepen your connections, and create a space where joy and grace can flourish!

Reflections ...

TODAY I AM GRATEFUL FOR ... _____

_____
_____
_____
_____
_____
_____

June 27
EPHESIANS 3:14–21

In Ephesians 3:14–21, Paul reminds us of the love, strength, and richness we receive through Christ. Paul's prayer speaks of the immeasurable love of God, who strengthens us and fills us with hope. Just as we celebrate the abundance of God's love, we can also celebrate the blessings of living in faith and trust in His promises.

An activity to help strengthen your relationship with God and one another could be to plan a couples' retreat or a personal study retreat. Whether it's a quiet weekend getaway or a dedicated time at home, this retreat can provide space for you to meditate on your faith, deepen your connection, and focus on nurturing both your relationship with God and with each other.

Reflections ...

TODAY I AM GRATEFUL FOR ... _____

_____
_____
_____
_____
_____

JOYOUS FAITH

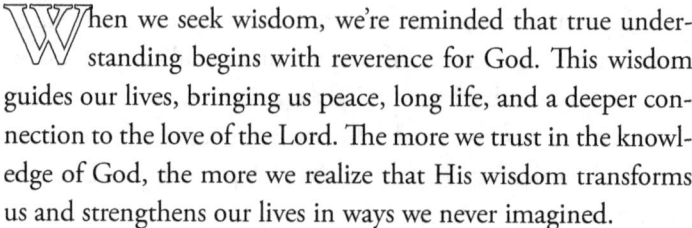

June 28
PROVERBS 9:10–12

When we seek wisdom, we're reminded that true understanding begins with reverence for God. This wisdom guides our lives, bringing us peace, long life, and a deeper connection to the love of the Lord. The more we trust in the knowledge of God, the more we realize that His wisdom transforms us and strengthens our lives in ways we never imagined.

A wonderful way to share this wisdom is by inviting someone to church. It could be a neighbour, a friend, or anyone you know who might benefit from hearing God's Word and experiencing the community and support of the church. Your invitation could be the spark that leads them to discover the peace and wisdom that comes from walking with God.

Reflections ...

TODAY I AM GRATEFUL FOR ... _____

_____
_____
_____
_____
_____
_____

June 29
Psalm 16:1–3

Seek refuge in the joy of God's presence and His people. The psalmist expresses confidence in God's care, proclaiming that their joy is found in the community of believers. When we gather with others in faith, we experience God's goodness together, and our hearts are lifted by the fellowship and love we share.

If your church has a baseball team, like our Pres-BAT-erians, maybe it's a good time to go and cheer them on! It makes our day when members of our congregation come out and support our team. It's a great way to live out the joy and community that Psalm 16 celebrates!

Reflections ...

TODAY I AM GRATEFUL FOR ... _____

_____
_____
_____
_____
_____
_____

June 30
Proverbs 3:1–12

Through today's Scripture reading, Solomon encourages us to trust in the Lord wholeheartedly and to seek wisdom as a guiding light in our lives. This passage highlights the importance of cultivating a deep relationship with God, where our trust in Him shapes our actions and decisions. When we embrace wisdom, we open ourselves to His guidance and care, allowing us to navigate life's challenges with grace and confidence.

We often set alarms on our phones for reminders throughout the day, but what if we used those notifications to nurture our spirits? Consider setting reminders with uplifting hymns that help keep you grounded in faith (a great one is "I Smile" by Kirk Franklin). Could setting a few reminders for yourself guide your heart and mind closer to God throughout your day? It couldn't hurt, could it?

Reflections ...

TODAY I AM GRATEFUL FOR ... _____

_____
_____
_____
_____
_____

July 1
Canada Day

Acts 2:42–47

In Acts 2:42–47, we see a beautiful picture of the early church, united in their devotion to teaching, fellowship, breaking bread, and prayer. Their commitment to these practices created a vibrant community where love and support flourished, and the impact of their faith was evident in their daily lives. As we read this passage, we're invited to consider how we, too, can foster such a spirit of devotion in our church community, creating an atmosphere where everyone feels valued, connected, and encouraged in their faith journey.

For Canada Day, I go all out. We wear red and white, enjoy a BBQ, and spend quality time with family? Celebrate the joy of community, and take a moment to consider how God's love has made this day even more meaningful. Whether it's watching fireworks or sharing a meal, could this be the reminder you need of the good gifts we have, both in our faith and our nation.

Reflections ...

Today I am grateful for ... _____
_____
_____
_____
_____
_____

July 2
Ephesians 4:1–6

This passage encourages us to live in a way that honours our calling by being humble, gentle, and patient with one another. It reminds us of the importance of maintaining peace and unity in the Spirit. Let these verses inspire you to build strong, loving relationships and to contribute positively to the community around you. This reading reminds me of "Humble and Kind" by Tim McGraw.

Is there someone you haven't spoken to in a while, whom you love deeply but have just been too busy to connect with? Now might be the perfect time to reach out and let them know how much you care. Taking a moment to rekindle that connection can be a beautiful way to show your love and strengthen your bond. A simple message or phone call can mean so much, and it's a wonderful way to bring a bit of joy into both your lives. Consider making that time today—it could brighten your day and theirs.

Reflections ...

TODAY I AM GRATEFUL FOR ... _____

_____

_____

_____

_____

July 3
COLOSSIANS 3:12–17

Paul encourages us to clothe ourselves with compassion, kindness, humility, gentleness, and patience, and above all, to let the peace of Christ rule in our hearts. This passage reminds us that as God's chosen people, we're called to live in harmony with one another, forgiving each other as Christ has forgiven us. When we embrace Christ's peace, it transforms our relationships and empowers us to live with love and gratitude.

Speaking of Christ's peace, during a women's retreat I was on, a minister presented from the book *The Nature Fix* by Florence Williams. This book beautifully reminds us of the profound impact nature has on our well-being. It encourages us to step outside and reconnect with the natural world, which can refresh our spirits and renew our sense of purpose. If you have opportunity to attend a women's retreat, I strongly encourage you to do so. Every time I go, I come back with something new that I've learned, or with a new idea or resource. Nature bathing was a new one for me, and it's the perfect opportunity to remember the peace God offers through His world, and to embrace the healing power of nature.

Reflections ...

TODAY I AM GRATEFUL FOR ... _____

_____

_____

_____

July 4
US Independence Day

MARK 10:13–16

Jesus welcomes the children with open arms, reminding us that the Kingdom of God belongs to those with a childlike heart—full of trust, wonder, and humility. He doesn't just allow the children to come to Him—He delights in it! It's a tender moment that beautifully shows us how deeply God values simplicity, sincerity, and openness. Let's strive to approach our faith the same way: with curiosity, joy, and the kind of trust that knows we are safe in His embrace.

If you have friends or family in the US, wish them a happy Independence Day! It's a great chance to connect, share a kind word, and say a prayer for our neighbours to the south—asking for peace, wisdom, and joy in their celebrations. Little acts of connection go a long way in showing God's love across borders!

Reflections ...

TODAY I AM GRATEFUL FOR ... _____

_____
_____
_____
_____
_____
_____
_____

July 5
James 3:1–12

Today's reading teaches us the power of our words, reminding us that they can either build up or tear down. Just as a small spark can set a great forest on fire, our words have the potential to greatly impact those around us. This passage encourages us to be mindful of what we say, striving for wisdom and kindness in all our conversations, using our words to mirror God's love and grace.

Keeping in mind this passage, let's use our words to further our relationships, maybe by inviting our in-laws over for dinner or taking someone out for a coffee. This is a great way to show others that we care. I am blessed to have two amazing in-laws, and I don't get to see them often enough. But simple acts of kindness like these help us live out the authenticity Christ calls for, echoing His love in our relationships and strengthening the bonds with those closest to us.

Reflections ...

TODAY I AM GRATEFUL FOR ... _____

July 6
GALATIANS 5:16–18

Paul encourages us to walk by the Spirit and not be driven by our own desires. When we live according to the Spirit, we're led away from selfishness and toward a life of love, kindness, and self-control. Let this passage remind you that the Holy Spirit is our guide, helping us live in alignment with God's will rather than being swayed by the world.

Volunteering for Vacation Bible Camp (VBC) is such a wonderful way to support the ministry that brings the message of God's love to children, many of whom may be hearing about Him for the first time. Consider baking some cookies or preparing a small treat to share with the volunteers and children—your kindness will be a sweet reminder of God's love. This simple act of support can make a big difference in creating a warm, welcoming environment where kids can grow in their faith.

Reflections ...

TODAY I AM GRATEFUL FOR ... _____

_____
_____
_____
_____
_____
_____

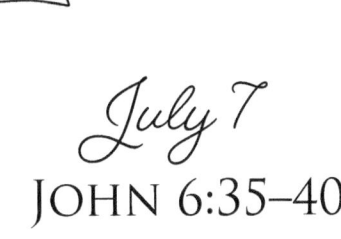

July 7
John 6:35–40

Jesus reminds us that He is the Bread of Life and that anyone who comes to Him will never go hungry or thirsty. He promises that those who come to Him will never hunger or thirst—not just physically, but spiritually. Isn't that such a comforting truth? No matter where we are in life, Jesus offers us a steady, sustaining presence that fills us with peace, purpose, and eternal hope. What a beautiful gift to know we are never alone and are always welcome at His table.

Think about someone in your life who could be encouraged by God's Word—maybe a young person, a friend new to faith, or someone going through a hard season. Gifting a Bible is such a heartfelt way to share the love and hope of Jesus. You could even include a note with your favourite verse!

Reflections ...

TODAY I AM GRATEFUL FOR ... _____

_____
_____
_____
_____
_____

July 8
Nehemiah 1:1–11

In this passage, we see Nehemiah's heartbroken prayer for his people and his city. He turns to God with humility and faith, seeking restoration not only for Jerusalem but for the hearts of those who have strayed. Nehemiah's deep concern and willingness to act remind us of the power of prayer paired with purpose. When we see something broken—whether in our community or within ourselves—we too can trust in God to lead us toward love and healing.

For volunteer work, I am more of a doer than a committee person. And there are so many beautiful and thoughtful activities you can do, like knitting prayer shawls or blankets for people undergoing chemotherapy or facing difficult circumstances. As you knit, pray over each stitch, asking God to bring peace and healing to whoever receives it. It's a heartfelt way to let someone know they are seen, loved, and surrounded by God's care—even in their hardest moments.

Reflections ...

TODAY I AM GRATEFUL FOR ... _____

_____

_____

_____

_____

July 9
PSALM 9:9–10

"*The Lord is a refuge for the oppressed, a stronghold in times of trouble. Those who know your name trust in you, for you, Lord, have never forsaken those who seek you.*" What a meaningful message that God is always our safe place. In every season—especially the hard ones—He is our steady anchor. These verses encourage us to place our full trust in Him, knowing that when we seek Him, He never turns us away. It's a comforting promise of His constant presence, strength, and love.

This brings to mind the joy of building community through something as simple and fun as pickleball! Just like our church team loves being part of the Christian baseball league, imagine organizing a Christian pickleball tournament. It's a fantastic way to enjoy the outdoors, connect with others, and shine Christ's love in a welcoming, laid-back setting. Whether you're rallying or just learning the game, it's all about growing together in faith and friendship!

Reflections ...

TODAY I AM GRATEFUL FOR ... _____

_____

_____

_____

July 10
Psalm 37:3–7

"*Trust in the Lord and do good; dwell in the land and enjoy safe pasture. Take delight in the Lord, and He will give you the desires of your heart*" (vv. 3–4). This beautiful passage reminds us to be still and patient, trusting that God is at work even when we can't yet see the outcome. It encourages us to stay rooted in goodness, finding joy in the Lord and His promises. When we place our hope in Him, we can rest confidently, knowing He is guiding every step with love and purpose.

With that in mind, what if you invited someone from your church community out for coffee this week? A session member and dear friend of mine recently came over and brought coffee for us to just sit and talk over. We had a beautiful conversation, and it meant the world to me that she took the time out of her day to stop and connect. It can be a beautiful way to build community, offer encouragement, and remind one another of God's faithful care.

Reflections ...

TODAY I AM GRATEFUL FOR ... _____

_____

_____

_____

_____

_____

July 11
ISAIAH 26:3–4

Did you know that the book of Isaiah is one of the major prophetic books in the Old Testament? Spanning sixty-six chapters, Isaiah is packed with powerful prophecies about both judgment and hope, providing insight into God's character, His plan for Israel, and even the coming of the Messiah, Jesus Christ. Many of its prophecies were fulfilled through the life, death, and resurrection of Jesus. In this passage, Isaiah calls us to trust in God's unshakable strength and peace. He reassures us that when we keep our minds focused on Him, we are granted perfect peace, no matter what life throws our way.

I love our local farmers market. It's easy to see God's work all around you—with the vibrant veggies and the smiling faces. It's a perfect opportunity to support local farmers, artisans, and businesses while soaking in the vibrant community atmosphere. I love to stroll through the market unhurried, and it's a lovely chance to connect with others, share a smile, and appreciate the abundance He has so generously placed in our world.

Reflections ...

TODAY I AM GRATEFUL FOR ... _____

_____

_____

_____

_____

July 12
JEREMIAH 17:7–8

Today's reading reminds us that when we place our trust in God, we are like trees planted by the water—strong, rooted, and able to thrive even during life's challenges. This passage brings such peace, knowing that when we focus on God, He nourishes and strengthens us, guiding us through every season of life. His words are a beautiful anchor for the soul, reminding us of God's faithfulness and our constant need for His grace.

Homemade popsicles are the best, made with fresh, seasonal fruits. It's a simple way to celebrate the sweetness of life and enjoy God's creation with your loved ones. What's your favourite flavour?

Reflections ...

TODAY I AM GRATEFUL FOR ... _____

_____
_____
_____
_____
_____
_____

July 13
ROMANS 10:9–13

In Romans 10:9–13, Paul speaks to the powerful truth that when we confess Jesus as Lord and believe in our hearts that God raised Him from the dead, we are saved! It's a gentle whisper of the simplicity and power of faith, that anyone—no matter who they are or where they come from—can call on the name of Jesus and be saved. This passage assures us that salvation is for all, and that the grace of God is freely offered to everyone who believes.

My son likes to challenge me by doing a Sudoku puzzle or a word search? These activities are a great way to keep your mind sharp and engaged, helping you maintain clarity and peace in your thoughts. Just as we nurture our faith, it's important to care for our mental health by staying sharp and focused on God's goodness.

Reflections ...

TODAY I AM GRATEFUL FOR ... _____

_____

_____

_____

_____

_____

HEBREWS 11:1–3

Have you ever wondered what it really means to live by faith? Hebrews 11:1–3 gives us a beautiful and grounding answer—it describes faith as the assurance of things we hope for and the conviction of things we can't see. These opening verses of what's often called the "Faith Hall of Fame" remind us that faith isn't just a feeling; it's a confident trust in God's unseen but ever-present hand in our lives. It's comforting to know that from the very beginning, God's Word brought everything into existence—and that same powerful Word continues to guide and sustain us.

Do you enjoy trying new things? Whether it's learning to crochet (I'm struggling, but I am learning.), offering to lead a Bible study (Ack! Heart palpitations!), or giving yoga a try (I really need to work on this), caring for both your body and spirit, doing something new can be a joyful way to stretch yourself and grow, knowing God is right there cheering you on in every fresh beginning!

Reflections ...

TODAY I AM GRATEFUL FOR ... _____

_____

_____

_____

_____

July 15
Psalm 56:3–4

Psalm 56:3–4 gently reminds us that when we're afraid, we can put our trust in God. It's a comforting invitation to shift our focus from fear to faith, knowing that God's Word and presence give us strength and courage. These verses are a promise that we are never alone—God is always near, holding us steady through every storm.

When we drive to visit my in-laws, I love to stop by a roadside stand to gather a few blooms. Bringing someone flowers is a simple act that can brighten someone's day and remind them of God's beauty and grace. It's a lovely way to share God's love and remind those around you that we're all part of His beautiful community!

Reflections ...

TODAY I AM GRATEFUL FOR ... _____

_____
_____
_____
_____
_____

July 16
Matthew 22:37–40

Jesus highlights the very heart of our faith: to love God with all our heart, soul, and mind, and to love our neighbours as ourselves. These two commandments are deeply connected—our love for God naturally overflows into how we treat others. It's a joyful invitation to become self-aware. How do we live out this love every day, growing in kindness, compassion, and grace in both our closest relationships and in simple encounters?

Maybe you have an outdoor music series in your area—like the ones we enjoy here! Our family loves packing up our patio chairs and soaking in the music under the open sky. It's a wonderful way to spend time together. How do you enjoy God's creation with your family and friends?

Reflections...

TODAY I AM GRATEFUL FOR ... _____

_____
_____
_____
_____
_____
_____

July 17
JAMES 3:13–18

Have you ever thought about what true wisdom looks like? In James 3:13–18, we're reminded that wisdom from above is pure, peace-loving, gentle, and full of mercy. It's not about knowing all the answers but about living with a humble heart and creating peace wherever we go. This kind of wisdom mirrors the heart of Christ and invites us to be peacemakers in our homes, communities, and relationships.

To celebrate this love-filled wisdom, it can be fun to snuggle up around a cozy fire pit for a fun s'mores night. It's such a simple, joyful way to gather with loved ones. One of my favourite things to roast over the campfire is strawberries. Laugh together, share stories, and let the glow of the fire reflect the light of Christ's love shining through you. And don't forget the strawberries—you'll thank me for it!

Reflections ...

TODAY I AM GRATEFUL FOR ... _____

_____
_____
_____
_____
_____

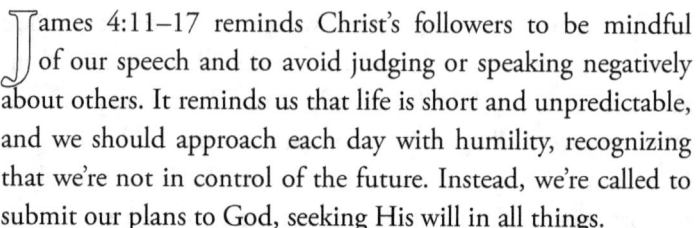

July 18
JAMES 4:11–17

James 4:11–17 reminds Christ's followers to be mindful of our speech and to avoid judging or speaking negatively about others. It reminds us that life is short and unpredictable, and we should approach each day with humility, recognizing that we're not in control of the future. Instead, we're called to submit our plans to God, seeking His will in all things.

A wonderful way to live out this reminder is by organizing a virtual family or friend reunion. Setting up a video call allows you to reconnect, share memories, and catch up with loved ones, all while fostering positive, encouraging conversations. During COVID, we did this often, and it's a great opportunity to focus on building each other up.

Reflections ...

TODAY I AM GRATEFUL FOR ... _____

_____
_____
_____
_____
_____
_____

July 19
JAMES 2:1–13

Today's reading challenges us to look beyond external appearances and to treat everyone with the same respect and love, regardless of their background or status. The passage reminds us that in God's eyes, we're all equal, and that favouritism has no place among believers. It calls us to examine our own biases and encourages us to embrace inclusivity, echoing the freedom found in the unconditional love of Christ in all our interactions.

A great way to connect with others and refresh your spirit is by planning a camping trip. Our church women's retreat is a time to get away, but we also enjoy family camping trips, where we can unplug from the distractions of everyday life and spend quality time in nature. Could this help you to recharge and deepen our relationships with both God and one another.

Reflections ...

TODAY I AM GRATEFUL FOR ... _____

July 20
MARK 9:23–24

Faith isn't always about having all the answers—it's about showing up with a heart open to God's power and presence. Mark 9:23–24 offers us such a moving picture of what it means to believe, even when we're struggling. Jesus reminds us that everything is possible for the one who believes, and the father's honest response—asking for help with his unbelief—is something many of us can relate to. It's an invitation from God and a reminder that He welcomes our questions, our hopes, and our faith, even when it feels fragile.

Could anyone else use a little musical therapy this week? Tune into music that stirs your heart—whether it's worship, instrumental, or something peaceful that lifts your spirit. Currently for me, this is belt-out-at-the-top-of-your-lungs Christian rock. But what resonates with you today? Let the lyrics or melodies move your soul and reconnect you with God's love and the quiet strength that comes with trusting Him.

Reflections ...

TODAY I AM GRATEFUL FOR ... _____

_____
_____
_____
_____
_____

July 21
LUKE 12:22–31

Jesus reminds us not to worry about our material needs—food, clothes, or even tomorrow—because God, who takes care of the birds and flowers, will surely care for us as His children. What's especially interesting is how Jesus points to nature as evidence of God's provision. If God provides for the simple things, how much more will He care for us who are made in His image?

How about a cozy movie night with someone special or a few friends? It's a simple, joyful way to relax and connect. Just like Jesus reminds us to focus on what really matters, spending quality time with loved ones brings peace and happiness. Enjoy the moment together!

Reflections ...

TODAY I AM GRATEFUL FOR ... _____

July 22
Proverbs 11:24–30

Today's reading highlights the blessings of generosity and the joy that comes from sharing with others. It teaches us that those who are generous will be richly rewarded, not only in material ways but with lasting joy and peace. In our service to others, we aim to reveal God's love and kindness, making the world a better place, one small act at a time. It's a reminder that true generosity is rooted in the heart, and it blesses both the giver and the receiver.

I love a peaceful moment by the water, whether it's a beach, lake, or river. Both my husband and I enjoy the quiet stillness of nature in the early morning. As you soak in the beauty around you, take a moment to consider how God's love has transformed you, washing away the old and bringing forth something new and beautiful. Maybe say a short prayer? "Dear Lord, as this water refreshed me, let your grace refresh my soul."

Reflections ...

TODAY I AM GRATEFUL FOR ... _____

_____
_____
_____
_____

July 23
Psalm 95

Psalm 95 beautifully invites us into worship, recognizing God's greatness and sovereignty over all creation. It calls us to bow down and kneel before Him, acknowledging that He is our Maker and Shepherd. The psalm also serves as a reminder not to harden our hearts like the Israelites did in the wilderness, but to trust in God's faithfulness and follow His ways with humility and faith.

Painting or taking a ceramics class with family or friends is a wonderful way to connect, unwind, and create something beautiful together. Just as God has given us the ability to create and appreciate beauty, this activity allows you to express yourself and enjoy the process while building lasting memories with loved ones.

Reflections ...

TODAY I AM GRATEFUL FOR ... _____

_____
_____
_____
_____
_____

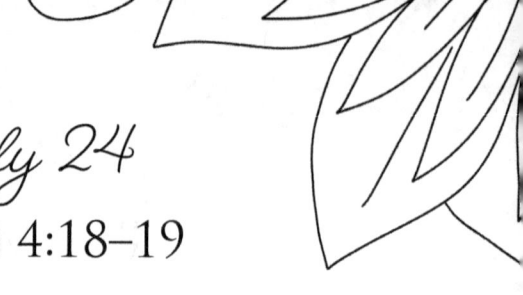

July 24
LUKE 4:18–19

How amazing would it have been to hear Jesus preach or read from the scrolls, declaring the good news and freedom He came to bring? In Luke 4:18–19, Jesus opens the Scriptures and speaks with authority and love, sharing His mission to bring hope to the broken-hearted, freedom to the oppressed, and healing to all. Jesus's message is one of renewal and restoration, a call for us to share His love and compassion with the world.

To embrace this teaching, let's try something new in the kitchen today. Perhaps it's baking a soufflé or mastering the art of a hollandaise sauce. I find that cooking with family is a fun, creative way to stretch your skills and enjoy the simple joy of trying something different.

Reflections ...

TODAY I AM GRATEFUL FOR ... _____

_____
_____
_____
_____
_____
_____

July 25
2 Corinthians 3:1–6

In this passage, Paul beautifully contrasts the old and new covenants, highlighting how the Holy Spirit empowers us to live in a deeper, more vibrant relationship with God. It's not about following rules but about experiencing God's grace and living out His truth in our everyday lives. We are living letters of Christ, meant to display His love to the world and share the freedom and hope found in the Spirit.

To share some of that joy, I like writing notes, and it's fun to write a heartfelt note of encouragement and tuck it into a Bible at your church? Imagine how uplifting it would be for someone to find your words of hope and warmth—a little reminder of God's love and grace. So let this small act of kindness be our little secret, and hopefully it can brighten someone's day and help spread the light of Christ in a beautiful, personal way.

Reflections ...

TODAY I AM GRATEFUL FOR ... _____

_____

_____

_____

_____

JOYOUS FAITH

July 26
1 John 3:1–3

This beautiful passage from 1 John reminds us of the amazing love God has for us, calling us His children. It encourages us to embrace that love and live with hope, knowing that one day we will be made like Him. As we consider this love, think about how you can share it with others, showing the same kindness and grace God has shown us.

Pray for the leaders in your church. Lift them up in prayer, asking God to guide their hearts and decisions so that they can continue to lead with wisdom, strength, and love. Praying for those who shepherd our faith community is a powerful way to support them and ensure they are empowered by the Spirit to serve well.

Reflections ...

TODAY I AM GRATEFUL FOR ... _____

_____
_____
_____
_____
_____
_____
_____

July 27
Ephesians 4:22-24

Paul encourages us to *"put off your old self"* and *"put on the new self, created to be like God in true righteousness and holiness."* This passage invites us into transformation, leaving behind the old ways of living and embrace what God has created for us in Christ. Just as sunshine tea relies on the warmth of the sun to bring out its best, we too are called to be filled with God's light and truth, allowing His presence to steep in our hearts and change us from the inside out.

To display this transformation, let's make one of my favs—sunshine tea. It's a simple, peaceful activity that reminds us of God's warmth and presence in our lives. As the tea brews in the sun, take a moment to consider how you're allowing God's light to refresh and renew you—just as the sun does for the tea!

Reflections ...

TODAY I AM GRATEFUL FOR ... _____

_____
_____
_____
_____
_____

July 28
GALATIANS 5:13–14

In Galatians 5:13–14, Paul reminds us that we are called to serve one another in love, echoing the greatest commandments: to love God and to love our neighbour as ourselves. This passage encourages us to live freely but with a heart of service, using our freedom not for selfishness but to build up those around us. It's a truth that love is not just a feeling but an action that brings us closer to one another and to God.

A wonderful way to live out this love is by working together on a seasonal puzzle. It's a fun, simple way to unplug from the distractions of life and connect with each other. As you piece it together, let it be a reminder of how we, too, come together in Christ to create something beautiful, piece by piece, through our love and service to others.

Reflections ...

TODAY I AM GRATEFUL FOR ... _____

_____
_____
_____
_____
_____
_____

July 29
COLOSSIANS 2:13–15

What a wonderful reminder we find in our passage today about the power of God's grace and the freedom we have in Christ. This passage celebrates how Jesus has forgiven us, disarmed the powers of sin, and made us alive through His sacrifice. It's empowering to think that no matter what challenges we face, we can walk in the victory He has won for us, living in the fullness of His love and forgiveness.

I like reading my Bible outside, finding a peaceful spot in nature—perhaps in my garden, at a nearby park, or just by a sunny bench—and meditating on God's goodness. When you read Scripture, take a moment to read and thank God for the blessings He's given you, and for the simple yet profound beauty of the world He's created.

Reflections ...

TODAY I AM GRATEFUL FOR ... _____

_____
_____
_____
_____
_____
_____

July 30
INTERNATIONAL DAY OF FRIENDSHIP

ROMANS 7:24–25

Have you ever felt torn between doing what's right and the struggle of your own human nature? In Romans 7:24–25, Paul opens up about this inner conflict, recognizing the battle between our desires and our imperfections. But here's the hope we cling to—thanks to Jesus Christ, we are no longer enslaved by this struggle. His grace ultimately gives us victory over our weaknesses.

For the International Day of Friendship, let's take a moment to reach out to a friend, whether near or far. A quick message, a phone call, or even a heartfelt prayer for them can brighten their day and strengthen the bond you share. Friendship is a precious gift from God, as are every one of my girlfriends!

Reflections ...

TODAY I AM GRATEFUL FOR ... _____

_____
_____
_____
_____
_____
_____
_____

July 31
2 Corinthians 3:12–18

Have you ever paused to consider the freedom we now have through Christ? In 2 Corinthians 3:12–18, Paul reminds us that through Jesus, the veil has been lifted, and we are invited to experience the full glory of God. It's a beautiful encouragement to know that as we grow in our relationship with Him, we're being transformed—day by day—into His likeness with ever-increasing glory.

To celebrate the end of summer, I enjoy hosting a BBQ with friends or family. In our area, corn on the cob is coming into season, and there's nothing better than enjoying fresh, in-season food while spending time together. Enjoy the day, celebrate God's blessings, and share the joy with those around you.

Reflections ...

TODAY I AM GRATEFUL FOR ... _____

_____
_____
_____
_____
_____
_____

August 1
Luke 11:2–4

Jesus offers us a tender and powerful model for prayer, reminding us to come to God with open hearts and childlike trust. This passage isn't just about the words we say—it's about the relationship we build. We're encouraged to centre our lives around God's presence, forgiveness, and provision, leaning into daily connection with our loving Father.

As August sets upon us, I like to make a list of things I'd like to accomplish. The summer goes so fast, and it's helpful for me to take stock of things. I include things that nurture my spirit, like praying outdoors and spending quality time with family. You could do this, too. Let's end summer with purpose and peace!

Reflections ...

Today I am grateful for ... _____

_____
_____
_____
_____
_____

August 2
Isaiah 1:10–18

In Isaiah 1:10–18, God invites us to move beyond hollow rituals and instead embrace sincere hearts and lives shaped by compassion. It's a powerful reminder that what God desires most is a relationship with us—one rooted in doing good, seeking justice, and caring for others. And the best part? He invites us to come to Him, no matter our past, promising that though our sins are like scarlet, they shall be white as snow. What an amazing promise of grace!

One of my favourite ways to enjoy the fruits of the season is making gazpacho! It's a refreshing, cold soup that uses ripe tomatoes, cucumbers, and peppers—perfect for a hot day. Try whipping up a batch and sharing it with a neighbour or friend. It's a delicious way to practise hospitality and celebrate the abundance God provides!

Reflections ...

TODAY I AM GRATEFUL FOR ... _____

_____
_____
_____
_____
_____
_____
_____

August 3
PROVERBS 8:1–10

Today, wisdom is personified as a voice calling out to us, offering guidance and understanding. It's a reminder that true wisdom comes from God, and it's always available to us if we are willing to listen. It's a beautiful call to seek wisdom and hold it close to our hearts, knowing that God's wisdom enriches our lives.

Take a moment to bring this message into your heart. Perhaps you can spend some time in nature, taking in the beauty around you and allowing yourself to listen for God's voice in the quiet. You could also reach out to a neighbour, offering a friendly chat or helping hand, sharing God's love through small acts of kindness.

Reflections ...

TODAY I AM GRATEFUL FOR ... _____

_____
_____
_____
_____
_____
_____

August 4
MICAH 4:1–5

In this beautiful vision, Micah speaks of a future where nations come together in peace, united under God's loving guidance. It's a promise of restoration, reminding us that no matter the challenges we face, God is always working toward our healing and wholeness. This message resonates deeply as we anticipate the birth of Jesus, the Prince of Peace.

Create a prayer board to help you focus on God's faithfulness. Gather some supplies like markers, sticky notes, or a corkboard and write down your prayer requests, answered prayers, and things you're thankful for. Could this simple act serve as a visual reminder of God's work in your life and keep you connected to His love and care?

Reflections ...

TODAY I AM GRATEFUL FOR ... _____

_____
_____
_____
_____
_____
_____
_____

August 5
PROVERBS 3:5–10

Today's reading reminds us to trust in the Lord with all our hearts, leaning not on our own understanding, but on His guidance. When we place our trust in Him, He promises to make our paths straight and fill our lives with abundance. It's a call to let go and let God lead, trusting that He'll provide for us in ways we never imagined.

As you enjoy the beauty of this season, this might be the perfect time to dive into a creative project. Crafting is a great outlet for me, as my imagination can run wild—whether it's a flower arranging, a painting, or woodworking. Let the act of creating serve as a reminder of the trust we place in God, knowing that He is working in every area of our lives, just like He works through our creativity!

Reflections ...

TODAY I AM GRATEFUL FOR ... _____

_____
_____
_____
_____
_____
_____

August 6
NEHEMIAH 4:14–20

Nehemiah is a book of rebuilding—of walls, of faith, and of community. In Nehemiah 4:14–20, we see a beautiful blend of courage and reliance on God. The people, facing threats and opposition, are reminded not to be afraid but to remember the Lord, who is great and awesome. They work with one hand and hold a weapon in the other, trusting that God will fight for them. It's an encouraging reminder that in the face of challenges, we are never alone—God stands with us, strengthening us for the work He has set before us. I don't know about you, but there is no one else I would rather have in my corner.

As you continue this devotional, I pray you will take a few moments to journal about what this experience has meant to you. Write down what's resonating most, where you've seen God at work in your life, and how you've grown.

Reflections ...

TODAY I AM GRATEFUL FOR ... _____

_____
_____
_____
_____
_____
_____

August 7
ROMANS 12:9–18

Paul teaches us to love genuinely, to serve one another in humility, and to seek peace with others. It challenges us to show kindness, even to those who may not expect it, and to love in a way that displays Christ's heart for all. When we serve selflessly, we not only bless others, but we also grow closer to the heart of God, who delights in our acts of love.

For an activity today, consider practising a breath prayer. It's a simple and peaceful way to centre yourself in God's presence. As you inhale, silently pray, "Lord, hear our prayers," and as you exhale, say, "Guide us in your truth." This short prayer can help you focus on God's guidance and open your heart to His will throughout your day.

Reflections ...

TODAY I AM GRATEFUL FOR ... _____

_____
_____
_____
_____
_____
_____

August 8
1 Timothy 3:1–16

Paul gives us valuable guidance on the qualities and characteristics of leaders in the church, emphasizing the importance of integrity, respect, and living a life that reflects the gospel. This passage reminds us that leadership comes with responsibility—leaders are called to serve with humility and devotion and to care for others. It's an inspiring message that the heart of Christian leadership is rooted in love, service, and teaching the truth of Christ.

For an activity, consider starting a tea ministry in your church or community. A tea ministry is a simple yet powerful way to connect with others, offer hospitality, and create space for meaningful conversations and prayer. You could begin by gathering a group of volunteers to host regular tea times, inviting those who might need encouragement or fellowship, and allowing God's love to flow through these moments of connection.

Reflections ...

TODAY I AM GRATEFUL FOR ... _____

_____
_____
_____
_____
_____
_____
_____

August 9
NATIONAL BOOK LOVERS DAY

PROVERBS 4:5–9

Wisdom, as described in Proverbs 4:5–9, isn't just something to be sought after; it's a treasure that protects and guides us, leading to a life of peace and success. Today's passage emphasizes that wisdom should be pursued with all our hearts, for it's more valuable than gold and brings us closer to God's will for our lives. When we gain understanding, it lights our path and shapes our decisions, giving us the ability to navigate life with confidence and grace.

For National Book Lovers Day, why not explore a Bible-based fiction book? I enjoy seeing how these novels bring the people and stories of the Bible to life, offering a new way to connect with God's Word and deepen your understanding. It's a great way to spend the day, letting your imagination soar while learning more about the rich history of scripture!

Reflections ...

TODAY I AM GRATEFUL FOR ... _____

_____
_____
_____
_____
_____

August 10
Luke 11:9–13

Jesus encourages us to ask, seek, and knock, assuring us that our loving Father will give us good gifts when we do. This passage is like a gentle tap on the shoulder, assuring us of God's generosity and the trust we can place in Him, knowing He will provide for our needs. Just as a parent delights in giving gifts to their children, God delights in blessing us with what is best for us.

I love a good games night! When was the last time you hosted a games night? Invite friends or family for an evening of fun with a spiritual twist—play Bible trivia, charades, or Pictionary with faith-based themes. Game nights are my favourite—so simple, but so fun. This could also be a fantastic activity for youth groups, blending fun, faith, and learning all in one!

Reflections ...

TODAY I AM GRATEFUL FOR ... _____

_____
_____
_____
_____
_____
_____

August 11
1 Peter 1:10–25

We are called to live our lives in a way that is worthy of the holiness of God. Peter calls us to set our hope fully on the grace of Jesus, inspiring us to cultivate attitudes of kindness, love, and integrity. As we read this passage, consider how your actions shine as a testament to our faith. Do they encourage others to experience the grace that transforms lives?

To celebrate this call to holiness in a fun way, you could let your vocals soar and host a karaoke party. Anytime I can put on some uplifting music, I'm in! This joyful activity not only brings your family closer but also serves as a beautiful inspiration of how God can be celebrated in everyday moments filled with love and laughter!

Reflections ...

TODAY I AM GRATEFUL FOR ... _____

_____
_____
_____
_____
_____
_____

August 12
2 Peter 3:1–18

In today's fast-paced world, it's easy to get caught up in the constant flow of information and distractions. In 2 Peter 3:1–18, Peter encourages us to be patient, to remember God's promises, and to live in a way that honours Him, knowing that He is faithful and His timing is perfect. Taking time to pause and move away from the noise helps us reconnect with what truly matters and strengthens our relationship with God.

Consider taking a break from technology this week. Unplugging for even a short time can help you refocus on the things that bring peace and joy, like spending time with family, reading Scripture, or simply enjoying the beauty of nature.

Reflections ...

TODAY I AM GRATEFUL FOR ... _____

_____
_____
_____
_____
_____
_____

August 13
2 Timothy 2:14–26

Second Timothy, the final letter written by the Apostle Paul, is one of the "Pastoral Epistles" and is filled with personal, heartfelt advice to Timothy. In this letter, Paul encourages Timothy to remain faithful, be a vessel of honour set apart for good works, and gently correct those in error. It serves as a tap on the shoulder reminding us to grow in grace, show kindness to others, and handle differences with gentleness and love.

As a different way to spread His message, it can be fun to paint rocks with uplifting Bible verses and place them along local trails. During COVID, I loved seeing this simple yet meaningful way to share encouragement and hope with others. As people stumble upon these little treasures, they'll be reminded of God's love and truth, making their walk a bit more joyful and uplifting.

Reflections ...

TODAY I AM GRATEFUL FOR ... _____

_____
_____
_____
_____
_____

August 14
2 Timothy 3:1–17

Paul reminds us of the challenges to come in the last days and guides believers to stay steadfast in their faith. He stresses the importance of holding firmly to Scripture, which is inspired by God and equips us for every good work. This passage encourages us to trust in God's Word for guidance, correction, and growth in righteousness.

A hiking trip is a great way to enjoy God's creation. Connect with nature, meditate on a scripture, and spend time in prayer, all while experiencing the beauty and peace that comes with the great outdoors.

Reflections ...

TODAY I AM GRATEFUL FOR ... _____

August 15
Assumption of Mary

Amos 5:14–15

Amos 5:14–15 encourages us to *"seek good, not evil, that you may live."* It's a call to make intentional choices that lead to justice, peace, and the flourishing of those around us. When we pursue goodness, we reveal God's heart for love and community, fostering environments where everyone can thrive.

The Assumption of Mary is a holiday celebrated primarily in the Roman Catholic Church and by some Orthodox Christians. The day highlights the unique role Mary plays in salvation history, and for Catholics, it emphasizes her purity and closeness to God.

Reflections ...

Today I am grateful for ... _____

_____
_____
_____
_____
_____
_____

August 16
Proverbs 10:8–14

The book of Proverbs is attributed mainly to King Solomon, and it's a treasure trove of wisdom for daily living, focusing on how to live a life that honours God. Proverbs 10:8–14 reminds us of the importance of wisdom and the value of building relationships with those around us. It tells us that *"The wise in heart accept commands,"* and that *"the mouth of the righteous is a fountain of life."* Through our words and actions, we can bless others and foster a community rooted in love and truth.

To bring this to life, could it be time to plan a church BBQ? Our church hosts a summer BBQ in June, and what a wonderful opportunity to build community and invite others to join in to plan some impromptu fun!. As you gather with friends, family, and fellow church members, take time to connect and encourage one another, just as Paul encourages us to do in his letters!

Reflections ...

Today I am grateful for ... _____

_____
_____
_____
_____
_____
_____

August 17
TITUS 1:1–16

Titus, whom Paul addresses in this letter, was a Greek believer and a trusted companion and fellow worker in the ministry. He played a key role in Paul's missionary work, particularly in organizing and strengthening churches in Crete. In these verses, Paul guides Titus on how to lead the church in Crete with integrity and a strong foundation in God's truth, encouraging the selection of trustworthy leaders and the importance of addressing false teachings so the church could stay rooted in God's love and wisdom.

Let's put this reading into action! consider supporting a local leader or mentor within your church by writing a note of encouragement or praying for them. Leadership, whether in the church or in our daily lives, can be challenging, and sometimes a simple word of support can make a big difference. Be intentional about lifting up those who guide us spiritually and lead with integrity!

Reflections ...

TODAY I AM GRATEFUL FOR ... _____

_____

_____

_____

_____

_____

August 18
Psalm 119:169–176

Psalm 119:169–176 is a heartfelt closing to the longest chapter in the Bible—a beautiful prayer from someone deeply in love with God's Word. The psalmist pleads for understanding, deliverance, and guidance, expressing a longing to stay close to God even when feeling lost, like a sheep without a shepherd. It's such a comforting and tender reminder that God always hears our cries, seeks us out in love, and delights when we draw near to Him.

To celebrate that closeness with God and each other, plan a group hike with friends! Whether it's a trail you've done before or a new spot on your list, being out in creation is a joyful way to connect—with God, with nature, and with your community. Pack some apples and water, and let the fresh air and laughter fill your soul with joy!

Reflections ...

TODAY I AM GRATEFUL FOR ... _____

_____
_____
_____
_____
_____
_____

August 19
World Humanitarian Day

2 Timothy 1:1–14

In today's passage, Paul is writing to Timothy to remind him to fan into flame the gift of God within him. It's a powerful encouragement to be bold in faith, grounded in love, and to never be ashamed of the gospel. Paul's words remind us that our faith is not just for private comfort but a courageous and living witness to God's grace, even in times of challenge.

In recognition of World Humanitarian Day—this can be the perfect opportunity to carry out a random act of kindness for someone in need. Whether it's volunteering at a shelter, donating to a local food bank, or helping a neighbour carry their groceries, isn't it spectacular to watch how these small gestures of love ripple out in big ways? You're not just doing good—you're living out the light of Christ in a world that deeply needs it. Let's spread that grace with open hearts!

Reflections ...

Today I am grateful for ... _____

_____
_____
_____
_____
_____

August 20
NATIONAL LEMONADE DAY

HEBREWS 13:1–17

In these verses, we're encouraged to live lives of love, hospitality, and integrity, always honouring God in our actions and relationships. Hebrews 13 also speaks to the importance of maintaining peace and gratitude, focusing on what is good, and having the wisdom to stay grounded in God's unwavering faithfulness. It reminds us that our daily choices—whether in how we treat others or in how we manage our own lives—should show the love and peace that God gives us.

Happy National Lemonade Day! I'm excited to share one of our favourite juicing recipes! Juice three peeled lemons, three apples, one beet, one cucumber, and a half-inch piece of ginger. Depending on the apples, you might want to adjust the sweetness by adding more or less of their juice. It's a refreshing and healthy twist on traditional lemonade, and I hope you enjoy it as much as we do!

Reflections ...

TODAY I AM GRATEFUL FOR ...

August 21
ROMANS 3:19–28

Romans 3:19–28 is a cornerstone of our understanding of grace. Paul reminds us that we are made right with God not by following the law perfectly, but through faith in Jesus Christ. This is such freeing and joyful news—our salvation isn't something we earn; it's a gift we receive! It's a beautiful invitation to rest in God's love, knowing that He sees us, forgives us, and welcomes us just as we are.

If your church has a backpack program for students, consider jumping in to help get kids ready for the school year. What a beautiful way to live out this message of grace! Whether you're gathering school supplies, packing backpacks, or simply sharing an encouraging word, your kindness reminds these young students—and their families—that they are seen, supported, and loved. Let's be the hands and feet of Christ in this season!

Reflections ...

TODAY I AM GRATEFUL FOR ... _____

_____
_____
_____
_____
_____
_____

August 22
Psalm 5

Psalm 5 is a heartfelt morning prayer in which David turns to God with trust and expectation. Through life's challenges, he confidently seeks God's guidance and protection, knowing that God delights in righteousness and surrounds His people with favour like a shield. What a comforting reminder that we can start each day grounded in God's love, bringing our hopes, worries, and praises to Him, knowing He hears us and walks with us.

As we move through the warmth of August, one of my favourite ways to savour the season is by gathering around a bonfire or heading out on a camping trip. For a fun and tasty twist, try roasting strawberries over the fire—just like marshmallows! It's a sweet, simple treat that feels like strawberry pie under the stars. Enjoy God's creation, the company of others, and the goodness that fills even the smallest of moments.

Reflections ...

TODAY I AM GRATEFUL FOR ... _____

_____
_____
_____
_____
_____
_____
_____

August 23
2 Timothy 4:6–8, 16–18

Have you ever looked back on a season of your life and felt a quiet sense of peace, knowing you gave your all for God? In 2 Timothy 4:6–8, 16–18, Paul reflects on his journey with deep assurance—he's fought the good fight, finished the race, and kept the faith. Even in hard moments, he trusted in God's presence and deliverance. His words encourage us to stay steady in our faith, knowing that God sees, strengthens, and rewards those who walk with Him.

Summer is the perfect time to enjoy the bright, refreshing flavours of lemon! My mom is a huge fan of lemon desserts, and I've inherited that love. So go ahead—treat yourself to a zesty lemon tart or a slice of pie, and as you savour each bite, thank God for the sweetness in your life and the joy that comes from walking with Him every day.

Reflections ...

TODAY I AM GRATEFUL FOR ... _____

_____
_____
_____
_____
_____
_____

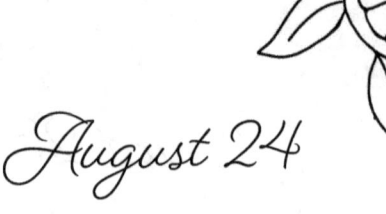

August 24
2 CORINTHIANS 1:3–4

Isn't it reassuring to know that God, in His boundless love, is the ultimate source of all comfort? In times of struggle, He comes alongside us to provide peace and healing and then guides us to share that same comfort with others. Just as He holds us in His arms, we are called to do the same for those around us, offering encouragement and kindness.

Did someone say picnic? Whether it's with close friends, family, or even a neighbour, gather together to enjoy good food and great company. It can be as simple as taking sandwiches down to the lake (my son's favourite) or enjoying a full-out catered extravaganza, but we can find comfort when we break bread with each other.

Reflections ...

TODAY I AM GRATEFUL FOR ... _____

_____
_____
_____
_____
_____
_____
_____

August 25
Proverbs 8:22–31

Our reading today offers a beautiful poetic vision, revealing wisdom as God's companion in creation—a joyful, present force in all He made. As we approach new seasons like the start of the school year, we're reminded that God's wisdom continues to guide and delight in the world He lovingly created.

With September fast approaching and the school year just around the corner, let's take a moment to pray for all the teachers and students preparing for a new year. Lifting them up in prayer is a beautiful way to support their journey and ask God to guide them in all they do. I want to reiterate that prayer can be simple. God knows what's in your heart, so opening the door to prayer can be short yet meaningful. "Dear God, please lift our students and teachers up and fill them with peace, wisdom, and strength as they face the challenges and joys of the year ahead."

Reflections ...

TODAY I AM GRATEFUL FOR ... _____

_____
_____
_____
_____
_____

August 26
JOHN 7:37–39

What a beautiful image Jesus gives us in John 7:37–39—offering living water to all who are thirsty. He promises the gift of the Holy Spirit, who refreshes, sustains, and flows within us like a life-giving stream. It's a joyful reminder that when we turn to Him, we are never left empty. His Spirit fills us with peace, strength, and purpose, even in the driest seasons of our lives.

Take a moment to enjoy the beauty of a sunrise or sunset today. As you watch the colours of the sky unfold, let it remind you of God's unchanging faithfulness and the hope we find in His promises. I love how the stillness of these moments can offer a chance to breathe and feel grounded in His love, knowing that just like the sun, God's faithfulness rises and sets with us every day.

Reflections ...

TODAY I AM GRATEFUL FOR ... _____

_____
_____
_____
_____
_____
_____

August 27
Psalm 32:8–9

Psalm 32:8–9 offers such a comforting promise—God assures us that He will instruct and teach us in the way we should go, guiding us with His loving eye upon us. What a joy to know we're not navigating life alone! Even when we feel uncertain, He's right there, gently leading us forward with wisdom and care.

Does your church do a blessing of the backpacks for students heading back to school? It's a meaningful tradition where we can pray for students, teachers, and families as they begin a new year. If your church doesn't have this tradition, it could be a wonderful way to come together as a community and lift up those who are preparing for the school year, asking God to bless them with wisdom, safety, and joy.

Reflections ...

Today I am grateful for ... _____

_____
_____
_____
_____
_____

August 28
LUKE 10:38–42

This story shows Martha busy with all the preparations for the meal, while Mary chooses to sit at Jesus's feet and listen to His wisdom and guidance. Jesus gently reminds Martha that sometimes the best way to honour those we love is by simply being present with them. This passage encourages us to slow down, take a breath, and cherish moments of connection over the hustle of daily life.

Invite a friend over for lunch or a simple meal and truly be present with one another, just as Mary was with Jesus. This is a beautiful opportunity to reconnect, enjoy meaningful conversation, and celebrate the joy of each other's company. Take a moment to appreciate the blessing of friendship and the joy that comes from sharing life together!

Reflections ...

TODAY I AM GRATEFUL FOR ... _____

_____
_____
_____
_____
_____
_____

August 29
JEREMIAH 29:11–13

Jeremiah 29:11–13 reminds us of God's incredible plans for our lives—plans to prosper us, give us hope, and a future. It's such a comforting thought that no matter what stage we're in, God has a good plan for us, one filled with purpose and promise. As we seek Him with all our hearts, we'll find Him, and His guidance will lead us toward the life He has for us.

As the end of August rolls around and gardens are bursting with produce, it's a great time to think about reaping what you've sown—both in your garden and in your life. Consider donating some of your harvest to those in need or sharing the fruits of your labour with a neighbour or friend. It's a beautiful way to give back, embodying the love and generosity God has shown us and spreading His goodness to others.

Reflections ...

TODAY I AM GRATEFUL FOR ... _____

_____
_____
_____
_____
_____
_____

August 30
John 14:25–27

As we look to the end of summer, we're reminded in John 14:25–27 that Jesus offers us a peace unlike anything the world can give. In times of worry or uncertainty, His peace remains steady, calming our hearts and allowing us to rest in His love. Jesus's gift of peace is a constant companion, reminding us that no matter what life throws our way, we can rely on His presence to guide and comfort us.

As summer winds down and you take stock of your garden, consider what you might want to do differently next year. Maybe you'd like to add a prayer bench, a quiet corner to reflect, or plant something new to symbolize hope and growth. This time is a wonderful opportunity to think about how your garden can be a place of peace, growth, and connection to God—just as Ruth's journey was a place of growth and new beginnings. Taking time to nurture this physical space can also nurture your spirit and bring you closer to God's peace.

Reflections ...

TODAY I AM GRATEFUL FOR ... _____

_____
_____
_____
_____
_____
_____

August 31
ECCLESIASTES 2:13–14

As we approach the end of summer, Ecclesiastes 2:13–14 reminds us that wisdom brings light to the things we do and see, just as the brightness of the day surpasses the darkness of night. It's a beautiful invitation to consider the wisdom we've gained this season—the lessons learned, the connections made, and the moments of peace found in God's creation. As we prepare for the transition into a new season, we can give thanks for the clarity and understanding that God's wisdom brings into our lives.

Make time to journal your gratitude for the summer, reflecting on the moments that have touched you most. Whether it's a special memory, a lesson learned, or the beauty of the season, writing down your thanks can help you recognize God's hand in every part of your life. Journaling gratitude helps us acknowledge His faithfulness and love, even in the everyday moments.

Reflections ...

TODAY I AM GRATEFUL FOR ... _____

_____
_____
_____
_____
_____
_____

September 1
PROVERBS 25:2–10

Proverbs 25:2–10 teaches us that there is wisdom in seeking out the deeper things, understanding that some things are meant to be discovered and revealed at the right time. Just as we search for wisdom and understanding, we're reminded that God's ways are not always immediate but are rich with purpose and goodness when we take the time to seek them out.

Making homemade bread, especially sourdough, can be a peaceful and grounding experience. I've been baking sourdough bread for years, long before the pandemic, and I find the process of mixing, kneading, and waiting for the dough to rise incredibly relaxing. As you bake, consider how the simple act of creating something from scratch parallels the wisdom we find when we take the time to patiently seek God's guidance. Just like the bread, the process of learning and growing in wisdom may take time, but the end result is always so fulfilling.

Reflections ...

TODAY I AM GRATEFUL FOR ... _____

_____
_____
_____
_____

September 2
PSALM 131

Psalm 131 speaks to a heart of quiet contentment and trust in God. The psalmist compares their soul to a weaned child, no longer anxious or striving, but resting peacefully in God's care. This meaningful message tells us to let go of our restless desires and embrace a childlike trust in God's will for our lives. When we surrender our worries and ambitions, we make space for true peace and contentment.

A wonderful way to ponder Psalm 131 is by doing a closet clean-out (yes, this is on my to-do list). Do you find that as the psalmist speaks of their gratitude to the Lord, cleaning out your closet can be a symbolic way of letting go of things that no longer serve you—whether it's physical clutter or emotional baggage? Take time to go through your clothes, donate items you no longer need, and create space for what truly brings you peace.

Reflections ...

TODAY I AM GRATEFUL FOR ... _____

_____

_____

_____

_____

_____

September 3
LUKE 8:1–3

Today's reading celebrates the incredible women who have shaped history and continue to inspire us. Luke reminds us of the important role women played in supporting Jesus's ministry, such as Mary Magdalene, Joanna, and Susanna. Their faithful service often went unnoticed, but their contributions were essential to Jesus's work, showing us that women have always been powerful agents of faith and change.

I've been lucky to have had many incredible female role models on my own spiritual journey. Who are the women in your life who have inspired your faith journey? Thank them for their influence and consider how you can be a source of encouragement and inspiration for a new generation of women walking in faith.

Reflections ...

TODAY I AM GRATEFUL FOR ... _____

_____
_____
_____
_____
_____

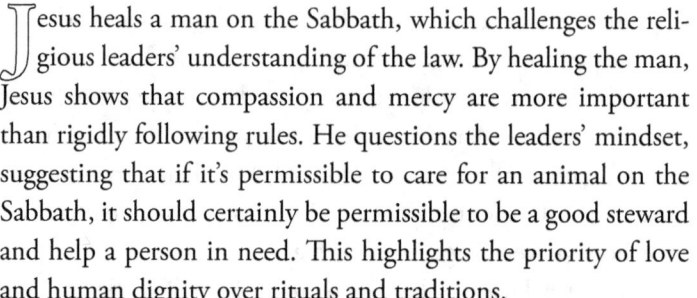

September 4
Luke 14:1–14

Jesus heals a man on the Sabbath, which challenges the religious leaders' understanding of the law. By healing the man, Jesus shows that compassion and mercy are more important than rigidly following rules. He questions the leaders' mindset, suggesting that if it's permissible to care for an animal on the Sabbath, it should certainly be permissible to be a good steward and help a person in need. This highlights the priority of love and human dignity over rituals and traditions.

A lovely way to embrace the remaining days of summer is by going for a bike ride. We love exploring our neighbourhood or riding through nature, biking offers a peaceful way to step away from the hustle and bustle, embrace the quiet, and consider Jesus's call to live humbly. As you ride, take a moment to think of how you can serve others with a heart of kindness, just as Jesus teaches in this passage.

Reflections …

TODAY I AM GRATEFUL FOR … _____
_____
_____
_____
_____
_____
_____

September 5
ACTS 4:32–35

In today's passage, we see the early church living in unity and generosity, sharing everything they had with one another. They cared deeply for each other, ensuring that no one was in need. The reading calls us to bear in mind the importance of community and selflessness, echoing God's love through our actions toward others.

Take the spirit of generosity into action by organizing a donation drive in your community. I do have to applaud our church, as they do a great job of gathering clothes, food, or supplies for those in need, this is a tangible way to share God's love with others. Don't you find that by serving others, we live out the beautiful message of unity and kindness shared in Acts 4:32–35?

Reflections ...

TODAY I AM GRATEFUL FOR ... _____

_____
_____
_____
_____
_____
_____

September 6
ACTS 8:26–40

Acts 8:26–40 is a powerful reminder of how God uses ordinary moments to transform lives. In this passage, Philip listens attentively to the Holy Spirit's guidance, leading him to an unexpected encounter with the Ethiopian eunuch. This encounter changes not only the eunuch's life but also shows us that when we remain open to God's direction, He leads us to places and people where we can share His love and salvation. It's a beautiful example of how God works through us to spread His hope in ways we might never anticipate.

As you look ahead to the fall, take a moment to explore the different groups your church offers. Whether it's a book club, a women's or men's group, or even something unique like a Christian baseball team (which is something I can really appreciate), these groups can be a great way to grow in your faith and build community. As you consider joining one of these groups, think about how they can help you persevere and grow in your relationship with God. You never know what opportunities may arise as you step into these spaces with an open heart!

Reflections ...

TODAY I AM GRATEFUL FOR ... _____

_____

_____

September 7
1 Timothy 1:1–20

In 1 Timothy 1:1–20, Paul writes to Timothy with heartfelt encouragement, urging him to remain firm in his faith and guard the teachings of Christ. He reflects on his own life, sharing how God's grace transformed him from a persecutor to a beloved servant, reminding us that no one is beyond the reach of God's redemptive love. This passage beautifully assures us that God's grace is abundant and available to all, regardless of our past mistakes. It's an encouraging call to embrace the transformative power of Christ's love and to hold fast to our faith.

With the changing seasons, I like to take a moment to check in with myself about my spiritual health. You can do this too, and ask yourself questions like, "How am I drawing closer to God lately?" or "Where can I strengthen my faith and trust in His plan for me?" I like to write these reflections down, as considering questions like these can help you pinpoint areas for growth, encouraging you to strengthen your relationship with God and live more fully in His love and grace.

Reflections ...

TODAY I AM GRATEFUL FOR ... _____

_____

_____

_____

September 8
1 Timothy 2:1–15

Paul emphasizes the importance of prayer in today's reading, urging believers to pray for all people, including leaders, so that we may live peaceful and godly lives. He also speaks about the dignity and role of women in the church, encouraging them to show God's beauty through humility and self-control. This passage reminds us that prayer is powerful and that we're called to both pray for others and live in a way that honours God in all things.

A beautiful way to embrace the peace and comfort we find in God is by spending time making something special, like canning your favourite summer recipes. One of my favourite things to do is make salsa with my in-laws' recipe, using the fresh produce from the garden. It's such a warm, fulfilling experience to preserve the goodness of the season and know that we can share these little gifts of love with others.

Reflections ...

TODAY I AM GRATEFUL FOR ... _____

_____

_____

_____

_____

_____

September 9
1 JOHN 4:1–6

In 1 John 4:1–6, we're reminded to test the spirits and be discerning about what we hear and believe. John encourages us to remain rooted in the truth of God's love and to be cautious of false teachings that can lead us astray. The passage invites us to grow in our relationship with God, knowing His voice and recognizing the Spirit of truth. It calls us to keep our hearts and minds aligned with the truth of Christ, especially in a world full of distractions.

For an activity, take some time for yourself and go to a spa? As I write this, my husband and I are enjoying some much-needed relaxation, and it's a wonderful way to refresh both body and spirit. Use the time to unwind and listen to God's voice in the stillness, allowing His peace to renew you.

Reflections ...

TODAY I AM GRATEFUL FOR ... _____

_____
_____
_____
_____
_____
_____

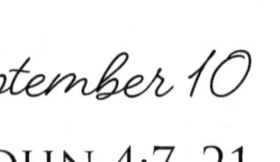

September 10
1 John 4:7–21

John reminds us that love comes from God, and if we truly know Him, love will naturally flow from us. This passage isn't just about being loved—it's about becoming love. When we live in God, His perfect love transforms us from the inside out, casting out fear and filling us with compassion for others. It's a powerful encouragement to not just know love, but to live it daily.

For a peaceful and creative way to consider these truths, I am regularly inspired by one of my girlfriends, who passed away—but oh how she loved to colour. A faith-themed colouring book is a simple way to remind us of God's love. As you colour, let the words and images sink into your heart, offering a calming space to pray and simply rest in God's love. It's a gentle and joyful way to connect with the Word and unwind your spirit.

Reflections ...

TODAY I AM GRATEFUL FOR ... _____

_____
_____
_____
_____

1 JOHN 5:1–12

1 John 5:1–12 reminds us that when we believe in Jesus as the Son of God, we are born of God—and with that comes a victorious, faith-filled life. This passage speaks to the assurance we have through Christ, that eternal life is not just a distant promise but a present reality lived in relationship with Him. God's testimony about His Son is trustworthy and life-giving, nurturing confidence and peace in every season.

I feel more in tune with God's Word the simpler I live. Living in this assurance, I like to dial back and enjoy the simple things in life. Try keeping a jug of water in the fridge with slices of cucumber, lemon, or your favourite fruit. It's a simple way to care for the body God gave you and a gentle reminder to keep filling up—not just with water, but with the living water of His Word every day.

Reflections ...

TODAY I AM GRATEFUL FOR ... _____

_____
_____
_____
_____
_____

JOYOUS FAITH

September 12
1 John 5:13–21

This reading brings us a beautiful assurance—John writes so that we may know we have eternal life through Jesus. It's not about guessing or hoping but about trusting fully in God's promise. He encourages us to remain rooted in truth, prayer, and love, turning away from anything that pulls us from God's light. This passage is a reminder of the deep confidence we can have in God's love and the strength that comes from living in His will.

As we read this passage, let's live it out! If you've planted extra vegetables in your garden, like we did, consider donating some to a local food bank or sharing with a neighbour. It's a beautiful way to pass along the blessings you've received and build a stronger, more caring community—just like John encourages us to do in our faith journey.

Reflections ...

TODAY I AM GRATEFUL FOR ... _____

_____
_____
_____
_____
_____
_____

September 13
2 John 1–13

Today we're reminded of the importance of walking in truth and love—two themes that beautifully mirror the heart of our faith. John encourages the church to hold fast to the teachings of Christ and to stay grounded in love, not just in word but in action. This short but heartfelt letter is a call to remain faithful and discerning, clinging to the truth of the gospel while continuing to care for one another deeply.

To carry that message with you wherever you go, set your car radio to a Christian music station and save it in your favourites. This is a simple way to fill my day with hope and encouragement. So blast those tunes and shine your light!

Reflections ...

TODAY I AM GRATEFUL FOR ... _____

_____
_____
_____
_____
_____
_____

September 14
3 JOHN 1–15

Third John 1–15 is a warm and personal letter from John, encouraging his friend Gaius to continue walking faithfully in truth and love. John celebrates hospitality, integrity, and support for fellow believers doing God's work—reminding us how important it is to lift each other up in service and sincerity. Like a gentle tap on the shoulder from a friend, John lovingly assures us that small acts of kindness and faithfulness matter deeply in the eyes of God.

To make your time with the Word a little more special today, treat yourself to a favourite coffee while you read—something just for you. I love enjoying an oat milk cappuccino when I take time to reflect and study; it feels like a little gift in the middle of a busy day. Find a cozy corner, open your Bible, and let the Word soak in as you sip something warm and comforting.

Reflections ...

TODAY I AM GRATEFUL FOR ... _____

_____
_____
_____
_____
_____

September 15
Genesis 4:1–15

Today's reading covers the story of Cain and Abel, a powerful reminder of the human heart and the choices we make. Though this passage deals with jealousy and consequence, it also shows God's continued presence and mercy—even in moments of failure. God's response to Cain reminds us that He sees our struggles and offers us the opportunity to turn back, grow, and live differently. It's a call to consider how we handle our emotions and how we treat one another.

As we move into a new season, take some time to make a list of things you'd like to accomplish this fall. And yes, I have pumpkin-themed notebooks for just such an occasion. Include spiritual goals, new routines, or ways you want to connect with others or deepen your faith. A fresh season brings fresh opportunities—let's walk into it with intention, grace, and hope.

Reflections ...

Today I am grateful for ... _____

_____
_____
_____
_____
_____

September 16
1 Timothy 6:1–21

This passage reminds us that our lives reflect the way we live out our faith. Paul speaks about honouring God through how we act, what we value, and how we respond to the gifts He's given us. Whether we have little or much, we're called to find contentment and focus on what truly matters—our relationship with God and how we treat others.

What does celebrating the gift of life mean to you? For me, it's often enjoying a peaceful walk in nature, spending time with loved ones, or simply pausing to consider the blessings in your life, do something that brings you joy. Remember, life itself is a reason to celebrate!

Reflections ...

TODAY I AM GRATEFUL FOR ... _____

_____

_____

_____

_____

_____

_____

Luke 6:27–36

Love our enemies, do good to those who hurt us, and extend mercy where it may not be deserved—it's not always easy, but it's one of the most beautiful ways we can mirror God's grace in the world. Jesus reminds us that we're called to love not just when it's easy, but especially when it's hard—because that's how He loves us.

With apple season right around the corner, plan a visit to a local orchard or farm. We are lucky enough to have a beautiful orchard close by, and they open their doors for our youth group. Visiting an orchard is a fun way to spend quality time with family or friends, and after picking, you can bake something delicious, like apple crisp, to share. We have the best youth group leaders, and after a Friday of picking apples, the youth make apple crisps for our church's Sunday coffee hour. It's a simple reminder of how sweet life can be.

Reflections ...

TODAY I AM GRATEFUL FOR ... _____

_____
_____
_____
_____

September 18
Proverbs 3:13–18

Have you ever stopped to think about the priceless value of wisdom in your life? Proverbs 3:13–18 paints a beautiful picture of wisdom as something more precious than silver or gold, offering long life, peace, and joy. When we seek God's wisdom, it becomes the foundation for living a life full of purpose, grace, and blessing. We are reminded that true happiness isn't found in possessions, but in following God's guidance.

I get a lot of enjoyment from music, and so often our music directors and organists are overlooked, and they work so hard. Let them know that they are a blessing by sending them a cheerful note. A heartfelt message to thank them for all the joy they bring through music can brighten their day and show appreciation for the powerful role they play in leading your worship community.

Reflections ...

TODAY I AM GRATEFUL FOR ... _____

_____
_____
_____
_____
_____
_____

September 19
Psalm 100:4–5

Psalm 100:4–5 invites us to enter God's presence with thanksgiving and praise, reminding us of His goodness, love, and faithfulness. Consider His many blessings. We are called to rejoice and be grateful, sharing His love with those around us.

Before the weather gets cool, gather friends or family for a friendly game of outdoor sports. Whether it's pickleball (Yes, please!), frisbee, or basketball, engaging in fun activities together is a great way to foster community and strengthen relationships.

Reflections ...

Today I am grateful for ... _____

_____

_____

_____

_____

_____

_____

September 20
Numbers 21:4–9

Today we read about the Israelites' journey through the wilderness and how, in their desperation, they were given hope through God's provision—a bronze serpent on a pole that brought healing to those who looked upon it. This story reminds us of God's grace and the importance of keeping our eyes focused on Him, even in challenging times. Just as the Israelites were given hope through their struggles, we too can find comfort in God's love and provision.

In the spirit of this inclusivity, now is the perfect time to share some blooms from your garden with friends? Our wedding was decorated with hydrangea blossoms in Mason jars—so simple and beautiful. Picking fresh flowers and gifting them is a lovely way to brighten someone's day and remind them of the beauty of God's creation.

Reflections ...

TODAY I AM GRATEFUL FOR ... _____

_____
_____
_____
_____
_____
_____

September 21
Psalm 104

The psalmist paints a picture of the natural world functioning under God's design, from the waters and the animals to the plants that sustain life. It encourages us to recognize God's hand in every detail of our lives and to trust in His faithfulness in providing for all our needs.

This psalm hits home for me. Trusting in God's design is hard at times—we are human, after all. But it's important to take time to consider if there's someone in your life you need to forgive, or perhaps someone from whom you should seek forgiveness. This can be a powerful step toward healing and reconciliation. Reach out to that person, whether it's through a heartfelt conversation or a simple note expressing your feelings. Remember, extending forgiveness not only enriches your relationships but also deepens your connection with God, who forgives us abundantly.

Reflections ...

TODAY I AM GRATEFUL FOR ... _____

_____
_____
_____
_____

September 22
2 Corinthians 9:6–8

Paul wrote 2 Corinthians to the Corinthian church to address several issues and follow up on his earlier request for a contribution to support the impoverished, famine-stricken, and persecuted believers in Jerusalem. Paul emphasized that God loves a cheerful giver, and when we give with a joyful heart, we reflect God's abundant grace and kindness. The verses also highlight that God provides for us in ways that allow us to be generous and bless others, and in doing so, we receive blessings in return.

Our families can often be the cheerful givers in our everyday lives. If you can, get together with loved ones and relive those precious moments by watching old home videos or flipping through photo albums. When our family goes down memory lane, I love hearing the stories and connecting to the joy of those times, and these memories are blessings from God, meant to be cherished.

Reflections ...

TODAY I AM GRATEFUL FOR ... _____

_____
_____
_____
_____
_____

September 23
Nehemiah 9:5–37

Nehemiah, a Jewish leader who served as the cupbearer to the Persian king Artaxerxes I, is a powerful example of resilience and faith. In Nehemiah 9:5–37, the people of Israel recount God's faithfulness throughout their history, acknowledging their shortcomings and celebrating His mercy and grace. Nehemiah's leadership during a challenging time shows how, even in difficult circumstances, God's faithfulness remains constant.

Think about how you can be a beacon of hope and encouragement in your own life. It can be intimidating, but consider sharing your faith story with someone or reaching out to a friend who might be going through a tough time. Isn't it humbling to think that your words and actions can uplift others and show them the power of resilience and faith, just as Nehemiah's example inspires us to stay steadfast and trust in God's plan, no matter what obstacles we face?

Reflections ...

TODAY I AM GRATEFUL FOR ... _____

_____
_____
_____
_____

September 24
Psalm 67

This psalm is a joyful and hope-filled prayer for God's blessing, not only for us but for all nations. It beautifully reminds us that when we receive God's grace, it's meant to be shared—so that His ways may be known and His love experienced far and wide. This psalm invites us to consider how our lives can shine His light and goodness into the world, just by living with gratitude, kindness, and praise in our hearts.

As a meaningful activity, take a moment to update your calendar with important dates—like family birthdays and anniversaries. I am bad for updating my calendar, but when you remember and celebrate these special moments, those small acts speak volumes. After all, many of us just want so badly to be seen.

Reflections ...

TODAY I AM GRATEFUL FOR ... _____

_____
_____
_____
_____
_____

September 25
NEHEMIAH 2:17–20

Nehemiah 2:17–20 captures a powerful moment when Nehemiah steps into his calling to help rebuild Jerusalem's broken walls. He doesn't just see the rubble—he sees the potential, and he inspires others to join him in the work. This passage reminds us that even when things seem overwhelming, with God's hand upon us and a heart full of faith, we can rise up and build something beautiful. Nehemiah's courage, leadership, and trust in God are a timeless encouragement to keep moving forward, even in the face of resistance.

For a simple, meaningful activity, take a bit of time this week to research the historical context of Nehemiah's life and the time he lived in. Okay, okay, I know—I love to read, but by learning about the Persian Empire, the return from exile, and the rebuilding of Jerusalem, you can deepen your understanding of just how faithful and bold Nehemiah truly was. And it's always pretty darn awesome whenever we can connect more deeply with Scripture!

Reflections ...

TODAY I AM GRATEFUL FOR ... _____

_____

_____

_____

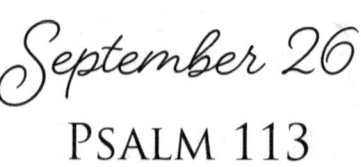

September 26
PSALM 113

Psalm 113 is a joyful celebration of God's majesty and tender care for the humble. It reminds us that the same God who is exalted above the heavens also bends low to lift up the poor and the needy. What an incredible image—our mighty God noticing and loving each of us so personally! This psalm encourages us to praise Him not only in grand ways but also in the everyday moments where His kindness and grace shine through.

I love baking in the fall! A simple classic is currant biscuits like my grandmother used to bake—they're simple, nostalgic, and full of love. Share them with family or neighbours. It's a warm and delicious way to spread love and gratitude!

Reflections ...

TODAY I AM GRATEFUL FOR ... _____

_____
_____
_____
_____
_____
_____
_____

September 27
1 John 2:18–29

We're reminded in 1 John 2:18–29 of the importance of staying rooted in Christ, especially in times of uncertainty or confusion. John encourages believers to remain faithful to what they've been taught and to let God's truth dwell deeply in their hearts. This passage reassures us that the anointing of the Holy Spirit helps guide and protect us, keeping us aligned with God's love and promises. What a comforting reminder that we're never walking this journey alone—God is with us, guiding us each step of the way!

So how about lifting your spirit and energizing your soul with some upbeat Christian tunes? I was recently listening to "A Wonderful Time Up There" by Pat Boone. This song is an oldie but a goody, and it's a foot tappin' smile enhancer. Check it out!

Reflections ...

TODAY I AM GRATEFUL FOR ... _____

_____
_____
_____
_____
_____
_____

JOYOUS FAITH

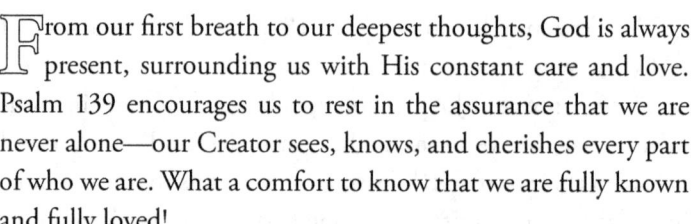

September 28
PSALM 139

From our first breath to our deepest thoughts, God is always present, surrounding us with His constant care and love. Psalm 139 encourages us to rest in the assurance that we are never alone—our Creator sees, knows, and cherishes every part of who we are. What a comfort to know that we are fully known and fully loved!

To live out that spirit of loving connection, be sure to call your parents or someone you care about but haven't spoken to in a while? One of my girlfriends moved out East, and even a short chat can bring joy and comfort, and it's a beautiful way to nurture the relationships God has blessed you with. Take a moment to check in, share a laugh, or simply say, "I'm thinking of you."

Reflections ...

TODAY I AM GRATEFUL FOR ... _____

_____
_____
_____
_____
_____
_____

September 29
Deuteronomy 8:1–10

Deuteronomy is essentially a series of farewell sermons delivered by Moses to the Israelites before they enter the Promised Land. He's not allowed to go with them, so he's giving them everything they need to stay faithful after he's gone. Deuteronomy 8:1–10 reminds us that even in seasons of challenge, God lovingly provides. As the Israelites journeyed through the wilderness, they learned to rely on His faithfulness, not their own strength.

Daily I try to set aside some quiet time to simply be still and meditate on God's goodness. I find a peaceful spot, close my eyes, and take a few deep breaths. By meditating on God's Word and what it means to trust the Lord fully, I can feel His peace settle into your heart, reminding me that He is right here beside me—guiding, providing, and lovingly leading me forward.

Reflections ...

TODAY I AM GRATEFUL FOR ... _____

_____
_____
_____
_____

September 30
Orange Shirt Day
(Canada)

PSALM 19:7–14

On Orange Shirt Day, we reflect on the importance of truth and reconciliation, acknowledging the painful history of residential schools in Canada. Psalm 19:7–14 reminds us of the beauty and power of God's Word, which is perfect and life-giving. Just as the psalmist speaks of God's law reviving the soul, we can look to God for healing, justice, and reconciliation in our own communities. His Word guides us, comforts us, and offers hope for restoration.

Observing today isn't just about wearing a shirt that's orange. It's about taking the time to contemplate the ways you can contribute to reconciliation—whether by learning more about this history, having a conversation, or extending kindness to those around you. Just as God's Word helps us grow, we can grow together as a community in love and understanding.

Reflections ...

TODAY I AM GRATEFUL FOR ... _____

_____
_____
_____
_____
_____

October 1
Psalm 91:1–13

Today's reading highlights the *promise* of God's protection and faithfulness. As we dwell in the shelter of the Most High, we find comfort and refuge under His wings. No matter what challenges come our way, we are assured that God is with us, guarding and guiding us with His unfailing love.

This week, take a moment to rest in God's protection and the ways He has kept you safe. You can also encourage someone else by offering a prayer or a kind word, reminding them that God's protection surrounds them too. Let's share the peace and security that comes from knowing we are held in His loving hands!

Reflections ...

TODAY I AM GRATEFUL FOR ... _____

_____
_____
_____
_____
_____
_____
_____

JOYOUS FAITH

October 2
2 Thessalonians 1:6–10

Today's reading comes from the second of two letters addressed to the Thessalonian church, and it addresses several key themes and concerns. Second Thessalonians 1:6–10 reminds us of the ultimate justice and rest that God will bring to those who are faithful to Him. Paul writes about how God will bring relief and vindication to His people, providing peace for those who endure hardship in His name. Truly this passage inspires us to live faithfully, knowing that God will reward us in the end.

Consider your favourite spiritual hymn and how it comforts and strengthens your faith. Is there a modern version or rendition of the hymn that brings new meaning to your heart? Go on a little musical treasure hunt, exploring different interpretations online or on your music platform, and let the song fill your spirit.

Reflections ...

TODAY I AM GRATEFUL FOR … _____

_____
_____
_____
_____
_____

October 3
2 Corinthians 1:3–7

Paul speaks of the comfort and encouragement we receive from God, which we're called to share with others. He reminds us that just as God comforts us in our struggles, we are to comfort and support others who are going through similar challenges. This passage speaks to the deep bond of fellowship we have in Christ, where our shared experiences of God's love and grace become a source of strength and hope for one another.

Rest and recharge—maybe indulge in a peaceful nap. Create a calm environment, perhaps with soft music or a cozy blanket, and allow yourself to simply be still. As you rest, ponder the importance of taking care of your body as part of your spiritual journey. Recognize that rest isn't just a physical necessity but a way to rejuvenate your spirit and remain connected to God's peace.

Reflections ...

TODAY I AM GRATEFUL FOR ... _____

_____
_____
_____
_____
_____

October 4
LUKE 21:5–24

Jesus speaks about the trials and challenges that will come, but He also encourages us to remain hopeful and trust in God's ultimate plan. His words remind us that even in the most difficult moments, God is with us, guiding us through every storm.

Create a prayer list for your community. As you write down the names of those in need of encouragement or healing, lift them up in prayer, asking God to cover them with peace and strength. This simple act of love not only supports others but also strengthens your own faith as you see the power of prayer at work!

Reflections ...

TODAY I AM GRATEFUL FOR ... _____

_____

_____

_____

_____

_____

_____

October 5
PSALM 62

David reminds us that our hope and trust are in God alone. He declares that God is our rock and salvation, a refuge in times of trouble. This powerful declaration of trust calls us to centre ourselves in God's faithfulness and rely on His unwavering support, especially when life feels uncertain or overwhelming.

Take a moment to share appreciation with those around you. Whether it's a family member, friend, or coworker, it's fun to let them know how much you value them and the good they bring to your life. Don't you find that a simple word of encouragement or gratitude can brighten someone's day?

Reflections ...

TODAY I AM GRATEFUL FOR ... _____

_____
_____
_____
_____
_____
_____

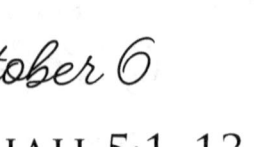

October 6
NEHEMIAH 5:1–13

Through this reading, we see Nehemiah's heart for justice as he confronts the unfair treatment of the poor among the Israelites. His action to restore fairness and protect his people reminds us that God calls us to live with compassion, fairness, and a sense of responsibility for one another. We are challenged here to think about the ways we can act justly and exhibit God's love through our actions.

Explore fresh ways to connect with God through prayer. Whether it's singing your favourite worship song, journaling your thoughts, or practising a simple breath prayer, make room for God in a way that feels authentic to you. Remember, just like Nehemiah's heart for his people, God cares deeply about our hearts, and prayer is one of the most intimate ways we can draw near to Him.

Reflections ...

TODAY I AM GRATEFUL FOR ... _____

_____

_____

_____

_____

_____

_____

October 7
LUKE 17:1–10

In Luke 17:1–10, Jesus teaches us about humility and faith, reminding us that even small acts of obedience can make a big impact when done with a heart that trusts in God. He calls us to serve selflessly and faithfully, knowing that our work is never in vain when it's done in His name. It's a gracious note that God doesn't look for grand gestures but a heart willing to serve, no matter how small or simple the task.

As you dive into fall decorating, let this be a fun celebration of the beauty and abundance God provides! Gather up some colourful autumn leaves, cute pumpkins, and warm-toned decorations to transform your home into a cozy haven. As you arrange each piece, consider how God's faithfulness fills your life with peace and joy, just like the warmth that fills your home this season.

Reflections ...

TODAY I AM GRATEFUL FOR ... _____

_____
_____
_____
_____
_____

October 8
Matthew 4:1–11

What a powerful reminder we find in Matthew 4:1–11, where Jesus, led by the Spirit into the wilderness, resists every temptation the enemy throws His way. Isn't it beautiful to know that even in our hardest, driest seasons, Jesus walks ahead of us, showing us how to lean fully on God's Word and trust in His provision? Matthew, a former tax collector turned disciple, wrote this Gospel. We're never alone in our struggles, and through Christ, we too can stand firm.

One of my favourite simple joys in the fall is picking up extra pumpkins for my front porch—I love everything about this, from going to the pumpkin patch to roasting the seeds for a crunchy snack. And don't forget to use the pumpkin itself for warm, cozy soups on a cold autumn day. This week, as you roast your pumpkin and savour the goodness, take a moment to meditate on God's daily provision. Thank Him for how He strengthens you in hard moments and ask Him to fill you with His Word like He filled Jesus in the wilderness. Let that warm bowl of soup remind you: God's love nourishes us deeply—body, mind, and soul.

Reflections ...

Today I am grateful for ... _____

_____

_____

October 9
Exodus 17:1–7

The book of Exodus invites us to consider how we can trust God's provision, even when we face difficult times and challenges. The Israelites were grumbling and complaining about their hardships in the desert, questioning God's provision. Yet despite their doubts and negativity, God still provided for them, showing His faithfulness and love.

Embrace positive life habits, like saving and budgeting. These bring a sense of peace and security into our lives, allowing us to manage resources wisely and focus on what truly matters. Contemplate your financial habits and consider setting a small, achievable goal to help bring more peace and stability into your life.

Reflections ...

TODAY I AM GRATEFUL FOR ... _____

_____
_____
_____
_____
_____
_____
_____

October 10
PROVERBS 4:23–27

Our reading today reminds us to guard our hearts above all else, for everything we do flows from it. The choices we make, the thoughts we entertain, and the actions we take are all shaped by the condition of our hearts. We are called to be intentional about what we allow to influence us, keeping our hearts aligned with God's wisdom, so that our lives display His love and peace.

To bring this reading to life, what more delicious way can there be than to bake fall cookies? Gather up your favourite autumn spices like cinnamon and nutmeg, and don't forget the seasonal goodies like pumpkin and apples! As you share these sweet treats, you're not just sharing a bite, but also spreading joy and kindness.

Reflections ...

TODAY I AM GRATEFUL FOR ... _____

_____
_____
_____
_____
_____
_____

October 11
John 6:16–21

In today's reading, we see Jesus walking on water to reach His disciples during a storm. In their fear, He calls out to them, *"It is I; don't be afraid"* (v. 20b). This powerful moment reminds us that no matter the storms we face in life, Jesus is always with us, offering strength and assurance. His presence in our lives can calm our fears and guide us through the most difficult times.

We love stopping to grab fresh blooms on the way to visit my in-laws. We don't get to visit as often as we'd like, but it lets them know how much we love them. Fall flowers are like God's art in bloom, reminding us of the beauty of creation and symbolizing the growth we seek in our spiritual lives.

Reflections ...

TODAY I AM GRATEFUL FOR ... _____

_____

_____

_____

_____

_____

October 12
Psalm 111

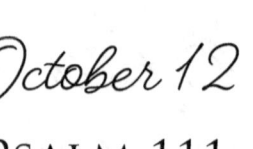

Psalm 111 is a joyful celebration of God's faithfulness, wisdom, and wondrous works. It reminds us to pause and praise the Lord with our whole hearts, especially in the company of others. This psalm highlights how God's righteousness and grace are remembered through the generations—and what better way to celebrate His goodness than by creating lasting, joy-filled memories with the people around us?

If you have young ones or are part of a youth group, gather for a meal where everyone uses a unique utensil from the kitchen instead of the usual forks and spoons – a utensil supper! Think whisks, spatulas, or even ladles—whatever sparks joy and laughter!

Reflections ...

TODAY I AM GRATEFUL FOR ... _____

_____

_____

_____

_____

_____

_____

October 13
Daniel 3:1–30

Shadrach, Meshach, and Abednego stood firm in their faith, refusing to bow to the king's golden image, even in the face of certain death. They remind us of the power of unwavering faith. God miraculously saved them from the fiery furnace, showing His protection and faithfulness to those who trust in Him—an important message of courage and strength.

Consider planting a fall garden or picking up some beautiful mums or other autumn plants that bring you joy. As you dig in the soil, take a moment to ponder the beauty of new beginnings—even in cooler seasons. And don't forget to tuck in a few crocus bulbs for spring! It's a lovely way to plant hope now and look forward to the blooms yet to come.

Reflections ...

TODAY I AM GRATEFUL FOR ... _____

_____
_____
_____
_____
_____
_____
_____

October 14
Psalm 31:1–5, 15–16

As we delve into Psalm 31, we see a heartfelt plea for God's protection, trust, and deliverance. The psalmist finds refuge in God, confident that He is a rock and a fortress in times of trouble. Just as we seek refuge in God, this passage reminds us that He is always our safe place, guiding and shielding us through every season of life.

Take a moment to step outside and connect with the beauty of God's creation. If weather permits, visit a local park or nature reserve. Being surrounded by the trees and greenery can be incredibly calming and uplifting.

Reflections ...

TODAY I AM GRATEFUL FOR ... _____

_____
_____
_____
_____
_____
_____
_____

October 15
JOHN 10:11–18

Jesus, the Good Shepherd, lovingly cares for us, guiding us with His protective presence and sacrificial love. Just as He laid down His life for His sheep, we're called to trust in His guidance and rest in the strength He offers. What a comfort to know that we're never alone but always held in His tender care, surrounded by His abundant love.

To show Christ's loving care, reach out to someone who may need a reminder of God's love. Send a thoughtful message or offer a listening ear. Your kindness can be a sign someone needs of the love and care Jesus shows to each of us, and it's sure to bring a smile to their face!

Reflections ...

TODAY I AM GRATEFUL FOR ... _____

_____
_____
_____
_____
_____
_____

October 16
ACTS 9:36–43

As we read the beautiful story of Tabitha, we see a woman full of good works and charity, who was raised from the dead by Peter's prayer. Her life was marked by kindness, generosity, and love for others, which made a lasting impact on her community. Like Tabitha, we're encouraged to live with hearts full of love and service, touching others with acts of kindness and care.

Is it too early to decorate pumpkins? If you paint them, you can decorate them early—and it's a cheerful way to celebrate the season and share some festive joy with neighbours and passersby.

Reflections ...

TODAY I AM GRATEFUL FOR ... _____

_____
_____
_____
_____
_____
_____

October 17
Psalm 47

Our reading today is a joyful declaration of God's sovereignty and His reign over all the earth. It invites us to clap our hands, shout with joy, and acknowledge that God is the King of all nations, deserving of our worship and praise. His greatness is unmatched, and we're called to respond with awe and gratitude for His love and faithfulness.

This week, take a moment to celebrate God's greatness in your own life. Whether through a song, a prayer, or simply pausing to reflect on His goodness, let your heart overflow with praise. Let's share His joy and invite others to join in worship, lifting up the name of our amazing King!

Reflections ...

Today I am grateful for ... _____

_____
_____
_____
_____
_____
_____

October 18
JAMES 4:1–10

This passage is a powerful reminder that true peace and joy come when we surrender our desires to God, submitting to His guidance and wisdom rather than seeking to control our circumstances. It's a call to humble ourselves before God, trust in His grace, and seek reconciliation in our relationships with others.

Who loves brunch? I do! A great way to put this into practice is by enjoying a brunch with family or friends. Take this opportunity to come together in peace, leaving any conflict or tension behind. As you share a meal, focus on fostering love and unity, encouraging open conversation and mutual respect.

Reflections ...

TODAY I AM GRATEFUL FOR ... _____

_____
_____
_____
_____
_____
_____
_____

October 19
EPHESIANS 6:10–18

Let's take a moment to understand the importance of standing firm in our faith, much like the message in Ephesians 6:10–18, where we're reminded to put on the full armour of God. This passage encourages us to be strong and steadfast, ready to face any challenges with faith and the strength God provides.

Is today a good day for a hike? You could collect fall leaves while you stroll through the trees. As you walk amidst the vibrant colours of autumn, contemplate the beauty of God's creation and the new beginnings He offers us. You might even consider creating a nature collage or a scrapbook page with the leaves as a visual reminder of the covenant and the promise of restoration in your own life.

Reflections ...

TODAY I AM GRATEFUL FOR ... _____

_____
_____
_____
_____
_____

October 20
1 Corinthians 10:12–13

In life, we're often faced with moments of temptation or difficulty. Yet we are reassured that God is always with us, offering strength and a way through. This reminder invites us to rely on His faithfulness in times of struggle, knowing that we're never alone and that He won't allow us to face more than we can bear. What a comfort to know that He provides us with the grace to overcome.

Making butter tarts is a great way to enjoy the fall season. As you bake, you can take a moment to consider how you seek God's wisdom in your life, especially during challenging situations. Butter tarts can nourish the soul and bring a smile to everyone you share them with!

Reflections ...

TODAY I AM GRATEFUL FOR ... _____

_____
_____
_____
_____
_____
_____
_____

October 21

2 Corinthians 4:16–18

Paul reminds us to have courage, even during life's challenges, for the things that are unseen are far more valuable than the things we can see. The temporary struggles we face pale in comparison to the eternal glory that awaits us. Just as we focus on what is eternal and lasting, we are invited to bring encouragement and joy to those around us, especially to children, who are so often in need of a little extra light in their lives.

I love sending cards, especially to our niece and nephews. It's so fun to brighten a child's day by sending a fun, sticker-filled letter. You can write a thoughtful note of encouragement, share a funny joke, or even include a Bible verse. The stickers will add a playful touch, and the letter will be a little reminder of the love and joy Jesus brings into our lives, helping to brighten their world and reminding them of the eternal hope we all share.

Reflections ...

TODAY I AM GRATEFUL FOR ... _____

October 22
PHILIPPIANS 3:13–14

Imagine starting each day with a sense of renewal, leaving behind what's already happened—good or bad—and moving forward with purpose and hope. That's exactly what Paul encourages us to do in this passage. He reminds us that the past doesn't define us; what matters is what lies ahead with Christ.

Baking a seasonal pie always reminds me of my mom, who's an incredible pie maker. It's such a simple, joyful way to celebrate the summer bounty God provides. You can bake a pie and share it with a loved one, just like my mom taught me—spreading kindness and enjoying God's gifts together.

Reflections ...

TODAY I AM GRATEFUL FOR ... _____

_____
_____
_____
_____
_____
_____
_____

October 23
MATTHEW 11:12–19

Matthew 11:12–19 reminds us that the kingdom of God is both powerful and often misunderstood. Jesus honours John the Baptist, recognizing his role in preparing hearts for the Messiah. It's a gentle nudge to stay rooted in grace and truth, even when the world feels noisy or confusing. Through it all, Jesus invites us into His wisdom and rest.

Focus on your mental health. Ponder how Christ empowers you to serve others while also caring for yourself. Consider journaling your thoughts on servant leadership—how can you embody this in your daily interactions, whether at work, home, or in your community? By nurturing your well-being, you create a healthier space to lead with humility and grace, allowing the hope found in Christ to shine through in all you do.

Reflections ...

TODAY I AM GRATEFUL FOR ... _____

_____
_____
_____
_____
_____

JOYOUS FAITH

October 24
ISAIAH 41:10–13

The beauty of this verse lies in God's constant presence and strength, offering peace amid fear and uncertainty. It's a reminder that we are never alone and that we can trust in God's protection and provision, no matter what trials come our way. His love is a constant source of strength, and in Him, we find the courage to face life's difficulties.

Declutter your inbox. Take a few moments to unsubscribe from email lists that no longer serve you or bring value. By letting go of these digital distractions, you can create a sense of peace and focus in your life. Just as we're encouraged to keep our hearts and actions pure, cleaning up your inbox can be a small but impactful step toward a more organized, peaceful, and intentional life.

Reflections ...

TODAY I AM GRATEFUL FOR ... _____

_____
_____
_____
_____
_____

October 25
Philippians 1:12–30

This passage from Philippians is such an uplifting reminder that joy and purpose can be found even in tough times. Paul shares how, despite his imprisonment, his struggles have helped spread the good news of Jesus, showing us that God can work through every situation. What's truly special here is how Paul's focus isn't on his own challenges but on how those challenges are being used to bring others closer to Christ. It's a lovely encouragement for us to trust that no matter what we're going through, God can give us the courage and strength we need.

Think of your life and how you're living out the person God created you to be. Are there areas where you feel like you're holding back or not fully embracing your potential? Ask yourself how you can step into the person God has designed you to be—without fear and with confidence, knowing that He's with you every step of the way. You might even want to jot down your thoughts in a journal and pray for the courage to live boldly in His purpose for you.

Reflections ...

TODAY I AM GRATEFUL FOR ... _____

_____

_____

_____

October 26
Joshua 1:8–9

The book of Joshua is named after its central figure—Joshua, the courageous leader who succeeded Moses and led the Israelites into the Promised Land. He was a faithful servant of God, known for his obedience, bravery, and deep trust in the Lord's promises. In Joshua 1:8–9, God lovingly reminds Joshua (and us) to stay grounded in His Word and to move forward with strength and courage, knowing He is always by our side.

Celebrate the season by making some sweet fall treats. Have you ever tried making homemade candy apples? I used to love making toffee apples and caramel corn in the fall, and there's just something so special about the smell of sugar bubbling and apples getting their glossy coating. It's a fun, nostalgic activity to do with loved ones, and a delicious reminder of the joy that can be found in even the simplest of moments.

Reflections ...

TODAY I AM GRATEFUL FOR ... _____

_____
_____
_____
_____
_____
_____

October 27
Titus 2:1–15

Paul offers guidance on living a life that honours God and supports those around us. He encourages older men and women to set an example of godly living, and challenges younger generations to follow these examples, embracing virtues like kindness, self-control, and purity. This passage reminds us that the grace of God empowers us to live righteously and with courage, and that our actions speak volumes about our faith.

To put this into action, consider volunteering with the next generation at your church, whether it's in Sunday school or youth group. By sharing your wisdom and example, you can help nurture the faith of young people and guide them to live lives that echo God's love and grace.

Reflections ...

TODAY I AM GRATEFUL FOR ... _____

_____

_____

_____

_____

_____

_____

October 28
2 Thessalonians 3:1–13

Paul reminds the church to stay diligent in doing good, even when the road gets tough. His encouragement speaks to the power of steadfastness, community, and love in action. As we walk in faith, we're called to support and uplift one another—not just in grand gestures, but in the small, meaningful ways that displays Christ's love in our everyday lives.

Making a concerted effort to say "I love you" more often is a beautiful way to embody this message. Whether it's with family, friends, or someone who just needs a bit of kindness today, share those three little words with intention and warmth. Write a note, send a text, or say it face-to-face—these simple moments of love and encouragement can create ripples of hope and joy all around you!

Reflections ...

TODAY I AM GRATEFUL FOR ... _____

_____
_____
_____
_____
_____
_____

October 29
PSALM 103:1–5

Psalm 103:1–5 is a lovely passage, telling us of God's endless love, compassion, and faithfulness. It invites us to praise Him for all His blessings, both big and small. The passage encourages us to consider how God has healed, redeemed, and renewed us, and it calls us to respond in gratitude for His goodness and mercy. As we meditate on His goodness, we can't help but feel our hearts swell with gratitude for all He has done.

To fully embrace the love captured in this psalm, I'd encourage you to listen to "Bless the Lord, O My Soul" by Matt Redman. This uplifting song beautifully expresses the joy and reverence we feel when we remember God's goodness. As you listen, let the music wash over you and inspire you to reflect on the blessings you've received.

Reflections ...

TODAY I AM GRATEFUL FOR ... _____

_____
_____
_____
_____
_____

October 30
2 Thessalonians 1:1–5

I marvel at how much Paul accomplished in his lifetime—today's reading has Paul offering encouragement to a community that is holding fast to their faith in the face of hardship. He praises their perseverance, love, and growing faith—reminding us that even in challenging times, our steadfastness speaks volumes about the strength God gives us. It's a heartfelt nudge to keep loving well, serving joyfully, and letting our lives reflect the grace we've been given.

How about whipping up a batch of homemade Halloween candy for your special friends and neighbours? I was lucky to grow up around a few wonderful women who would make homemade treats at Halloween—and what a treat it was! I always ate that candy first! It's such a fun, thoughtful way to spread joy and care, wrapped in sweetness and love. So go ahead—share a little homemade kindness this season!

Reflections ...

TODAY I AM GRATEFUL FOR ... _____

_____
_____
_____
_____
_____

October 31

HALLOWEEN

PSALM 34:17–19

Have you ever felt overwhelmed or heartbroken, wondering if anyone truly sees your pain? Psalm 34:17–19 assures us that God not only sees us—He is *near* to us in those moments. He hears our cries, offers comfort to the broken-hearted, and brings healing and hope when we feel crushed in spirit.

This Halloween, embrace the joy and lightheartedness of the season with open arms! I love walking my dog, Joy, while soaking in the laughter and creativity of little ones dressed up and running around our neighbourhood. Set out a bowl of treats on your steps—maybe even a few treats for furry friends—and include a cheerful note encouraging kindness. Then you can partake in the joy and laughter.

Reflections ...

TODAY I AM GRATEFUL FOR ... _____

_____
_____
_____
_____
_____
_____

November

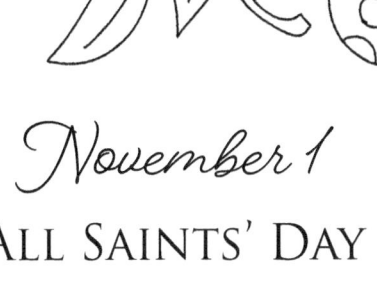

November 1
All Saints' Day

Psalm 27:7–14

Psalm 27:7–14 is a profoundly meaningful message, as it shows us God's unwavering presence in our lives, especially when we face challenges. The psalmist calls out to God, expressing deep trust in His protection and guidance, even when others may turn away. We can find comfort in the knowledge that God hears us, guides us, and is with us through all circumstances, offering us strength and hope in His promises.

All Saints' Day, celebrated on November 1 by many Christian denominations, honours all the saints—known and unknown—who have gone before us in faith. It's a time to contemplate their lives, their contributions to our faith, and the legacy they leave behind. This year, take a moment to list the loved ones in your life who have inspired your faith journey. In doing so, you can express your gratitude to God for the community of believers who have impacted your life and continue to guide you in your walk with Him.

Reflections ...

Today I am grateful for ... _____

_____

_____

_____

_____

November 2

All Souls' Day

2 Timothy 4:1–22

Our reading today encourages us to stay faithful in our mission, share the good news of Christ, and continue to do good work no matter the challenges. Paul speaks about his own journey, offering a strong reminder to keep pressing forward, even in the face of trials, and to serve God with perseverance.

Consider spending time in conversation with a loved one, sharing stories about how faith has shaped your journey. You might find inspiration in the legacy of those who've influenced your walk with God, like my great aunt, who devoted her life to mission work, and my grandmother, whose love for God was evident in everything she did.

Reflections ...

TODAY I AM GRATEFUL FOR ... _____

_____
_____
_____
_____
_____
_____

November 3
Philemon 1–25

The book of Philemon is one of the shortest letters in the New Testament, yet it carries a powerful message about forgiveness, reconciliation, and the transformative power of Christian love. It's a personal letter from Paul to Philemon, urging him to forgive and welcome back Onesimus, a runaway slave who has become a believer. It highlights how the gospel redefines relationships and calls us to extend grace and love beyond what the world might expect.

What better way to embrace the beauty of this season than by capturing it with your loved ones? Arrange a fall photo shoot, whether with a professional or just using your phone, and enjoy the vibrant colours of autumn. As you take pictures, take moments to express gratitude for the time spent together, the warmth of family, and the beauty of creation around you.

Reflections ...

TODAY I AM GRATEFUL FOR ... _____

_____
_____
_____
_____
_____
_____

November 4
Zephaniah 3:14–20

Isn't it beautiful to know that God's heart is always set on restoring us and bringing joy into our lives? Zephaniah 3:14–20 reminds us that God is not only with us during the struggles but is also working to lift us up and fill us with peace and celebration. He offers us the hope of restoration, no matter what we've gone through. What a wonderful reminder that His joy and love can transform even the hardest of times!

Simple things that bring me joy include raking leaves. It reminds me of times with my dad. Raking leaves for a neighbour is a simple yet thoughtful way to spread kindness and brighten someone's day. Plus, it's a lovely way to enjoy the season and give back to your community!

Reflections ...

TODAY I AM GRATEFUL FOR ... _____
_____
_____
_____
_____
_____
_____

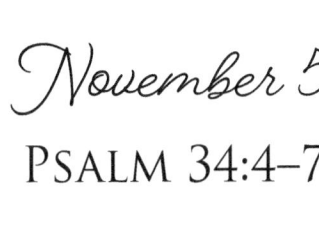

November 5
Psalm 34:4–7

In this passage, the psalmist shares the comforting truth that when we seek God, He hears our cries and delivers us from all our fears. The imagery of God's presence being with us in times of trouble assures us that we are never alone, no matter what we face. When we turn to God, He responds with love, protection, and guidance, offering us peace even in difficult times.

As you consider how God has guided you, it could be time to start preparing for a Christmas float if your church is participating in a local parade. Our parade runs at the end of November, so time to get moving! This can be a wonderful opportunity to come together with your community, share your faith, and spread joy during the festive season. You might want to engage your youth group or the congregation to brainstorm ideas, but let it serve as a reminder of the hope we have in Christ.

Reflections ...

Today I am grateful for ... _____

_____
_____
_____
_____
_____

November 6
ISAIAH 66:1–24

Today's reading offers a sweeping and hope-filled conclusion to the book of Isaiah, reminding us of God's greatness and the promise of restoration for His people. It's a powerful passage that encourages us to remain faithful, humble, and attentive to God's presence in both the grand and ordinary moments of life. God's care extends to every corner of creation, and He delights in hearts that seek Him with sincerity.

Now's a great time to start crafting those meaningful homemade Christmas gifts! Whether you're crocheting a nativity scene, like I've been doing (which turned out to be a much bigger project than I expected), a woodworking project, or canning, giving yourself lots of time makes it more joyful and less stressful. These heartfelt gifts display the thoughtfulness and love of Christ—and bless both the giver and the receiver!

Reflections ...

TODAY I AM GRATEFUL FOR ... _____

_____
_____
_____
_____
_____

November 7
1 Thessalonians 5:1–28

Through today's reading, Paul reminds us to stay alert and prepared for the return of the Lord, living in peace and joy as we wait for His coming. He encourages us to encourage one another, building each other up with love and grace, staying mindful of the presence of God in our lives.

Focus on developing your inner peace. Try to avoid negative self-talk; instead, take time to meditate in prayer. You could even try an herbal tea or listen to calming music, creating a peaceful atmosphere for yourself.

Reflections ...

TODAY I AM GRATEFUL FOR ... _____

_____
_____
_____
_____
_____
_____

November 8
1 Timothy 5:1–25

Today's passage speaks to how we are to care for one another in the family of faith, whether that's by showing respect, offering support, or ensuring that we're looking out for each other. Paul highlights how important it is for us to honour those around us. Have you heard the saying "the grass is greener where you water it"? It's our responsibility to water and cultivate these deep and loving relationships.

Start your day with a morning ritual that helps you connect with God. Whether it's a peaceful walk with some uplifting music, a quiet moment of prayer while sipping tea (love!), or sitting outside with your Bible, make that time your own to pray, and start the day centred in God's presence.

Reflections ...

TODAY I AM GRATEFUL FOR ... _____

_____
_____
_____
_____
_____
_____
_____

November 9
2 Thessalonians 1:11–12

In 2 Thessalonians 1:11–12, Paul prays that God would make the believers worthy of His calling and empower them to live out their faith with goodness and purpose. It's humbling to know that it's not by our strength, but by God's grace and power that we are equipped to do good and bring Him glory. As we trust in Him, He works through us to shine His light and love into the world, making His name known through our lives.

Looking ahead, can you set some time aside to do something that relaxes you—before the Christmas season sneaks up and your calendar fills up? Planning ahead for a little rest can be a great way to make sure you have time to recharge during what can be a joyful but busy season. Giving yourself space to pause and restore not only refreshes your body but also renews your spirit so you can share God's love with energy and grace.

Reflections ...

TODAY I AM GRATEFUL FOR ... _____

_____
_____
_____
_____
_____
_____

November 10
Exodus 3:1–15

Exodus 3:1–15 tells the powerful story of Moses encountering God in the burning bush—an extraordinary moment where the ordinary becomes sacred. In this passage, God reveals His name—I AM—affirming His eternal presence and faithfulness. It's a reminder that God meets us where we are, often in the middle of our daily routines, and invites us into something greater. Just like Moses, we may feel unprepared, but God equips and walks with us every step of the way.

Embrace the beauty of the season with a peaceful fall car ride. Take the scenic route and soak in the vibrant colours of the trees. The smell of the crisp fall air is invigorating! Let the changing leaves remind you of God's presence in every season.

Reflections ...

TODAY I AM GRATEFUL FOR ... _____

_____
_____
_____
_____
_____
_____

November 11
Remembrance Day
(Canadian)
/Veterans Day
(US)

Psalm 148

Psalm 148 is a glorious call to all of creation to praise the Lord—from the heavens and the earth to the mountains, animals, and people of every age. It's a reminder that we're all part of a much bigger story, united in our purpose to glorify God. On a day like Remembrance Day, this psalm feels especially meaningful as we honour those who have served and sacrificed for peace and freedom. Their courage and selflessness display the kind of strength and love that echoes God's own care for His people.

Be sure to wear your poppy today as a sign of remembrance and gratitude. It's a small gesture with a big message—honouring those who gave so much and acknowledging the importance of peace in our world.

Reflections ...

Today I am grateful for ... _____

_____
_____
_____
_____

November 12
2 Thessalonians 2:1–8, 13–17

Today's reading encourages us to stand firm in our faith, even when uncertainty or confusion creeps in. Paul reminds the believers that they are loved and chosen by God, and that His truth offers strength and comfort in challenging times. This passage is a beautiful affirmation that, even when the world feels shaky, we can hold tightly to God's promises and encourage one another along the way.

Consider sending an anonymous thank-you note to a friend who has made a positive impact in your life. How have they shown you kindness or support? Let your gratitude flow freely as you write—and trust that this simple, thoughtful gesture will bless them in just the right way.

Reflections ...

TODAY I AM GRATEFUL FOR ... _____

_____
_____
_____
_____
_____
_____

November 13
Luke 20:27–40

Jesus reminds us of the eternal nature of God's promises and the hope we have beyond this life. When questioned about resurrection, He beautifully affirms that God is not the God of the dead, but of the living—for to Him, all are alive. It's a comforting reminder that our faith anchors us not only in this life but also in the life to come, where love and connection continue in God's presence.

As the days get cooler, take a moment to slow down and enjoy a warm mug of mulled apple cider. Whether you're making it from scratch or heating up a favourite blend, let the comforting spices and sweetness remind you of the warmth of God's love. Sip slowly, breathe deeply, and reflect on the joy of life lived with eternal hope. Apple harvest season is the best!

Reflections ...

TODAY I AM GRATEFUL FOR ... _____
_____
_____
_____
_____
_____

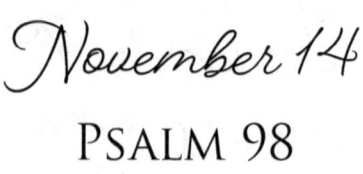

November 14
Psalm 98

Psalm 98 is a joyful celebration of God's marvellous deeds—calling all creation to sing, shout, and praise the Lord! This psalm reminds us that God's righteousness and steadfast love are not only reasons to rejoice but also reasons to move our bodies and lift our spirits in gratitude.

Try a chair yoga—yes, you can even do it at your desk! Stretching your arms in praise, rolling your shoulders, and taking a few deep breaths can help centre your mind and body in God's goodness. Let each gentle movement be a quiet act of worship and thankfulness.

Reflections ...

TODAY I AM GRATEFUL FOR ... _____

_____
_____
_____
_____
_____
_____

November 15
Psalm 150

Have you ever stopped to think about all the ways we can worship and praise God? Psalm 150 bursts with praise, inviting everything that has breath to worship the Lord with joyful noise and celebration! This psalm is a kind truth that worship can be expressed through music, movement, and everyday moments.

Whether with instruments, dancing, or simply your voice, God delights in our heartfelt praise. Make time today to listen to something new to you – "It's a beautiful Day" by Jamie Grace is a great song to soak in. 'Cause it is a beautiful day!

Reflections ...

TODAY I AM GRATEFUL FOR ... _____

_____
_____
_____
_____
_____
_____
_____

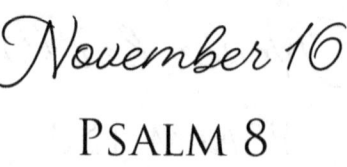

November 16
PSALM 8

Psalm 8 beautifully shows the majesty of God and His care for humanity. The psalmist marvels at the vastness of creation and wonders why God, in all His glory, would care for mankind. Yet it's in His love and grace that we are entrusted with such a special place in His creation, crowned with glory and honour.

As we prepare for the Advent season, it's a wonderful time to create a bucket list filled with meaningful activities that embody the spirit of faith and anticipation. Consider including items that reflect your values, such as volunteering for those in need, spending time with loved ones, or engaging in daily acts of kindness.

Reflections ...

TODAY I AM GRATEFUL FOR ... _____

_____
_____
_____
_____
_____
_____
_____

November 17
Proverbs 16:1–9

Proverbs 16:1–9 reminds us that while we make plans, it is ultimately the Lord who directs our steps. His wisdom and guidance are key in shaping our choices, leading us to purpose and peace. This passage encourages us to trust in God's plan, knowing He is always working through us to bring about good.

Does your area have a Christmas hamper or a shoebox project? It's a wonderful way to put your plans into action and bless others during the holiday season. By giving of your time and resources, you're not only bringing joy to those in need but also aligning your heart with God's love and generosity.

Reflections ...

TODAY I AM GRATEFUL FOR … _____

_____
_____
_____
_____
_____
_____

November 18
Proverbs 10:1–7

Proverbs 10:1–7 highlights the value of wisdom, righteousness, and kindness. It reminds us that our actions, whether big or small, can have a lasting impact and bring joy to others. Just like a wise son brings joy to a father's heart, our thoughtful acts can bring light to those who need it most.

Consider sending Christmas cards to our brave military personnel. This small act of kindness not only uplifts those serving far from home but also echoes the love and care that Jesus exemplified. You can find the addresses online, and I love picking cards that depict our beautiful country—it's a personal touch that makes the holiday season a little brighter for those who sacrifice so much for us.

Reflections ...

TODAY I AM GRATEFUL FOR ... _____

_____
_____
_____
_____
_____
_____

November 19
Luke 18:9–17

Humility and a childlike heart are central to Jesus's teachings. In Luke 18:9–17, Jesus reminds us that true greatness in God's eyes isn't about status or achievements but about approaching Him with the openness, trust, and humility that children naturally possess. It's a beautiful invitation to come to God just as we are, not striving to prove ourselves but simply resting in His love and grace.

How about organizing a cookie exchange with friends? Set the date before their calendars fill up with holiday bookings and parties! The season rushes by so fast that booking this early ensures you make time for those close to you.

Reflections ...

TODAY I AM GRATEFUL FOR ... _____

_____
_____
_____
_____
_____

November 20
Psalm 27:1–6

Psalm 27:1–6 is a sacred truth that God is our light and salvation, a constant source of strength and protection. In times of fear or uncertainty, we can find courage in knowing that God is always with us, guiding us through life's challenges. David's confidence in God's care and provision invites us to trust deeply in His unwavering presence and love, finding peace even in difficult circumstances.

How about participating in a Secret Santa (or Angel of Gratitude) program at your church? It's a joyful way to spread kindness, build deeper connections with your church family, and display God's love through thoughtful giving. If your church doesn't have one, consider starting this tradition yourself—it's a wonderful opportunity to foster community and share the spirit of the season.

Reflections ...

TODAY I AM GRATEFUL FOR ... _____

_____
_____
_____
_____
_____
_____

November 21
Proverbs 31:10–12

Proverbs 31:10–12 paints a picture of a woman who is trustworthy, hardworking, and full of wisdom, someone whose actions bring strength and peace to her household. This passage encourages us to contemplate how we, too, can embody these qualities in our own lives. It reminds us to be intentional in our relationships and mindful of how we use our time, ensuring that we prioritize what truly matters and brings peace to our hearts and homes.

Heading into this busy season, consider taking a break from social media for a week. It's a refreshing way to refocus on the things that truly matter—whether it's spending quality time with loved ones or nurturing your own well-being. This simple act of stepping back can help you recharge and re-centre your life.

Reflections ...

TODAY I AM GRATEFUL FOR ... _____

_____
_____
_____
_____
_____
_____

November 22
ROMANS 5:1–5

This reading reminds us that through our faith in Christ, we have peace with God and hope in His promises. It's a gracious assurance that our suffering, though difficult, leads to perseverance, character, and ultimately, hope. The love of God has been poured into our hearts through the Holy Spirit, and this gives us strength and encouragement, no matter what life brings our way.

It's the perfect time to bring out the flannel sheets! If you're in need of a new set, consider investing in some with a fun pattern that makes you smile—perhaps featuring dogs or skiers. As you snuggle into warmth and comfort, remember the peace and hope that God's love provides in your life, knowing He is with you through every season.

Reflections ...

TODAY I AM GRATEFUL FOR ... _____

_____
_____
_____
_____
_____
_____
_____

PROVERBS 2:1–10

Diving into Proverbs 2:1–10, we're reminded of the value of wisdom and that it's something we should seek and cherish, just like a treasure. The passage speaks about the importance of actively seeking understanding, as it will lead to a deeper relationship with God, who fills us with knowledge and insight. This wisdom, like a guiding light, can lead us to make good decisions in every area of our lives, including how we prepare for and celebrate the holidays.

For a fun and meaningful activity, take a moment to decorate your home for the holidays with intention and joy. As you hang your ornaments or arrange festive decorations, think about how the wisdom and love of Christ can fill your home this season. You can even incorporate special items that remind you of blessings and lessons learned, making each decoration a symbol of God's presence in your life.

Reflections ...

TODAY I AM GRATEFUL FOR ... _____

_____
_____
_____
_____
_____

November 24
Psalm 149

Today's reading invites us to rejoice and find delight in the Lord, singing praises and celebrating Him in all that we do. This psalm calls us to find joy in worship and to approach each day with a heart full of praise, recognizing God's greatness in every moment. Just as the psalmist celebrates God's goodness, we're reminded to embrace His presence and allow His joy to fill our hearts, especially in this season.

Make a list of your intentions for this season. Whether it's embracing more gratitude, finding time to connect with others, or strengthening your relationship with God, set some simple, intentional goals that will help you stay centred on His love and joy throughout the busy days ahead. Consider doing this as a family so you can help each other stay focused on the true reason for the season!

Reflections ...

TODAY I AM GRATEFUL FOR ... _____

_____
_____
_____
_____
_____
_____

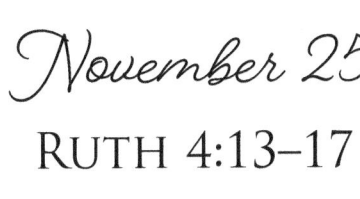

November 25
RUTH 4:13–17

Ruth's story in these verses is a beautiful testimony to God's faithfulness and the rewards of loyalty. Even in the hardest of circumstances, Ruth's steadfastness is richly rewarded. Through her faithfulness, God brings about not only personal blessing but also plays a part in His grand plan for redemption. It's a reminder that, like Ruth, we too can trust in God's timing and His ability to turn our trials into blessings.

As you prepare for the Advent season, consider making or using a reusable Advent calendar. Each day, you can include a reminder of God's love, a scripture from the Christmas story, or even an encouragement to trust in His plan.

Reflections ...

TODAY I AM GRATEFUL FOR ... _____

_____
_____
_____
_____
_____
_____

November 26
Psalm 122

Are you ready to fill your home with the peace and joy of Christ this Christmas season? Psalm 122 reminds us of the joy we find in coming together in God's presence, and what better way to prepare our hearts for the season than through music that lifts us up and draws us closer to Him?

I love creating a new Christmas playlist filled with spiritual songs that inspire my heart and bring me into a spirit of worship. Choose a blend of traditional hymns and contemporary Christmas songs, each reminding you of the miracle of Christ's birth.

Reflections ...

TODAY I AM GRATEFUL FOR ... _____

_____
_____
_____
_____
_____
_____
_____

November 27
MARK 5:21–24

In this passage, we see a beautiful display of faith and urgency as people approach Jesus with their concerns, trusting that He can make a difference in their lives.

This season goes so fast, so let's take this message to heart. Prioritize time with family and friends—those precious moments matter more than the hustle and bustle. Set aside time for what's truly important this season: love, connection, and building relationships. Make it a point to reach out to loved ones, share in their joy, and create lasting memories.

Reflections ...

TODAY I AM GRATEFUL FOR ... _____

_____
_____
_____
_____
_____
_____

JOYOUS FAITH

November 28
PSALM 84

Psalm 84 paints such a warm and inviting picture of God's presence—like a sanctuary for the soul. The psalmist speaks of longing to dwell in the house of the Lord, where even a single day is better than a thousand elsewhere. It's a reminder that true peace and joy are found when we rest in God, no matter where we are.

As the temperature drops, treat yourself to a peaceful evening soak in a hot tub (or a warm bath if that's more your style). Let the snow fall gently around you as you hold onto God's goodness and draw near to His comforting presence.

Reflections ...

TODAY I AM GRATEFUL FOR ... _____

_____
_____
_____
_____
_____
_____
_____

PSALM 25:1–10

Psalm 25:1–10 is a beautiful expression of trust and guidance. In it, David lifts his soul to God, seeking truth, mercy, and direction. It's a heartfelt reminder that when we humbly turn to God, He leads us in love and faithfulness. Especially in seasons of waiting and preparation—like Advent—this passage encourages us to seek Him with open hearts.

Perhaps you might initiate a nightly Advent reading with your family, lighting a candle and sharing reflections on the meaning of each week. This simple ritual can become a cherished tradition, drawing everyone closer to God and to one another as you focus on hope, peace, joy, and love.

Reflections ...

TODAY I AM GRATEFUL FOR … _____

_____
_____
_____
_____
_____
_____

November 30
1 Thessalonians 3:9–13

First Thessalonians 3:9–13 overflows with Paul's heartfelt gratitude and deep love for the believers. His joy is evident as he prays earnestly for their growth in faith and love, and for the day they will stand blameless before God. This can be a warm and uplifting reminder of how powerful it is to encourage one another and to grow together in love, rooted in Christ's grace.

Who doesn't love cuddling into a warm blanket and a good book? Create a cozy space where you can unwind and connect with God through literature that inspires your faith. Pick a beautiful book centred on the Christmas season—perhaps a devotional, a touching novel, or a retelling of the nativity—to gently prepare your heart for the joy of Christ's coming.

Reflections ...

TODAY I AM GRATEFUL FOR ... _____
_____
_____
_____
_____
_____
_____

December 1
Isaiah 9:2–7

Isn't it amazing how Isaiah 9:2–7, written centuries before Jesus was born, shines with such hope and joy? This beautiful prophecy bursts with promise—the light breaking into darkness, the birth of a child who will be called *Wonderful Counsellor, Mighty God, Everlasting Father, Prince of Peace.* What a breathtaking reminder that God's love story with us has been unfolding all along, and Christmas is the celebration of that love arriving in the most tender, miraculous way!

How about we kick off this beautiful season with joy in our hearts by creating an Advent wreath together! Gather some evergreens, candles, and a few meaningful touches to make it your own. Traditionally, the first candle (Hope) is lit on the first Sunday of Advent, followed by Peace (Week 2), Joy (Week 3—the pink candle!), and Love (Week 4). As you light each candle, pause to reflect on Christ's light in your life and how you might share that love with the world around you. Let each candle bring a little more warmth to your heart as we journey closer to the miracle of Christmas!

Reflections ...

TODAY I AM GRATEFUL FOR ... _____

_____
_____
_____
_____

December 2
Isaiah 60:1–6

Isaiah 60:1–6 is a glorious prophecy that truly resonates with Christmas joy! It paints the most beautiful picture of light breaking into darkness—a promise fulfilled in the birth of Jesus. This passage reminds us that God's love shines bright, even in the dimmest moments, and that we, too, are invited to carry and display His radiant light into the world. What a reason to celebrate! The long-awaited Saviour has come, and His light fills our hearts with joy, peace, and unshakable hope!

Let's turn your home into a living Advent story! Place Mary and Joseph together and move them a little closer to the stable each day, travelling across your home toward the manger under the Christmas tree. Let baby Jesus appear on Christmas morning, and the wisemen arrive on Epiphany. It's a heartwarming and visual way to build anticipation, centre your days in the meaning of the season, and remind everyone in your home that Christmas is all about Christ coming near. Oh! And don't forget the shepherds—place them out in the "fields" nearby, keeping watch over their sheep until the angel brings them good news!

Reflections ...

Today I am grateful for ... _____

_____

_____

_____

_____

December 3

International Day of Persons with Disabilities

MALACHI 3:1–7

Oh, the joy and wonder of Advent! This passage bursts with the excitement of a promise—God is sending a messenger to prepare the way! During this beautiful season, we're not only celebrating the birth of Jesus, but we're also joyfully looking forward to His return, when peace and goodness will reign. Even when the world feels broken, God is lovingly at work, shaping hearts and lives for His kingdom. Isn't that just the kind of hope we need this season?

And today, on the *International Day of Persons with Disabilities,* let's let our hearts be extra tender. Advent reminds us that Jesus came for *everyone*—bringing healing, wholeness, and deep, unshakable love. Let's reflect His heart by creating spaces of belonging, kindness, and joy for all God's children, each one fearfully and wonderfully made.

Add an extra bit of love this Advent by including everyone in your Christmas preparations! Whether it's baking cookies with a friend or writing an encouraging card to someone who might feel left out this season—your small acts of inclusion shine big with God's love. Let's make room in our hearts and homes this Advent, just like God has made room for each of us.

Reflections ...

TODAY I AM GRATEFUL FOR ... _____

_____

_____

_____

December 4
Micah 5:2-5

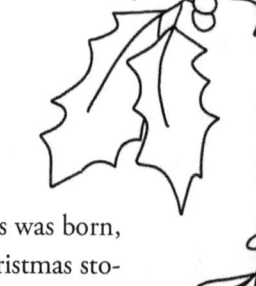

Isn't it amazing that hundreds of years before Jesus was born, God had already written Bethlehem into the Christmas story? This sweet little town—so small it was barely noticed—became the birthplace of the greatest gift the world has ever received! Micah's prophecy sparkles with hope, painting a picture of our coming Saviour: a gentle shepherd, a bringer of peace, and a ruler whose strength comes from the heart of God. What a humbling reminder that God uses the quiet and humble places to unfold His most powerful plans!

Let's fill your home with laughter and joy! Gather your loved ones and host a Christmas charades night—acting out nativity scenes, holiday songs, or even your favourite Christmas treats! It's a fun and festive way to celebrate the joy of Christ's birth, while creating memories that shine as bright as the star over Bethlehem. Go ahead—laugh, play, and let that holiday cheer bubble over with love!

Reflections ...

TODAY I AM GRATEFUL FOR ...

December 5
Philippians 1:2–11

Isn't it amazing how much love and warmth Paul shares in this passage? His joyful words remind us of the heart of the Christmas season—gratitude, love, and a deep hope for what's to come. As we journey through Advent, Paul's prayer encourages us to open our hearts wider, grow in love and kindness, and prepare room for Jesus with anticipation and joy. Christmas isn't just about waiting—it's about growing in grace and being transformed by His light.

Anyone up for a Christmas movie night? The hardest part will be deciding which one to watch first! Grab your fluffiest blanket, your favourite festive snacks, and settle in with loved ones for a night of laughter, wonder, and Christmas cheer! Let the joy of the season fill your home as you make memories together.

Reflections ...

Today I am grateful for ... _____

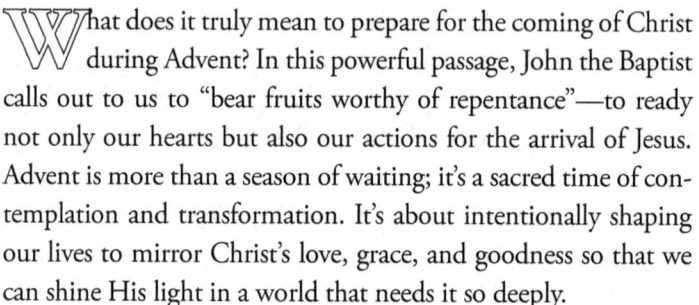

December 6
Luke 3:1–14

What does it truly mean to prepare for the coming of Christ during Advent? In this powerful passage, John the Baptist calls out to us to "bear fruits worthy of repentance"—to ready not only our hearts but also our actions for the arrival of Jesus. Advent is more than a season of waiting; it's a sacred time of contemplation and transformation. It's about intentionally shaping our lives to mirror Christ's love, grace, and goodness so that we can shine His light in a world that needs it so deeply.

What if we live out the message of John the Baptist by stepping into service this season? Whether you volunteer at a soup kitchen, help with a toy drive, or lend a hand to a neighbour in need, your kindness and care can make the way for Jesus to enter into someone's life today. These acts of love and generosity are your own special way of preparing the world for the coming of Christ—one smile, one gift, one helping hand at a time. Let's fill this Advent season with action, heart, and joyful giving!

Reflections ...

TODAY I AM GRATEFUL FOR ... _____

_____
_____
_____
_____
_____

Zephaniah 3:14–20

What a joyful, hope-filled message we find in Zephaniah today! This Advent passage is like a warm hug from God—a reminder that He delights in us, sings over us with gladness, and promises restoration and peace. As we prepare our hearts for Christmas, let's take in the beauty of this truth: no matter where we are in life, God is gently, lovingly at work bringing new beginnings and joy into our lives. What a reason to rejoice!

This year, instead of wrapping up more stuff for under the tree, why not focus on creating memories? Gifting experiences—like a fun winter outing, tickets to a concert, or even a cozy afternoon tea date—can be such a meaningful way to celebrate. One year I surprised my son with a dog sledding adventure. Talk about lasting memories! The hardest part? Choosing just one!

Reflections ...

TODAY I AM GRATEFUL FOR ... _____

_____
_____
_____
_____
_____

December 8
PSALM 85

Oh, what a beautiful way to enter the heart of the Christmas season—with a psalm that was written like a carol of hope. Psalm 85 is filled with longing for peace, restoration, and joy—the very things Advent promises. As we wait for the celebration of Jesus's birth, we're reminded that God is always near, working in the quiet places of our lives to bring healing and love. Just like twinkling lights in the dark, His mercy and faithfulness shine through, guiding us closer to the joy of Christmas morning.

Why don't we add a little Christmas magic to your evenings with a nativity puzzle? Set it out on the coffee table with a plate of holiday cookies and a mug of hot cocoa nearby. As you and your family work together piece by piece, talk about the incredible story of Jesus's birth. It's a sweet way to stay connected to the true meaning of Christmas while creating quiet, joy-filled memories that warm the heart—just like the season itself.

Reflections ...

TODAY I AM GRATEFUL FOR ... _____

_____
_____
_____
_____
_____

December 9
Philippians 4:4–7

"*Rejoice in the Lord always*" (v. 4a). What a joyful reminder as we journey through Advent. Amid all the twinkling lights, carols, and cozy gatherings, Paul's message gently calls us back to what matters most—resting in God's peace and letting our hearts be filled with His joy. Even when the season gets a little hectic, we're reminded to pause, breathe, and trust that the Lord is near. And isn't that what Christmas is all about? The nearness of God, wrapped in love and hope.

This season, gift your loved ones a board or card game and plan a special Christmas game night! Whether it's a classic family favourite or something new and silly, gathering around the table to laugh and play is a beautiful way to make memories and share joy. There are so many festive games to choose from—the hardest part might be picking which one to play first! Let the fun remind you of the peace and connection we find in Christ and in each other.

Reflections ...

TODAY I AM GRATEFUL FOR ... _____

_____
_____
_____
_____
_____

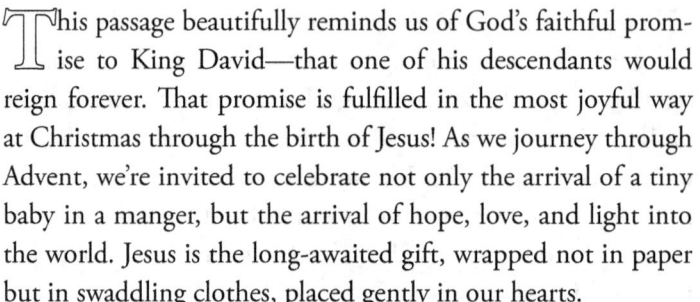

December 10
Psalm 132:11–18

This passage beautifully reminds us of God's faithful promise to King David—that one of his descendants would reign forever. That promise is fulfilled in the most joyful way at Christmas through the birth of Jesus! As we journey through Advent, we're invited to celebrate not only the arrival of a tiny baby in a manger, but the arrival of hope, love, and light into the world. Jesus is the long-awaited gift, wrapped not in paper but in swaddling clothes, placed gently in our hearts.

Bring a little something to your Advent season by starting a matching Christmas pajama tradition with your family or friends! It's a fun way to feel connected and festive—perfect for cozy movie nights, baking cookies, or lighting the Advent candles together. Snap a photo, sip some hot chocolate, and celebrate the joy of Jesus's coming with warmth, laughter, and love!

Reflections ...

Today I am grateful for ... _____

_____
_____
_____
_____
_____
_____
_____

December 11
Psalm 2:1–6

Even as the world bustles with Christmas preparations, Psalm 2:1–6 offers us a quiet moment to remember the true King we celebrate. This powerful passage points to the coming of Jesus—the long-awaited Messiah, born in a humble stable, yet holding divine authority. His birth fulfilled ancient prophecies and ushered in a Kingdom of peace, joy, and everlasting light. In the twinkling lights and joyful music of the season, we catch a glimpse of the hope and majesty that Christ brings. As we prepare our hearts this Advent season, we can rest in the assurance that Christ is in control, and His light shines bright in even the darkest of times.

To celebrate: Gather your family for a fun afternoon of making homemade wrapping paper! Use brown kraft paper, cut out star shapes from raw potatoes, and dip them in colourful paint to create your own festive designs. Not only are you making memories together, but it looks absolutely beautiful under the tree—and it's made with love, creativity, and Christmas cheer!

Reflections ...

Today I am grateful for ... _____

_____
_____
_____
_____
_____

December 12
MATTHEW 1:1–17

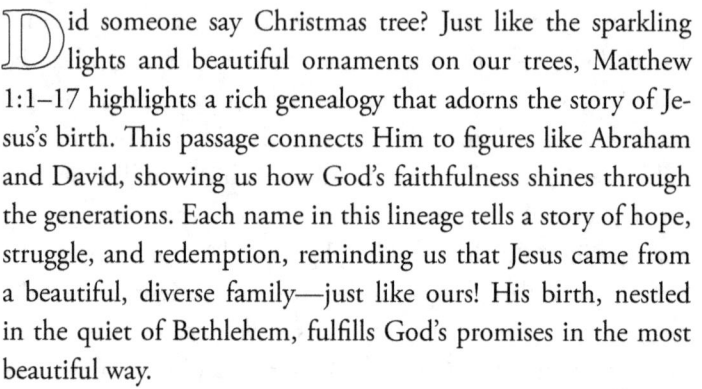

Did someone say Christmas tree? Just like the sparkling lights and beautiful ornaments on our trees, Matthew 1:1–17 highlights a rich genealogy that adorns the story of Jesus's birth. This passage connects Him to figures like Abraham and David, showing us how God's faithfulness shines through the generations. Each name in this lineage tells a story of hope, struggle, and redemption, reminding us that Jesus came from a beautiful, diverse family—just like ours! His birth, nestled in the quiet of Bethlehem, fulfills God's promises in the most beautiful way.

Gather around the Christmas tree with your loved ones for a cozy eggnog or nut-nog tasting party! It's the perfect way to sip on some festive drinks, share laughs, and make wonderful memories together. As you taste, take a moment to reflect on the gift of Christ's birth, knowing that God's perfect plan continues to unfold through the joy of the season.

Reflections ...

TODAY I AM GRATEFUL FOR ... _____

_____
_____
_____
_____
_____
_____

December 13
Micah 5:2–5

Micah 5:2–5 is a beautiful prophecy about the birth of Jesus, foretelling that the Messiah would come from the humble little town of Bethlehem. Despite its small size, Bethlehem was chosen to cradle the greatest miracle of all time. Born in the quiet stillness of Bethlehem, Jesus arrived—our Prince of Peace—fulfilling God's promise to send a Shepherd who would bring comfort, guidance, and everlasting peace to His people. We are reminded that even in the most unexpected places, God is at work bringing forth His light and love.

Is there someone in your life who might be finding the holiday season a little overwhelming? Offer to help with their Christmas prep—maybe it's wrapping gifts, picking up groceries, or helping them hang lights. A simple act of service can display the very heart of Christ's peace and kindness. Let's be His hands and feet this Christmas, sharing joy wherever we go!

Reflections ...

Today I am grateful for ...

_____

_____

_____

_____

_____

_____

December 14
Isaiah 11:1–10

Long before the twinkling lights and joyful carols, the birth of Jesus was long-awaited—foretold through a sleigh-full of Old Testament prophecies, each one carrying the promise of His arrival, including this beautiful one in Isaiah. It speaks of a shoot from the stump of Jesse, a promise that from David's family line would come a new kind of King—full of wisdom, peace, and righteousness. Born in humble circumstances, Jesus fulfilled these ancient words, bringing light into a world that had been waiting in darkness. This Advent, we celebrate not just His arrival, but the incredible faithfulness of God through the generations. Isn't it amazing how the Christmas story was written across centuries?

It's time to bring out the gumdrops and icing—let's build a gingerbread house! And save extra gumdrops for me! This classic Christmas tradition is the perfect way to gather with your family. As you decorate your house, think about how Jesus came to build something even more lasting: a kingdom of peace, love, and joy. A gingerbread house kit also makes a heartfelt gift for another family—because sharing joy is what this season is all about!

Reflections ...

TODAY I AM GRATEFUL FOR ... _____

_____

_____

_____

_____

December 15
Isaiah 40:1–11

Isaiah 40 brings a heartwarming message of hope, comfort, and preparation. It calls us to ready our hearts for the arrival of the Lord, reminding us of His everlasting love, forgiveness, and the promise of redemption. As we celebrate Advent, we're invited to make space in our lives for God's incredible gift of salvation, knowing that He is coming to bring peace, joy, and restoration. These words of comfort are a sweet reminder that the season is about more than just waiting—it's about eagerly preparing for the wonderful gift of Christ, our Saviour, who brings us everlasting joy.

Get ready for some Christmas fun with a *Christmas sweater competition*! Gather your loved ones and let the holiday spirit shine as you put on your most festive, funny, or creative Christmas sweaters. The fun and laughter you'll share together will fill your hearts with joy, and as you celebrate in this silly, cozy way, think about how Christ's love fills our hearts with warmth and light during this beautiful season. You'll have memories to cherish for years to come!

Reflections ...

TODAY I AM GRATEFUL FOR ... _____

_____
_____
_____
_____

December 16
Luke 1:26–38

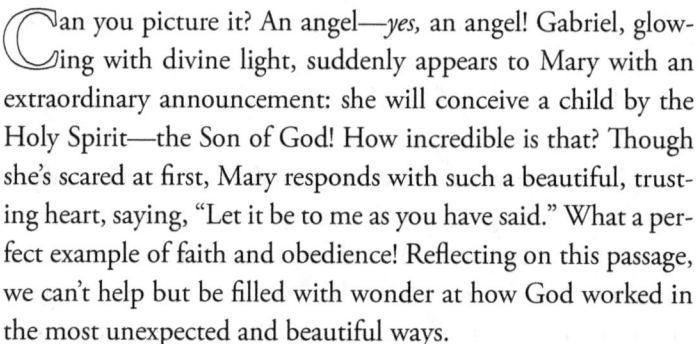

Can you picture it? An angel—*yes,* an angel! Gabriel, glowing with divine light, suddenly appears to Mary with an extraordinary announcement: she will conceive a child by the Holy Spirit—the Son of God! How incredible is that? Though she's scared at first, Mary responds with such a beautiful, trusting heart, saying, "Let it be to me as you have said." What a perfect example of faith and obedience! Reflecting on this passage, we can't help but be filled with wonder at how God worked in the most unexpected and beautiful ways.

Let's fill our homes with the magic of Christmas music! Create a Christmas playlist with your favourite carols, joyful hymns, and merry songs that bring warmth and cheer into your home. Whether you're trimming the tree or enjoying a cup of cocoa, let the music fill the air and remind you of the amazing gift of Jesus. As you listen, think of Mary's joy and the excitement of waiting for Jesus's arrival—just like we do now, with hearts full of love and anticipation!

Reflections ...

TODAY I AM GRATEFUL FOR ... _____

_____
_____
_____
_____
_____

December 17
Luke 1:39–45

What a beautiful and joyful moment this passage brings! Mary, full of excitement and love, visits her cousin Elizabeth, who is also miraculously expecting. As soon as Elizabeth hears Mary's greeting, the baby in her womb leaps for joy, and Elizabeth is filled with the Holy Spirit. She praises Mary for her faith, acknowledging the incredible blessing that is about to unfold for the world. This moment shows us how God works in surprising ways, bringing joy and wonder to all those who believe. As we prepare for Christ's birth, may we too, like Mary and Elizabeth, rejoice in the incredible gift of Jesus and share our joy with others!

I love Christmas concerts! Whether it's a local performance, a church service, or a festive musical gathering, it's a beautiful way to experience the joy of Christmas through song. As you listen to the music, let it fill your heart with the same joy and praise that Elizabeth expressed as she welcomed the Saviour's arrival. What a wonderful way to celebrate the season with loved ones!

Reflections ...

Today I am grateful for ... _____

_____
_____
_____
_____

December 18
LUKE 1:46–56

Mary's song of praise, the Magnificat, overflows with joy for God's faithfulness and mercy. As she considers the miracle within her, she celebrates how God lifts up the humble and fulfills His promises to His people. This beautiful passage reminds us to rejoice in God's goodness, for He is always at work in our lives, turning the ordinary into something extraordinary. Just as Mary rejoiced in the coming Saviour, we too can sing His praises this Advent season, knowing that God's love and faithfulness are with us, now and always.

What is more spectacular than a cozy drive during the Advent season to enjoy the magic of Christmas lights? Find a route in your neighbourhood or a nearby town where the lights are twinkling and let the beauty of the season fill your heart. Maybe grab a warm peppermint hot chocolate to enjoy on the way—perfect for sipping as you soak in the sights and bask in the joy and wonder of God's love this Christmas!

Reflections ...

TODAY I AM GRATEFUL FOR ... _____

_____
_____
_____
_____
_____
_____

December 19
Luke 1:57–66

In this beautiful passage, we see the birth of John the Baptist. Zechariah and Elizabeth, who had longed for a child, finally receive their son. As they celebrate, Zechariah is filled with the Holy Spirit and bursts into praise, prophesying that his son will help prepare the way for the Messiah. This joyful moment reminds us of the anticipation we feel as we await the arrival of Christ at Christmas. Just as the birth of John marked the beginning of God's great plan of redemption, so too does the birth of Jesus bring the fulfillment of God's promise to us.

Get into the Christmas spirit by baking cinnamon buns with your family. You could get creative by shaping them like a Christmas tree. It's a fun way to add a bit of festive flair to your baking, and it will fill your home with the sweet smells of the season! As you bake and decorate together, take time to talk about the joy of anticipation—just as Zechariah and Elizabeth rejoiced in the fulfillment of God's promises, we too can rejoice in the coming of Jesus! Enjoy a sweet treat and create memories that will last for years to come!

Reflections ...

TODAY I AM GRATEFUL FOR ... _____

_____

_____

_____

_____

December 20
Luke 1:67–80

Zechariah, filled with the Holy Spirit, sings a song of praise overflowing with joy and gratitude for the fulfillment of God's promises. Zechariah recognizes that his son's life will point to the greater hope—the arrival of Jesus, who will bring salvation and light to the world. As we read this passage during Advent, I can't even fathom how excited they must have been for Jesus's birth!

With the excitement of Christmas, it's important to remember that this isn't an easy time for all of us. If you or someone you know struggles during this time, know that it's okay to feel sadness, loneliness, and loss, but also know that you're not alone.

Reflections ...

TODAY I AM GRATEFUL FOR ... _____

_____
_____
_____
_____
_____
_____

December 21
Matthew 1:18–20

Just days before Christmas, we pause to understand the quiet strength of Joseph. Faced with uncertainty and questions, Joseph chooses faith. When the angel appears and reveals God's miraculous plan, he doesn't run—he trusts. His loving obedience reminds us that God often calls us into something greater than we can see. As we wait for the celebration of Christ's birth, Joseph's courage and kindness inspire us to listen for God's voice and respond with trust, love, and grace.

This close to Christmas, I like to slow down and spread some heartfelt love. Take a few peaceful moments to write personal letters to family or friends—sharing encouragement, gratitude, or sweet Christmas memories—and tuck them under the tree. It's a simple but meaningful way to reflect the love Joseph showed and remind your loved ones just how cherished they are. Let your words become little gifts of joy and blessing this Christmas!

Reflections ...

TODAY I AM GRATEFUL FOR ... _____

_____
_____
_____
_____
_____

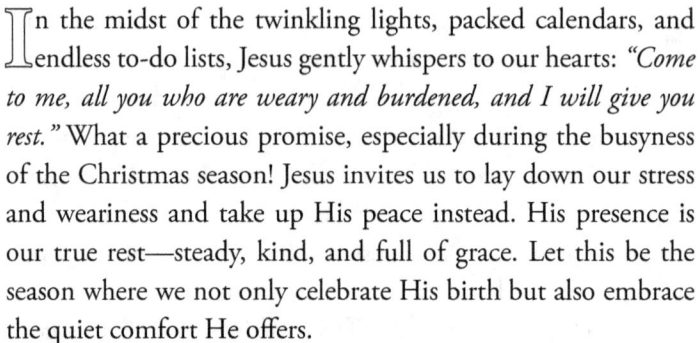

December 22
Matthew 11:28–30

In the midst of the twinkling lights, packed calendars, and endless to-do lists, Jesus gently whispers to our hearts: *"Come to me, all you who are weary and burdened, and I will give you rest."* What a precious promise, especially during the busyness of the Christmas season! Jesus invites us to lay down our stress and weariness and take up His peace instead. His presence is our true rest—steady, kind, and full of grace. Let this be the season where we not only celebrate His birth but also embrace the quiet comfort He offers.

Spread the peace and joy of Christ with your neighbours by arranging a night of Christmas caroling! Gather a few friends or family members, bundle up in scarves and mittens, and sing your favourite carols under the stars, or maybe dazzle the residents with songs of joy in a nursing home! It's a beautiful way to share the message of hope and rest with others—and trust us, the smiles you receive will warm your heart more than any cup of cocoa!

Reflections ...

TODAY I AM GRATEFUL FOR ... _____

_____
_____
_____
_____
_____

December 23
Matthew 1:21–25

Today we circle back to the angel's message to Joseph, reassuring him not to fear taking Mary as his wife, for the child she carries is the Saviour, the promised Messiah. This moment is like a sacred whisper of God's deep love for us—He sent Jesus to bring us peace, forgiveness, and the hope of salvation. Joseph's obedient trust in God's plan gives us a powerful example of faith, and we're invited to rest in the assurance that God's promises are always fulfilled, even in the unexpected.

This Advent, take time to rest and find peace amidst the busyness. Create a cozy, quiet space in your home where you can pray, giving thanks for the hope and rest that Christ brings. Whether it's with a cup of warm cocoa, a comfy blanket, or a quiet moment alone, allow yourself to rest in the joy of knowing that Jesus has come to offer us peace, hope, and redemption. What a beautiful way to centre your heart on Christ this Christmas season!

Reflections ...

TODAY I AM GRATEFUL FOR ... _____

_____
_____
_____
_____
_____

December 24
Luke 2:1–5

Did someone say Christmas Eve? As we read Luke 2:1–5, our hearts are filled with wonder imagining Mary and Joseph making their way to Bethlehem, trusting God's plan every step of the way. Though the journey was long, and the accommodations humble, it marked the beginning of the most miraculous story ever told—our Saviour, born in a stable, bringing light, love, and joy to the world.

On this magical Christmas Eve, gather your loved ones and head to a Christmas Eve service together. There's something incredibly heartwarming about singing carols by candlelight, feeling the hush of holy night settle in, and letting your heart soak up the joy of Jesus's arrival. Let this sacred time bring you peace, renew your hope, and wrap you in the love of Christ.

Wishing you and your family a Christmas Eve filled with all the warmth, wonder, and love your heart can hold!

Reflections ...

TODAY I AM GRATEFUL FOR ... _____

_____
_____
_____
_____
_____
_____

December 25
CHRISTMAS DAY

LUKE 2:6–7

Have you ever stopped to imagine the quiet, holy moment when Jesus was born? In Luke 2:6–7, we're invited into the tender scene of the Saviour of the world entering the humblest of places—a simple manger, with Mary and Joseph by His side. This precious moment reminds us that God's love for us isn't about grandeur or perfection; it's about His presence in the smallest, most humble corners of our lives. As we journey through Advent, let's open our hearts to this deep, pure love of Christ Jesus.

From my family to yours, Merry Christmas! Twelve Days of Christmas: Today celebrates the first day of Christmas. As we delve into these days, let's reflect on the beautiful symbolism in the first verse of that famous song: partridge in a pear tree. Could it be pointing to the greatest gift we've ever received—the birth of baby Jesus? Just as the partridge guards its young, God sent His Son to protect and save us, giving us the most precious gift of all.

Reflections ...

TODAY I AM GRATEFUL FOR ... _____

_____
_____
_____
_____

December 26
Boxing Day

Luke 2:8–15

As we continue our journey through the beautiful story of Jesus's birth, let's take a moment to reflect on Luke 2:8–15. The shepherds were the first to hear the angels' joyful announcement of Christ's birth. Imagine the wonder and awe they must have felt as they were chosen to witness such a miraculous event! In their humble state, they were the first to receive the good news that a Saviour had been born. Just like the shepherds, everyone is invited to come and see the wonder of Christ, no matter where we are in life.

Happy Day Two of the Twelve Days of Christmas! The second day of Christmas celebrates St. Stephen's Day. St. Stephen was the first Christian martyr.

On this second day, we remember the two turtle doves in the popular song and give thanks to Mary and Joseph—the loving parents who humbly cared for and protected baby Jesus. Just as the turtle doves are gentle and devoted, so too were Mary and Joseph in their obedience to God's call, bringing their child into the world with hearts full of faith and sacrifice. As we think about their quiet yet powerful role in the Christmas story, let's remember how we, too, can offer ourselves to God in love and humility this season.

Reflections ...

TODAY I AM GRATEFUL FOR ... _____

_____

_____

December 27
1 Corinthians 13:13

The third day of Christmas celebrates St. John the Apostle's Day. It commemorates St. John, the beloved disciple of Jesus. On this day, we remember the core virtues of our faith: faith, hope, and charity (or love). These three virtues are beautifully captured in 1 Corinthians 13:13, where Paul reminds us that *"the greatest of these is love."*

As I read this verse, I'm inspired to take a moment to think about how to live out faith, hope, and love more deeply this season. Every so often, we need a reminder to shine Christ's love to those around us. May your heart overflow with faith, hope, and love today and always!

Reflections ...

TODAY I AM GRATEFUL FOR ... _____

_____

_____

_____

_____

_____

December 28
LUKE 2:21

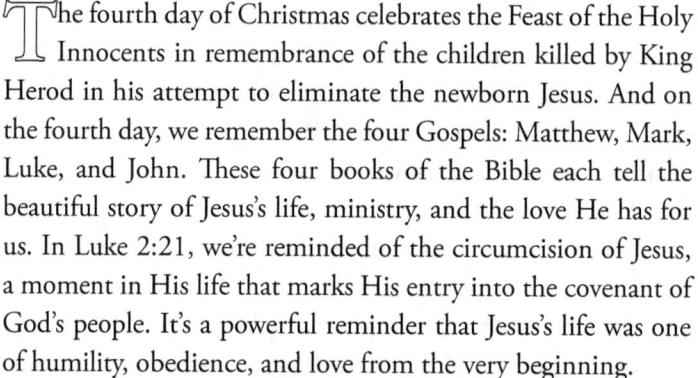

The fourth day of Christmas celebrates the Feast of the Holy Innocents in remembrance of the children killed by King Herod in his attempt to eliminate the newborn Jesus. And on the fourth day, we remember the four Gospels: Matthew, Mark, Luke, and John. These four books of the Bible each tell the beautiful story of Jesus's life, ministry, and the love He has for us. In Luke 2:21, we're reminded of the circumcision of Jesus, a moment in His life that marks His entry into the covenant of God's people. It's a powerful reminder that Jesus's life was one of humility, obedience, and love from the very beginning.

As you reflect on the Gospels, consider how they reveal the heart of Christ, His teachings, and His sacrifices for us. What message of hope or peace can you carry into your day from these precious books? May you be blessed as you journey through this time with the words of the Gospels guiding your heart.

Reflections ...

TODAY I AM GRATEFUL FOR ... _____

_____
_____
_____
_____
_____
_____

December 29
NUMBERS 6:22–27

Happy Day Five! The fifth day of Christmas is St. Thomas Becket's Day. It commemorates the martyrdom of Thomas Becket, the Archbishop of Canterbury. Today we can celebrate the five books of the Torah, or Pentateuch: Genesis, Exodus, Leviticus, Numbers, and Deuteronomy. These foundational books lay the groundwork for our understanding of God's covenant with His people, His laws, and His promises. Numbers 6:22–27 is a powerful reminder that God desires to bless His people, to be with them, and to give them peace.

Reading from a portion of the Torah today, think about how God's love and faithfulness are woven through each page. What blessings can you thank God for? How can you carry this peace into your relationships with others during this Christmas season?

Reflections ...

TODAY I AM GRATEFUL FOR ... _____

_____
_____
_____
_____
_____

December 30
Exodus 20:1

The sixth day of Christmas is the Feast of the Holy Family. It honours the Holy Family of Jesus, Mary, and Joseph. On this day, let's reflect on the six days of creation described in Genesis 1:11–27. Just as God spoke the world into being, creating light, land, sea, creatures, and humanity, the creation story reminds us of His power and goodness. It's through His will and purpose that everything came into existence, and He saw that it was good!

Going about your day today, think about how God is still creating, still bringing new life and hope into the world. What new beginnings are you looking forward to in this season of Advent? How can you bring a little more light and love into your world, just as God did during creation? Wishing you a blessed Day Six of Christmas!

Reflections ...

Today I am grateful for ... _____

December 31
New Year's Eve

Isaiah 11:2–3

No surprise here—the seventh day of Christmas is New Years Eve! On this day we celebrate the seven gifts of the Holy Spirit found in Isaiah 11:2–3. These gifts—wisdom, understanding, counsel, might, knowledge, fear of the Lord, and delight in the fear of the Lord—are given to us by the Holy Spirit to help us grow closer to God and serve others with love and grace. As we read earlier this month, Isaiah prophesied about the coming Messiah, and these gifts are the very qualities Jesus displayed during His earthly ministry.

Consider how you can ask for these gifts in your daily life. Pray for wisdom in your decisions, understanding in your relationships, and courage to follow where God leads you. These gifts are not only for us to treasure but for us to share, shining light to the world as we prepare for the birth of Christ.

Reflections ...

TODAY I AM GRATEFUL FOR ... _____

_____
_____
_____
_____
_____
_____

Readings for Special Days

Shrove Tuesday
(Pancake Tuesday)

JOEL 2:12–17

In this reading, we hear a powerful call from God to return to Him with all our hearts. As we move through this season of reflection, we come before God, acknowledging our need for His mercy and grace. It's a time to pause and open ourselves to God's forgiveness, knowing He is always ready to receive us with love and compassion. This isn't about guilt but about the joy of renewing our hearts and souls in God's presence.

I am so excited! Today as we prepare for the season of Lent, let's celebrate Shrove Tuesday, also known as Pancake Day! This tradition is a beautiful way to mark the day before Ash Wednesday by enjoying one last feast before the fasting season of Lent begins. It's a time to gather with loved ones and enjoy a simple yet joyful meal together.

In the spirit of the tradition, plan a pancake dinner with your family or friends to mirror the richness of God's blessings. Many churches organize pancake suppers as a way to come together in community, and we were so happy to have ours going again last year to enjoy fellowship and raise money for those in need. Use this time to talk about the significance of the season, sharing your hopes and prayers for the journey ahead. Enjoy this moment of feasting, knowing it sets the stage for a meaningful and transformative Lenten season!

Reflections ...

TODAY I AM GRATEFUL FOR ... _____

_____

_____

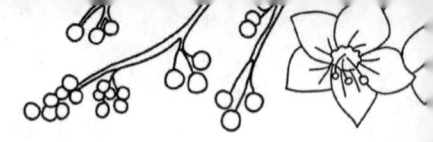

Lent

As we journey through Lent together, I've included both weekends and Easter in our readings, so while Lent traditionally spans forty days (excluding Sundays), you'll find a special adjustment here to ensure a reading for each day of this meaningful season.

Lent Day One
—Ash Wednesday

Matthew 6:1–6

Through today's reading, Jesus teaches us about the importance of humility in our faith practices. He reminds us that our acts of worship, prayer, and fasting should not be for the approval of others, but for God alone. True treasures aren't found in earthly possessions but in the intimate relationship we build with God. By examining this reading, we're encouraged to focus on what truly matters—aligning our hearts with God's will and storing up treasures in heaven through acts of faith and love.

Lent is a forty-day season (excluding Sundays) leading up to Easter, symbolizing the forty days Jesus spent fasting and praying in the wilderness. It's a tradition for all Christians to observe, focusing on repentance, prayer, and spiritual growth. The season begins on Ash Wednesday and ends on Holy Saturday, the day before Easter Sunday.

As we begin this Lenten journey, take a quiet moment for personal reflection and repentance. Spend some time in prayer, asking God to search your heart and show you areas where you can grow closer to Him. During this time, I like to light a candle, find a peaceful corner, or research Lenten traditions and give thanks for His mercy and grace, and set the tone for a season of transformation.

Reflections ...

Today I am grateful for ... _____

_____

_____

_____

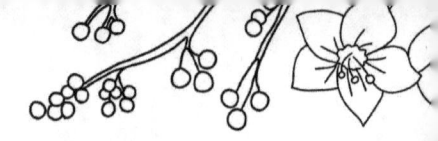

Lent Day Two
MATTHEW 6:16–21

Jesus teaches us the importance of sincerity in our spiritual practices, especially when it comes to fasting and acts of devotion. He warns against seeking attention or praise from others and instead encourages us to focus on our relationship with God. True treasure, He says, is found not in earthly possessions but in storing up treasures in heaven, where our hearts truly belong. This reminder calls us to humble ourselves, seek God in secret, and allow our actions to reflect His love—not for the praise of others, but for His glory.

For Lent, commit to ten, twenty, or even thirty days of small acts of kindness. Each day, do something kind—whether it's offering a word of encouragement, helping someone in need, or simply sharing a smile. Track your kindness in a journal or share it with a friend to inspire and support each other. This simple challenge will help you display Jesus's love in tangible ways and transform the world one act at a time. As you serve others in secret, you'll find that these small gestures create treasures in heaven, not seen by the world, but deeply known by God.

Reflections ...

TODAY I AM GRATEFUL FOR ... _____

_____

_____

_____

Lent Day Three
2 Corinthians 5:20–6:10

Paul calls us to be ambassadors for Christ, living out the message of reconciliation with God through Christ. Ass followers of Jesus, we're called to embody His love, grace, and truth in every area of our lives. We're encouraged to live with joy, purpose, and intentionality, even in difficult circumstances, knowing that God is at work within us.

Get ready to have some fun and start prepping for Lenten Bingo! Whether at your church or with family and friends, you can include simple acts like going to church or donating to a food bank. You can even create a kids' version to include them in the spirit of giving. It's a joyful way to bring meaning to the season of Lent while having fun together!

Reflections ...

TODAY I AM GRATEFUL FOR ... _____

_____
_____
_____
_____
_____
_____

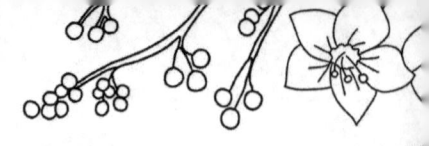

Lent Day Four
Isaiah 58:1–12

God calls His people to a genuine fast—one that isn't just about abstaining from food but about changing the way we live and care for others. Today's passage speaks about true worship, which involves justice, compassion, and sharing with those in need. God reminds the Israelites that when we align our actions with His heart, our fasting and offerings are pleasing to Him. This encourages us to focus on selflessness, humility, and bringing light to others, not just through actions, but through our words and attitudes.

This Lent, consider fasting from negative language. Choose to refrain from complaining or speaking negatively, and instead focus on using your words to encourage, uplift, and express gratitude. Just as God provided for the Israelites in times of need, we can offer words of grace and kindness, bringing light and encouragement to those around us. By changing our speech, we reflect God's love and cultivate a heart that trusts in His provision during this season of Lent.

Reflections ...

Today I am grateful for ... _____

_____
_____
_____
_____
_____

Lent Day Five
Exodus 14:10–31

The Israelites experienced an incredible act of God's salvation as He parted the Red Sea, rescuing them from certain defeat. The story of Exodus reminds us that no matter how impossible our circumstances may seem, God is always able to make a way and deliver us. It reminds us to trust in His power and faithfulness, even when the path ahead looks uncertain.

Who's up for a Lenten movie night! Gather your family or friends and choose a film that inspires hope and reminds you of God's ability to rescue and bring light into dark situations. Just like the Israelites, we can be reminded that God is always working behind the scenes, bringing us through challenges with His love and strength. Don't forget the popcorn!

Reflections ...

TODAY I AM GRATEFUL FOR ... _____

_____
_____
_____
_____
_____
_____

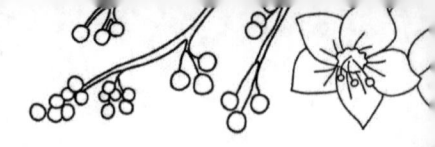

Lent Day Six
Genesis 22:1–14

God tested Abraham's faith by asking him to sacrifice his beloved son, Isaac. But in His great mercy and provision, God provided a ram as a substitute, demonstrating His unwavering care and faithfulness. This powerful moment reminds us of the trust we can place in God, knowing that even in times of trial, He's always there to provide for us and guide us with His love.

This Lent, write a heartfelt letter to each of your family members, expressing how much you appreciate them. Share specific moments when they've made a positive impact on your life, and let them know how grateful you are for their love and support. A handwritten note is a beautiful, personal way to show your love and create lasting memories that remind them of God's love in your life.

Reflections ...

TODAY I AM GRATEFUL FOR ... _____

_____
_____
_____
_____
_____

Lent Day Seven
GENESIS 24:1–28

We see God's faithfulness in this reading, guiding the servant to find the perfect match for Isaac. We're reminded that God is always actively involved in our lives, providing direction and care in both the big and small decisions. During Lent, we're called to pause and reflect on how God leads us and how His provision, even in unexpected ways, is always aligned with His perfect plan for our lives.

Think of something truly thoughtful you could do for a friend or loved one during this season of Lent. Whether it's writing a heartfelt note, preparing a simple meal, or just offering a listening ear, these small acts of kindness speak to God's love and are a beautiful way to serve others.

Reflections ...

TODAY I AM GRATEFUL FOR ... _____

_____
_____
_____
_____
_____

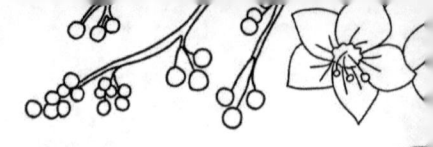

Lent Day Eight
Genesis 25:19–34

Lent is a season in which we reflect on our own choices, seek repentance, and turn back to God with a renewed trust in His will. Just like the story of Jacob and Esau, we're invited to acknowledge that even in times of uncertainty, God's sovereignty remains, and He is continually working to bring about His good purpose for us. Lent is a wonderful opportunity to trust that God's plan for us is perfect, even when it's hard to see in the moment.

As a family, consider committing to fasting or eating simpler meals together during Lent. Whether it's choosing meatless meals on Fridays or simplifying your regular meals, this can be a beautiful way to focus on the spiritual discipline of fasting and grow closer to God throughout this season.

Reflections ...

TODAY I AM GRATEFUL FOR ... _____

_____
_____
_____
_____
_____
_____

Lent Day Nine
GENESIS 29:1–14

In today's reading, we see how God's plan unfolds through the relationships in our lives, just as in the beautiful connection between Jacob and Rachel. Genesis reminds us that God is at work even in the midst of our everyday interactions, providing opportunities for love, growth, and connection. Lent reminds us to trust in God's timing and His purpose, even when things seem to unfold slowly or unexpectedly. Just as Jacob's journey had its challenges, our Lenten journey calls us to embrace patience and faith, trusting that God is guiding us toward deeper relationships with Him and others.

Let's create a "family bucket list" together! Sit down as a family and dream up some fun activities or experiences you'd love to share together in the future. This is not only a way to build lasting memories but also to show how much you value spending time with each other and strengthening your bond. We did this years ago, and it was amazing how simple and doable many of the ideas were—so much so that we started incorporating them into our everyday lives!

Reflections ...

TODAY I AM GRATEFUL FOR … _____

_____

_____

_____

_____

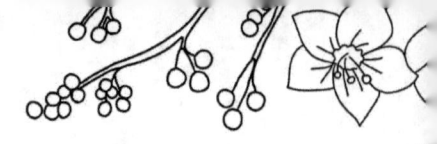

Lent Day Ten
Genesis 32:22–32

In today's passage, Jacob wrestles with God, and through this struggle, he is transformed and given a new name—Israel. This powerful moment highlights how our faith journey often involves wrestling with challenges, doubts, and struggles, but through them, God shapes and transforms us. As we move through Lent, this story reminds us that even in times of hardship, God is refining us and bringing us closer to His purpose. Just as Jacob was forever changed by his encounter with God, we too can experience growth and transformation as we seek a deeper connection with Him during this season.

Make time to compliment each family member in a meaningful way. Go around the house and tell each person something you truly admire about them—whether it's their kindness, their hard work, or the joy they bring to your life. This simple act of encouragement will not only make them feel seen and valued but will also deepen your family's bond and uplift their spirits, reminding them of their own unique beauty and worth in God's eyes.

Reflections ...

TODAY I AM GRATEFUL FOR ... _____

_____

_____

_____

_____

Lent Day Eleven
Jeremiah 17:5–10

Today, we're reminded of the stark contrast between trusting in human strength and putting our faith in God. The passage calls us to examine where we place our trust and to recognize that true hope and security are found in the Lord alone. During Lent, this scripture invites us to look into our own hearts and how we can grow closer to God by relying fully on His guidance and grace.

A great way to focus on this during Lent is by joining or organizing a Bible study group. Choose a study that embraces the themes of Lent, such as the Stations of the Cross, Lenten devotions, or Scripture studies focused on repentance. This shared time of growth with others can be a powerful way to seek God's strength and deepen your faith during this season.

Reflections ...

TODAY I AM GRATEFUL FOR ... _____

_____
_____
_____
_____
_____

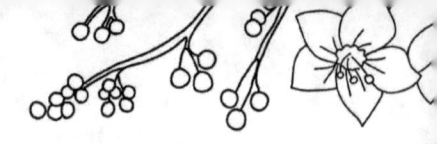

Lent Day Twelve
DEUTERONOMY 30:15–20

God offers us the choice between life and death, calling us to choose life by loving Him and following His ways. As we journey through Lent, this passage encourages us to consider the choices we make. Lent is a time to turn away from what distracts us and choose to walk more closely with God, trusting His guidance for true life.

To nurture your spiritual growth this Lent, set aside some time each week for family devotions. Pick a meaningful passage (like this one), reflect on its message together, and lift your voices in prayer as a family. Focus on themes of repentance and sacrifice, and watch how it strengthens your bond and deepens your faith.

Reflections ...

TODAY I AM GRATEFUL FOR ... _____

_____
_____
_____
_____
_____
_____

Lent Day Thirteen
Isaiah 58:1–9

In today's reading, God calls us to show love and mercy through our actions, reminding us that true fasting is not just about sacrifice but serving others with a compassionate heart. It's a wonderful Lenten reminder of how we can live out our faith through acts of service, drawing closer to God by caring for His people.

Lent is a great time to engage in a family service project. You could make care packages for the homeless, visit a nursing home, or help out with a local charity. Not only does this teach the importance of giving, but it also brings your family together in love and compassion, just as God intended!

Reflections ...

Today I am grateful for ... _____

_____

_____

_____

_____

_____

_____

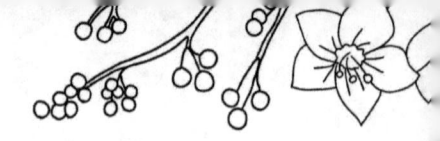

Lent Day Fourteen
Ezekiel 36:24–28

Today's reading invites us to reflect on God's desire for spiritual transformation, which aligns beautifully with the Lenten season. God promises to cleanse His people, give them a new heart, and put His Spirit within them. Just as God promised to restore His people, Lent is a time for us to allow God to renew and purify our hearts as we draw closer to Him in repentance, prayer, and contemplation.

Participating in daily Lenten reflections or journaling is a wonderful way to invite God's transformation into your life. By contemplating Scripture, journaling your thoughts, or using a guide from your church (or a super awesome devotional book ☺), you can stay focused on the theme of spiritual growth during this sacred season. Let this practice help open your heart to God's work in your life as He shapes you into the person He has called you to be.

Reflections ...

TODAY I AM GRATEFUL FOR ... _____

_____
_____
_____
_____
_____
_____

Lent Day Fifteen
1 Samuel 16:1–13

God calls Samuel to anoint David as the future king of Israel in 1 Samual, reminding us that God looks at the heart, not outward appearances. This passage encourages us to focus on the inner transformation God desires for us. As we seek a closer relationship with Him throughout Lent, we're reminded that He is working in us, shaping our hearts and guiding us toward His purpose.

Creating a family prayer jar is a beautiful way to focus on prayer together during Lent. Have each family member write down their prayer requests and place them in the jar. Each day, choose one to pray for together, strengthening your family's bond in prayer while allowing God to shape your hearts and deepen your faith.

Reflections ...

TODAY I AM GRATEFUL FOR ... _____

_____
_____
_____
_____
_____

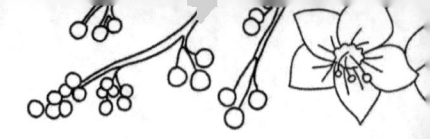

Lent Day Sixteen
LUKE 13:1–9

Jesus calls us to reflect on our lives and make changes where needed, just as He urged the people to bear good fruit. His message reminds us that repentance and transformation are key to living a life pleasing to God. As we move through Lent, it's a wonderful time to examine our hearts and seek growth in faith and action.

For a Lenten activity, gather with family or friends and do some crafting together that focuses on the cross or other symbols of Lent. You can make a simple Lenten wreath to remind your family of this reflective season. Crafting not only engages creativity but can also provide a meaningful way to talk about repentance and the importance of forgiveness.

Reflections …

TODAY I AM GRATEFUL FOR … _____

_____
_____
_____
_____
_____
_____
_____

Lent Day Seventeen
Matthew 7:7–12

Through our reading in Matthew, Jesus invites us to ask, seek, and knock, assuring us that God will provide for our needs. The season of Lent reminds us to trust God's generosity and to approach Him with faith. It also calls us to live out the Golden Rule, treating others with kindness, as God has shown us His grace. Let this season be a time to ponder God's provision and extend His love to those around us.

For this Lenten movie night, gather your family or friends and choose a Christian film that highlights themes of sacrifice, redemption, or the life of Jesus, such as *The Passion of the Christ*. Note that this movie does include a graphic representation of the crucifixion and may not be suitable for your children. After the movie, have a heartfelt discussion about how the story connects to the Lenten season, focusing on the lessons of sacrifice, love, and forgiveness that guide us.

Reflections ...

Today I am grateful for ... _____

_____
_____
_____
_____
_____

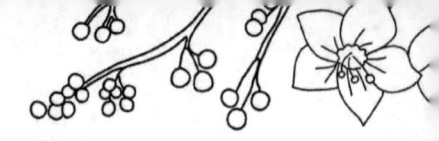

Lent Day Eighteen
Matthew 20:17–28

Matthew tells us the story of how Jesus predicts His own death, speaking openly about the suffering He will endure for the salvation of humanity. He reveals that He will be handed over to the authorities, mocked, and crucified, yet He teaches His disciples that true greatness comes through serving others, not seeking power. We're challenged to reflect on the ultimate sacrifice Jesus made and how we can follow His example by serving others with humility and love.

For Lent, practise mindful giving by setting aside time or money each week to support a cause or ministry. This thoughtful act of generosity allows us to serve others and deepen our connection with God, reminding us of the importance of living with a heart of humility and love.

Reflections ...

Today I am grateful for ... _____

_____
_____
_____
_____
_____
_____
_____

Lent Day Nineteen
Luke 9:28–36

When Jesus is transfigured before His disciples in this passage, His divine glory shines through, and He's seen speaking with Moses and Elijah about His upcoming departure in Jerusalem. This moment is a powerful revelation of Jesus as the fulfillment of God's promises through the Law and the Prophets. As we journey through Lent, we're invited to reflect on this glimpse of Christ's glory and prepare our hearts for the sacrifice He made. It reminds us of the importance of trusting in God's greater plan, even when it leads us toward the cross.

Lent is one of my favourite seasons—we talk a lot about reflection during Lent, as it's important. Lent is often not celebrated as much as Christmas. To help bring the meaning of this season into your home, order palm leaves from a florist for your table this Palm Sunday. If you have kids, you could make these out of construction paper. It's a beautiful and simple way to display your thankfulness and to honour Jesus's journey to the cross. As you set the table, take a moment to praise His glory and sacrifice, making the season even more meaningful for you and your loved ones.

Reflections ...

Today I am grateful for ... _____

_____

_____

_____

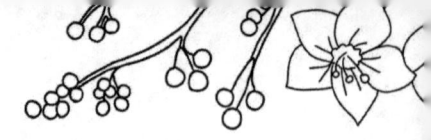

Lent Day Twenty
Isaiah 61:1–4

Isaiah 61:1–4 is such an uplifting reminder of God's incredible love and purpose for us! In these verses, God promises to bring good news to the oppressed, comfort those who mourn, and restore what was lost. As we continue through our Lenten readings, this is a beautiful call to share that hope and joy with others, knowing that God's purpose for us is one of healing, restoration, and freedom.

A great way to embrace fasting during Lent is by partnering with a friend or family member as your fasting accountability partner. Share your goals and challenges with each other, whether it's fasting from food, technology, or certain habits. Check in regularly, encourage each other, and pray together, supporting each other through the fast. Fasting can be tough, but with someone to walk alongside you, it becomes a journey of growth and shared strength, deepening your relationship with God and with each other too!

Reflections ...

TODAY I AM GRATEFUL FOR ... _____

_____
_____
_____
_____
_____
_____

Lent Day Twenty-One
Isaiah 42:1–9

This reading beautifully describes the servant of the Lord, chosen to bring justice and light to the nations. God promises to uphold and support His servant, guiding him with gentleness and love. This passage calls us to consider God's mission of healing and redemption in the world, reminding us that through Jesus, God's light shines into the darkness, bringing hope and transformation.

I love a good ringtone! Choose a special Lenten ringtone to keep you focused on God's love and presence. Each time your phone rings, let it be a gentle reminder of God's presence and a call to reflect on His justice, mercy, and grace throughout your day. It's a simple but meaningful way to keep your heart attuned to the Lenten season and God's guiding light.

Reflections ...

TODAY I AM GRATEFUL FOR ... _____

_____
_____
_____
_____
_____
_____

Lent Day Twenty-Two
JEREMIAH 29:11–14

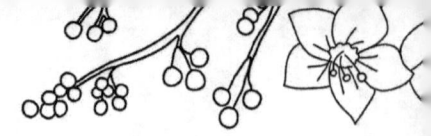

Jeremiah 29:11–14 is an inspiring reminder that God has a plan for us—a plan full of hope and a future. We're called to seek God with all our hearts, knowing that when we do, He promises to listen and draw near. This is especially relevant as we journey toward the resurrection, a time to give thanks for God's faithfulness and to trust in His good plans for our lives.

In that spirit, create a Lenten playlist to enjoy over this time. Music is a wonderful way to connect with God's promises throughout this season. One song I highly recommend is Dolly Parton's "*He's Alive.*" It's a powerful reminder of Christ's resurrection and the hope we have in Him. Let each song you choose be a gentle nudge toward deeper faith and trust in God's plan for you this Lent.

Reflections ...

TODAY I AM GRATEFUL FOR ... _____
_____
_____
_____
_____
_____
_____

Lent Day Twenty-Three
MARK 4:35–41

Jesus calms the storm, showing His authority over nature and reminding us that He's always in control, even in the midst of life's most turbulent moments. The disciples were terrified, but Jesus gently asks, "Why are you afraid? Do you still have no faith?" This story speaks to our fears and challenges, inviting us to trust Jesus to bring peace and calm to the storms in our lives.

For a powerful Lenten activity, consider creating a Lenten trust challenge with your family or friends. Throughout the season, share moments when you've seen God's peace in the midst of chaos. Each time you face a challenge, pause to pray and trust God to bring calm, just as He calmed the storm for His disciples. Reflect on how God is always with us, no matter what storm we face.

Reflections ...

TODAY I AM GRATEFUL FOR ... _____

_____
_____
_____
_____
_____

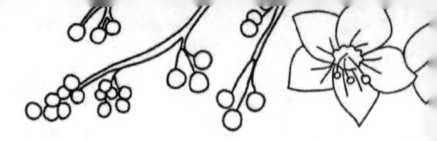

Lent Day Twenty-Four
Psalm 103:8–14

Psalm 103:8–14 is a passage that shows us God's immense mercy and compassion, qualities that are especially meaningful during Lent. In this passage, God is described as slow to anger, abounding in love, and full of grace. His kindness and forgiveness are available to us, even when we fall short. This passage is perfect for Lent, as it encourages reflection on God's tender-hearted care for us, offering an opportunity to repent, receive His forgiveness, and grow in gratitude for His unshakable love.

Baking bread is a favourite pastime of mine. I love the smells wafting from the kitchen, and challah bread is on my list! This traditional Jewish bread, often braided, symbolizes unity, connection, and the abundance of God's provision. While making the dough and braiding it, think about how God has woven His grace into your life, especially during this Lenten season. Each step in the process can serve as a reminder of His forgiveness and love. Once baked, enjoy the bread with loved ones, and thank God for His endless mercy and the redemption He offers through Christ.

Reflections ...

Today I am grateful for ... _____

_____

_____

_____

Lent Day Twenty-Five
Isaiah 58:1–9

God invites us to embrace a deeper kind of fasting—one that focuses on justice, compassion, and helping others. It's not about outward rituals but about how we live our lives and care for those around us. This passage challenges us to look beyond ourselves and ask how we can share God's love through acts of kindness and service. As we reflect on this, we're reminded that true worship is found in our hearts and in the way we treat others.

In keeping with the spirit of reflection and sacrifice during Lent, consider observing a meatless Friday. This small act of fasting can be a wonderful way to honour God and consider the sacrifice of Jesus. Try preparing a delicious meat-free meal, like a vegetable stir-fry or a hearty soup, and enjoy the time spent together in gratitude. It's a wonderful reminder of God's provision and an opportunity to focus on kindness, simplicity, and mindful eating.

Reflections ...

TODAY I AM GRATEFUL FOR ... _____

_____
_____
_____
_____
_____

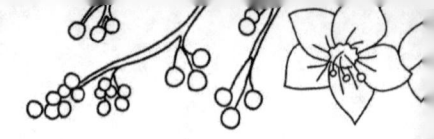

Lent Day Twenty-Six
Isaiah 58:10–14

In today's reading, God invites us to live out His love and compassion through acts of selflessness and service. When we care for others—especially the hungry, the poor, and those in need—God promises to bless us with His presence and guidance. We are called to reflect His light in the world by choosing to live with generosity and kindness, which is no small task. How do you feel called upon to show God's love today? As we care for others, we also experience God's blessings and experience deeper joy and peace.

After reading of Isaiah's call to live out love and compassion, wouldn't it be fun to create a simple Easter craft to celebrate the season? A resurrection garden is a beautiful, hands-on way to symbolize the new life and hope we have in Christ. A girlfriend of mine showed me how to make these, and this cute craft is something you can with others. This quiet activity can be a gentle reminder of the new beginnings and blessings that come when we follow God's example of love.

Reflections ...

Today I am grateful for ... _____

_____
_____
_____
_____
_____
_____

LENT

Lent Day Twenty-Seven
Psalm 86:1–11

In today's reading, David calls out to God for mercy, guidance, and help in times of distress. He acknowledges God's greatness and faithfulness, asking for a heart that is devoted to Him and willing to follow His ways. This passage is a truth and shows us that God is always near, ready to listen to our prayers and help us grow in faith. David's heartfelt plea for God's guidance and steadfast love teaches us to seek God with sincerity and trust, knowing He will lead us on the right path.

Choose a scripture that has personal meaning to you—a verse that brings comfort, peace, or encouragement. It could be part of Psalm 86 or any other passage that resonates with your heart. Take time to memorize it over the next few days by writing it down, saying it out loud, or praying it. Let it be a source of strength as you reflect on God's promises, and allow His Word to guide your thoughts and actions.

Reflections …

TODAY I AM GRATEFUL FOR … _____

_____

_____

_____

_____

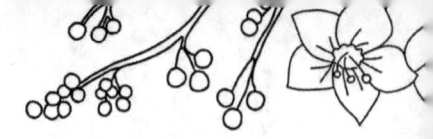

Lent Day Twenty-Eight
Luke 5:27–32

When Jesus calls Levi, a tax collector, to follow Him, it's a beautiful picture of grace in action. Levi leaves behind his comfortable life to follow Jesus, showing that no matter our past, Jesus welcomes us with open arms. This story invites us to consider how Jesus calls each of us into a deeper relationship with Him, not because we're perfect, but because He desires transformation in our hearts.

During Lent, take some quiet moments each day to reflect on what this season means for you personally. Whether it's through prayer, journaling, or reading Scripture, allow yourself to truly listen for how God is calling you to grow. Just as Levi left his old life behind to follow Jesus, consider what you might need to release this Lent in order to follow Christ more closely.

Reflections ...

TODAY I AM GRATEFUL FOR ... _____

_____
_____
_____
_____
_____
_____

Lent Day Twenty-Nine
MATTHEW 4:1–11

Matthew 4:1–11 recounts the story of Jesus being tempted in the wilderness, where He fasted for forty days and resisted the devil's temptations. This passage is particularly meaningful for Lent, because it mirrors the forty days of fasting and reflection we practise during this season. Just as Jesus resisted temptation and focused on God's Word, Lent provides us with the opportunity to turn away from distractions and strengthen our relationship with God. Jesus's response to each temptation reminds us that true strength comes from trusting in God and relying on His Word. This passage helps us refocus during Lent, encouraging us to grow spiritually and to resist the temptations that may pull us away from God's presence.

To deepen your Lenten reflection, why not bake some delicious fougasse? This traditional bread, which resembles a palm leaf, is a wonderful way to connect with the season, symbolizing both the temptations Jesus faced and the hope of His victory over them. As you bake, think about how Jesus, during His forty days in the wilderness, relied on God's strength, and consider how you can grow in your own trust and dependence on God throughout this Lenten season.

Reflections ...

TODAY I AM GRATEFUL FOR ... _____
_____
_____
_____

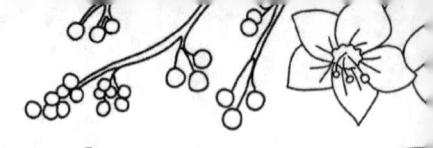

Lent Day Thirty
Psalm 41

The psalmist in Psalm 41 speaks of the blessings and care that come to those who are compassionate and considerate of others, especially those who are suffering. It reminds us that God's favour rests on those who show kindness, and in times of trouble, He is our refuge and strength. This passage is particularly meaningful during Lent, as it invites us to focus on caring for others and reflect on the ways we can serve and love those around us. Lent is a time to grow in compassion and to remember that our actions—small or large—reflect God's love for us.

An activity that may deepen your Lenten journey is by gathering your family for a meal and discussing what Lent means to each of you. Sharing thoughts, and even struggles, can be a meaningful way to connect with one another and strengthen your faith together.

Reflections ...

Today I am grateful for ... _____

_____
_____
_____
_____
_____
_____
_____

Lent Day Thirty-One
Psalm 44

Psalm 44 is a heartfelt prayer in which the psalmist reflects on times of distress and feels as though God is silent in the midst of suffering. Despite this, the psalmist remains hopeful, trusting in God's past faithfulness and calling on Him to intervene. It's a reminder that even in our darkest moments, we can hold on to the truth that God has been with us before, and He will continue to be our refuge and strength.

A wonderful way to echo the spirit of Psalm 44 during Lent is by practising a "pay it forward" act of kindness. If you see someone in line at a coffee shop or grocery store, consider offering to pay for their purchase. This simple, spontaneous gesture not only brightens someone's day but also spreads kindness and love in a world that can sometimes feel heavy. Just as we rely on God's love and faithfulness, we can mirror His generosity and grace by sharing a little of that love with others in unexpected ways. It's a tender reminder that, even when life feels uncertain, we can still make the world around us a little brighter with small acts of kindness.

Reflections ...

TODAY I AM GRATEFUL FOR ... _____

_____

_____

_____

_____

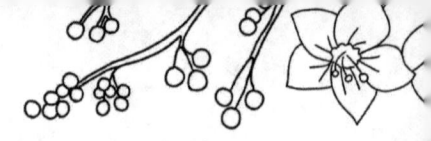

Lent Day Thirty-Two
Psalm 52

David contrasts the destructive nature of those who do evil with the steadfast love of God, who ultimately protects and nurtures His people. The psalm reminds us that God's love and faithfulness are a refuge, and it encourages us to remain rooted in His goodness. We're reminded of how God's love is meant to flow through us, touching the lives of others in meaningful ways.

This week, open your home to friends, family, or even strangers. Inviting others in for a meal or a simple conversation is a beautiful way to build community, strengthen relationships, and share the love of Christ. Whether it's inviting someone over for a cup of tea or hosting a small dinner, this simple act fosters love and connection.

Reflections ...

TODAY I AM GRATEFUL FOR ... _____

_____
_____
_____
_____
_____
_____

Lent Day Thirty-Three
Deuteronomy 8:11–20

Have you ever stopped to think about how easy it is to forget God's provision when life is going well? In Deuteronomy 8:11–20, Moses reminds the Israelites not to forget the Lord when they are blessed with abundance and success. He urges them to remember that it's God who gives them strength and prosperity. It's a call to reflect on God's faithfulness and to always acknowledge His role in our blessings, no matter where we are in life.

Start a prayer jar at your church where people can drop in their prayer requests and others can randomly select one to pray for. This can be a wonderful way to build community and encourage one another in prayer. Just as Deuteronomy encourages us to stay mindful of God's provision and love, a prayer jar helps us come together, acknowledging our dependence on God and supporting each other in our journeys of faith.

Reflections ...

Today I am grateful for ... _____

_____
_____
_____
_____
_____

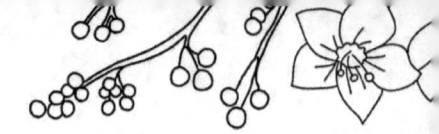

Lent Day Thirty-Four
JOHN 2:1–12

Today we read about Jesus performing His first miracle: turning water into wine at a wedding in Cana. This miracle shows His power to transform ordinary moments into something extraordinary, and it reminds us that Jesus brings joy and abundance into our lives. Just as He turned the water into something beautiful and celebratory, Jesus continues to transform our hearts and lives with His love and grace. This season of Lent is a perfect opportunity to reflect on how God can turn our challenges into moments of beauty and joy.

Have you ever made homemade hot cross buns? These sweet, spiced buns are a delicious tradition for Easter, and their simple cross design reminds us of the sacrifice of Jesus. As you mix, knead, and bake, think about how Jesus brings joy and transformation into your life, just like He did with the water at Cana. It's a wonderful way to enjoy a delicious treat and celebrate the sweetness of the season while remembering God's goodness and the joy He brings to our lives. Plus, they're perfect to share with family and friends as a way to spread some Easter joy!

Reflections ...

TODAY I AM GRATEFUL FOR ... _____

_____

_____

_____

Lent Day Thirty-Five
John 2:13–22

In John 2:13–22, Jesus cleanses the temple, driving out the money changers and those selling animals for sacrifices. His actions demonstrate His passion for the holiness of God's house and His desire for true worship, free from distractions and exploitation. Jesus's declaration that He is the true temple points to His own body, revealing the deeper connection between His mission and the ultimate sacrifice He would make for us. The reading calls us to reflect on our own lives, asking if we're honouring God with pure hearts and if our worship is focused on Him alone.

As you read this passage, take time to consider the sacred spaces in your life. This could be a physical space, like a quiet corner for prayer. Consider how you can make the space intentional and focused on worship and connection with God. You might even take a few moments to clear away distractions from your surroundings or your heart, making space for God's presence in a deeper way.

Reflections ...

TODAY I AM GRATEFUL FOR ... _____

_____
_____
_____
_____
_____

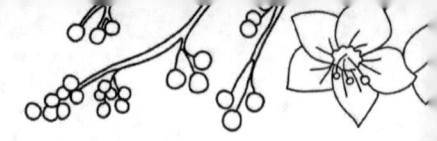

Lent Day Thirty-Six
Deuteronomy 9:4–12

Moses reminds the Israelites that their success in the Promised Land is not because of their righteousness, but because of God's faithfulness and mercy. He highlights how, despite their failures, God's grace has been evident in their journey. This passage is a powerful reminder of God's constant presence and His patience with us, even in our imperfections—not just over Lent, but always. Just as the Israelites were called to remember God's faithfulness, we too are invited to reflect on God's mercy and grace as we prepare for the celebration of Easter.

A great way to enhance your Lenten journey is by reading a book on Lent. Our church librarian is a wealth of knowledge on this subject. There are many insightful books that explore the spiritual significance of this season, offering prayers and meditations to help deepen your faith. By dedicating time to read and reflect, you can better understand the meaning of God's mercy.

Reflections ...

TODAY I AM GRATEFUL FOR ... _____

_____
_____
_____
_____
_____
_____

Lent Day Thirty-Seven
Deuteronomy 9:13–21

Moses reminds the Israelites of their stubbornness and how, despite their disobedience, God showed mercy and spared them. This passage serves as a powerful reminder of God's patience and grace, even when we fall short. During Lent, it calls us to examine our own hearts, repent for our shortcomings, and turn toward God's forgiveness and grace, just as the Israelites were given another chance despite their failings.

To deepen your connection to God during Lent, you may feel called to go on a Lenten retreat. Whether in person or virtually, retreats offer a peaceful space to reflect on God's mercy, practise prayer, and spiritually recharge. Taking time away from your daily routine can help you draw closer to God, just as the Israelites were called to return to Him with humble hearts.

Reflections ...

Today I am grateful for … _____

_____
_____
_____
_____
_____

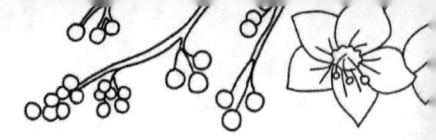

Lent Day Thirty-Eight
Deuteronomy 10:12–22

Moses reminds the Israelites of God's great love and faithfulness, and the importance of loving Him with all their heart, soul, and strength. This passage speaks to the deep covenantal relationship between God and His people, highlighting His justice and mercy. For Lent, this passage is a beautiful reflection on the love and grace we experience through the resurrection of Jesus. Just as God showed His steadfast love to the Israelites, He demonstrated the ultimate expression of love by sending His Son to die and rise again for us.

One meaningful way to share God's love this Easter is by sending Easter cards to friends, family, or those in need of encouragement. Just as God's love was extended to us, sending a card is a small, heartfelt way to spread joy and remind others of the hope that Easter brings. Whether it's a simple note of encouragement or a message of Easter joy, this simple activity can help you connect with others and share the good news of Christ's resurrection. It's a loving gesture that echoes the spirit of Easter.

Reflections ...

TODAY I AM GRATEFUL FOR ... _____

_____
_____
_____
_____

Lent Day Thirty-Nine
MATTHEW 21:1–5

In preparation for Palm Sunday, we read Matthew 21:1–5 which focuses on Jesus's instructions to His disciples to go into the village and bring back a donkey and its colt. This simple act fulfilled the prophecy in Zechariah 9:9, showing that Jesus's kingship was not one of earthly power, but of humility and peace. By choosing a donkey instead of a mighty horse, He displayed His mission to bring peace, not conquest, to the world.

As you prepare for the change of seasons and warmer weather, use this time to clean out your closet and donate the clothes you no longer need. Jesus's humble request for the donkey invites us to live with open hands and hearts, offering what we have to help others. Let Lent be a reminder of how small acts of kindness and humility can make a big impact.

Reflections ...

TODAY I AM GRATEFUL FOR ... _____

_____
_____
_____
_____
_____

JOYOUS FAITH

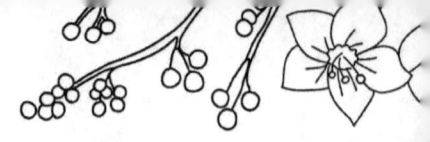

Lent Day Forty
Palm Sunday

MATTHEW 21:6–9

It's Palm Sunday! Matthew paints an exciting picture for us of Jesus entering Jerusalem with all the fanfare and celebration! The crowds eagerly laid down their cloaks and waved palm branches, joyfully shouting, *"Hosanna to the Son of David!"* It's a triumphant moment that shows us not only Jesus as the victorious King but also His incredible humility—a King who came to serve and love us rather than be served. Consider how you can welcome Jesus into your life today with the same excitement and joy. It is Palm Sunday, after all!

For Palm Sunday, let's get ready to celebrate in style! Gather with loved ones and share a special meal, filling the room with love, laughter, and gratitude. As you consider Jesus's grand and humble entry into Jerusalem, think about how you can invite Him into your heart in an even deeper way. This is your chance to really embrace the joy of the season and remember that Jesus, our King, offers us His love and grace with open arms!

Reflections ...

TODAY I AM GRATEFUL FOR ... _____

_____
_____
_____
_____
_____

Lent Day Forty-One
Matthew 21:12–17

Cleansing the Temple

Lent is an opportunity for us to reflect on the areas in our lives that need purification, allowing His love to transform us. Matthew 21:12–17 records a powerful moment when Jesus cleanses the temple, driving out those who had turned it into a marketplace instead of a house of prayer. This act of purification reminds us that Jesus desires to cleanse our hearts as well.

The passion that Jesus shows in this reading is inspiring. By donating to a food bank, we can keep our hearts focused on God's Word and show kindness and support to those in need. Take a few moments to gather non-perishable items from your pantry, or make a monetary donation to help provide meals for others in your community. By sharing what you have, you're not only offering physical sustenance but also spreading love and care in a meaningful way over Lent.

Reflections ...

Today I am grateful for ... _____

_____
_____
_____
_____
_____
_____
_____

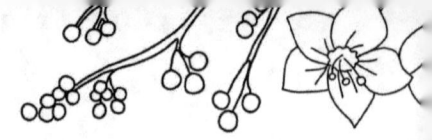

Lent Day Forty-Two
MATTHEW 22:15–22

Paying Taxes to Caesar

As we continue delving into the Easter story, we read Matthew 22:15–22, which presents Jesus's teaching on giving to Caesar what is Caesar's, and to God what is God's. In this passage, Jesus calls us to consider our dual responsibilities—both as citizens of this world and as followers of Christ. It's a powerful reminder to live with integrity, balancing our obligations in society with our ultimate calling to honour and serve God.

Living out Christ's commandments is no small feat, and it can be overwhelming at times. By gathering together, I can draw on others and reflect on the blessings that life has to offer. I pray that you too can find moments to reflect on God's love. Insider information: I would *love* to organize a fish fry at our church next year. Fingers crossed!

Reflections ...

TODAY I AM GRATEFUL FOR ... _____

_____
_____
_____
_____
_____
_____

Lent Day Forty-Three
MATTHEW 26:6–13

During Lent, we reflect on how we serve and love God. In this passage, a woman anointed Jesus with expensive perfume, showing deep devotion. Jesus acknowledged her act of love, reminding those present that He wouldn't be with them much longer. It's a call to offer our hearts fully, even in simple or sacrificial ways, while we have the chance.

Making homemade pretzels is a wonderful way to connect with the theme of prayer, as their shape resembles arms crossed in prayer. Take some time to knead the dough, forming each pretzel with love and intention, remembering the moments of prayer and reflection in your life. As you bake them, let the aroma fill your home, and consider offering a prayer for those you love, just as the pretzel symbolizes arms reaching out in connection and faith.

Reflections ...

TODAY I AM GRATEFUL FOR ... _____

_____
_____
_____
_____
_____
_____

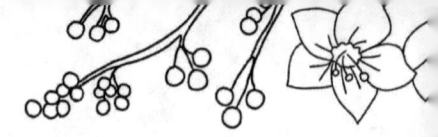

Lent Day Forty-Four
MAUNDY THURSDAY

Luke 22:19–20, The Last Supper

On Maundy Thursday, we remember Jesus's final meal with His disciples, the Last Supper. In this sacred moment, Jesus instituted the sacrament of Holy Communion, sharing the bread and wine with His disciples, symbolizing His body and blood, given for the forgiveness of sins. This act of love and sacrifice points to the deeper meaning of the Passover, where Jesus, as the Lamb of God, fulfills the ultimate act of deliverance for all humanity.

I enjoy researching the meaning behind the Passover meal, focusing on the symbolism of unleavened bread, bitter herbs, and lamb. This can help deepen your understanding of the connection between the Passover and the Last Supper. Consider incorporating some of these elements into your own meal and reflect on how Jesus fulfilled the Passover in His sacrifice.

Reflections ...

Today I am grateful for ... _____

Lent Day Forty-Five
Good Friday

Matthew 27:27–60, The Crucifixion of Jesus

Through Jesus's crucifixion, we're reminded of His immense love and sacrifice for all of humanity. This painful and powerful moment in history reveals the depths of God's grace and forgiveness. It calls us to pause and deeply consider the cost of our salvation and the depth of Jesus's love.

On Good Friday, take time to read about Jesus's crucifixion. There are many powerful books that portray this pivotal event. Allow these reflections to deepen your understanding of Jesus's sacrifice and draw you closer to Him.

Reflections ...

Today I am grateful for ... _____

_____
_____
_____
_____
_____
_____
_____

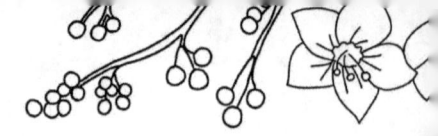

Lent Day Forty-Six
Matthew 27:62–66

The Guard at the Tomb

As we read about the guards being placed at Jesus's tomb, we're reminded of the lengths people will go to out of fear. Despite these efforts, God's plan could not be stopped. This moment invites us to consider the power of God's promises, knowing that even when obstacles arise, His will prevails.

Get ready for an egg-citing Easter celebration! I love decorating eggs with family and friends—and don't forget to sneak in some Bible verses or messages of God's love inside the plastic eggs, along with a little chocolate treat. As you decorate, remember that the egg symbolizes life—just like the incredible inspiration we experience through Jesus's resurrection. It's a great way to celebrate the victory of life over death and the pure joy of Easter!

Reflections ...

Today I am grateful for … _____

_____
_____
_____
_____
_____
_____

Easter Sunday
Matthew 28:5–7

The Resurrection of Jesus

In Matthew 28, the angel proclaims the glorious news that Jesus has risen from the dead, just as He said He would. This moment of triumph marks the victory over sin and death, and it brings us the incredible hope of eternal life. As we celebrate the resurrection, let's rejoice in the rebirth we have in Christ.

Before heading to church, enjoy a fun Easter egg hunt! If your church has one, join in the celebration. Each egg represents Jesus's resurrection. It's a playful way to share in the excitement of Easter and reflect on the miracle of Christ's victory over the grave!

Reflections ...

Today I am grateful for ... _____

_____
_____
_____
_____
_____
_____
_____

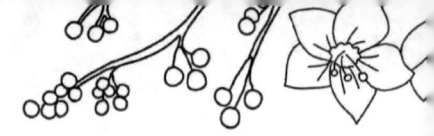

Easter Monday
JOHN 20:11–18

JESUS APPEARS TO MARY MAGDALENE

After the resurrection, Jesus appeared to Mary Magdalene, calling her by name and offering her comfort in her grief. In the same way, Jesus knows each of us personally and offers us hope, peace, and love. As we continue celebrating Easter, let's reflect on how Jesus meets us in our own moments of sorrow and transforms them into joy.

To spread some Easter joy, surprise a friend with a beautiful bouquet of flowers. Just like Jesus brought joy to Mary, your small gesture of kindness can brighten someone's day and remind them of God's love and the hope that Easter brings.

Reflections ...

TODAY I AM GRATEFUL FOR ... _____

_____
_____
_____
_____
_____
_____
_____

Other Important Days
PURIM

ESTHER 4:13–17

Purim celebrates the deliverance of the Jewish people in the story of Esther. In Esther 4:13–17, we see Esther's courageous decision to stand up for her people, even when it means risking her own life. This passage beautifully reminds us that sometimes God calls us to step out in faith and trust in His timing, no matter how daunting the challenge may seem. Just as Esther's bravery brought about deliverance, we're encouraged to trust in God's plan for us and step into our own moments of purpose with courage and love.

Bring justice and kindness into your day. Whether it's offering a helping hand, being patient with others, or standing up for someone in need, these acts of love echo God's heart. Let's be a light in the world through our actions, just as Esther chose to be for her people!

Reflections...

TODAY I AM GRATEFUL FOR ... _____

_____
_____
_____
_____
_____

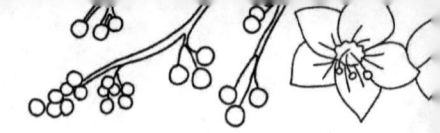

World Day of Prayer
Matthew 6:9–13

What better way to celebrate the World Day of Prayer than by embracing the perfect prayer that Jesus gave us—the Lord's Prayer. This beautiful prayer guides us to seek God's kingdom, ask for our daily provision, and forgive others as we've been forgiven. It connects us to God, reminding us of His deep love and faithfulness, and it's a powerful way to deepen our spiritual journey.

With the Lord's Prayer no longer recited in our public schools, many people may not have it memorized. Take this opportunity this week to memorize the Lord's Prayer, either as a family or individually. This practice can strengthen your connection with God and align your heart with His will.

Reflections...

Today I am grateful for ... _____

_____
_____
_____
_____
_____
_____

OTHER IMPORTANT DAYS

Passover

NEW TESTAMENT READING: MATTHEW 26:17–28
OLD TESTAMENT READING: EXODUS 12:1–14

On this day, we have two readings that connect the significance of Passover in the Old Testament with Jesus celebrating Passover in the New Testament. Exodus 12:1–14 recounts the first Passover, where God instructed the Israelites to sacrifice a lamb and mark their doorposts with its blood, symbolizing God's protection and deliverance from Egypt. This tradition was an important part of Jesus's heritage. But how would Jesus have celebrated Passover?

The traditional Seder meal was celebrated with prayers, rituals, and the recounting of the Exodus story. They ate matzah (unleavened bread), which symbolized the haste with which the Israelites left Egypt, and bitter herbs, likely horseradish or chicory, which symbolized the bitterness of slavery. While observing the customs, Jesus would have infused the meal with deeper meaning, pointing to Himself as the sacrificial Lamb preparing to fulfill the prophecy and establish a new covenant. How humbling to think of this profound moment in history!

Through Matthew 26:17–28, we see how Jesus celebrated the Passover with His disciples (the Last Supper), using the bread and wine to symbolize His body and blood. This moment redefines the Passover meal, pointing to Jesus's sacrifice and establishing the new covenant of salvation through Him. These readings remind us of God's faithfulness in delivering His people, both in the past and through Jesus's ultimate act of love.

A great way to connect with the Passover story is by making matzah ball soup, a traditional dish often served during the Seder meal. The matzah balls (or *kneidlach*) are made from matzah meal, which represents the unleavened bread the Israelites ate

during their hasty departure from Egypt. Enjoying this meal can deepen your connection to the Passover story and Jesus's ultimate sacrifice.

Reflections ...

TODAY I AM GRATEFUL FOR ... _____

_____
_____
_____
_____
_____
_____
_____

Mother's Day
JUDGES 4:4–16

On Mother's Day, we're reminded of the powerful example of Deborah, a woman who courageously led Israel with faith and wisdom. In Judges 4:4–5, we see how Deborah served as a judge, prophetess, and guide, offering strength and guidance to her people in times of need. Her leadership wasn't defined by force but by a deep trust in God's provision. Just like Deborah, many mothers serve as leaders, counsellors, and guides to their families, helping to make decisions, settle disputes, and offer wisdom in times of uncertainty.

For Mother's Day, consider how you can lead with courage and wisdom in your own life. Whether it's supporting a friend, guiding your family, or offering a kind word, let's share the strength and love that comes from trusting in God's call for us. I love to get my mom a corsage for Mother's Day. It's a tradition my grandmother handed down to us (a white flower for yourself if your mother has passed, and a colourful flower for your mother if she's still alive).

Reflections ...

TODAY I AM GRATEFUL FOR ... _____

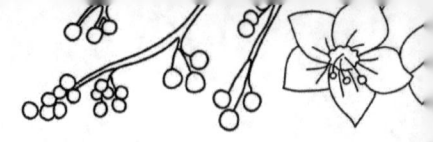

Shavuot, Feast of Weeks
(LASTS FOR TWO DAYS)

Exodus 19:1–8

Shavuot, also known as the Feast of Weeks, celebrates the giving of the Torah to the Israelites at Mount Sinai, a powerful moment when God made a covenant with His people. In Exodus 19:1–8, we read about God's call to the Israelites to be His treasured possession, preparing them to receive His commandments. This passage shows us God's desire for a close relationship with His people and His invitation to walk in His ways—an invitation that still stands for us today as we seek to follow His guidance and love.

In the spirit of deepening our understanding of our faith, let's investigate Shavuot and its significance! This special holiday celebrates the giving of the Torah at Mount Sinai, marking a pivotal moment for our own faith. As we explore Shavuot, let's reflect on how being rooted in Christ aligns with the themes of covenant and commitment.

Reflections ...

TODAY I AM GRATEFUL FOR ... _____

Pentecost
ACTS 2:14–41

Pentecost is the Christian celebration of the Holy Spirit's descent upon the apostles, marking the birth of the Church and the empowerment of believers to spread the gospel. Peter's sermon on Pentecost powerfully demonstrates the transformative impact of the gospel message, leading to the conversion of thousands. This moment reminds us that the message of Christ is alive and dynamic, capable of changing hearts and lives even today. Let's embrace the joy of this message and consider how we can be vessels of God's love and grace in our communities.

If inviting someone to church feels intimidating, start by inviting them to a church dinner or a fun activity, say church baseball game. (lol) These more casual settings can create a welcoming atmosphere for those who may be curious about faith but unsure about attending a service. Share a meal, enjoy some fellowship, and let them experience the warmth and kindness of your church community.

Reflections ...

TODAY I AM GRATEFUL FOR ... _____

_____
_____
_____
_____
_____

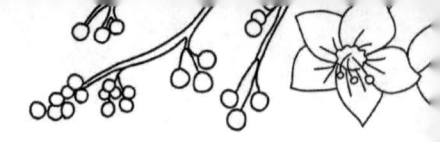

Trinity Sunday
Ephesians 3:14–21

Trinity Sunday celebrates the mystery of God's nature as three-in-one—Father, Son, and Holy Spirit. In this beautiful passage, Paul speaks of God's immeasurable love and strength, qualities that mirror the very heart of the Trinity. This same love empowers and strengthens us, inviting us to grow in our relationship with God and one another.

To honour this beautiful day, take a quiet moment to reflect on the depth of God's love and the unity of the Trinity. Perhaps spend a few peaceful moments in prayer, inviting God to gently strengthen your faith and draw you closer to His loving embrace. It's a special opportunity to feel His presence and deepen your connection with Him.

Reflections ...

TODAY I AM GRATEFUL FOR ... _____

_____
_____
_____
_____
_____
_____

OTHER IMPORTANT DAYS

Father's Day
Deuteronomy 6:4–9

On this Father's Day, we're reminded through our reading of the importance of teaching and passing down our faith to the next generation. The passage calls us to love the Lord with all our heart, soul, and strength, and to impress these commands upon our children. The foundation of faith, love, and respect begins at home and is nurtured by those who lead with wisdom and love—whether it's fathers, grandfathers, or anyone who steps into a guiding role.

Instead of giving a physical gift this Father's Day, consider gifting an experience that will create lasting memories. Whether it's tickets to a sports game, a fishing trip, or a fun cooking class, experiences bring families closer together and create moments that will be cherished forever. The role of a father or father figure can be filled in many different ways—through guidance, love, support, and shared adventures. An experience gift gives the opportunity to not only enjoy a fun activity together but also to strengthen those bonds and make new, meaningful memories.

Reflections ...

Today I am grateful for ... _____

_____

_____

_____

_____

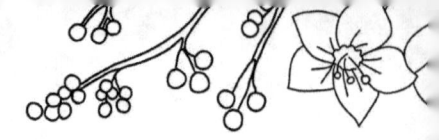

Rosh Hashanah
(LASTS FOR TWO DAYS)

Psalm 90, Moses's prayer

Genesis 21 and 22

Rosh Hashanah, the Jewish New Year, is a deeply significant holiday marked by prayer, self-inspection, and a time of renewal. It lasts for two days and begins with the setting of the sun on the evening of the first day. During this sacred period, Jews remember God's creation of the world and look ahead with hope to the year to come.

Day One: Psalm 90—Moses's Prayer: On the first day of Rosh Hashanah, Psalm 90 is often read. It's a powerful prayer written by Moses that highlights the brevity of life and the eternal nature of God's presence. It's a reminder that despite the passage of time, God is our refuge and source of strength. As we reflect on the past year and seek God's guidance for the year ahead, this psalm invites us to consider how we live our lives in light of God's eternity.

Day Two: Genesis 21 and Genesis 22: On the second day, two passages from Genesis are traditionally read. Genesis 21 recounts the birth of Isaac, the fulfillment of God's promise to Abraham and Sarah, marking a significant moment of joy and new beginnings. Genesis 22 tells the story of Abraham's faith and obedience when God asks him to sacrifice Isaac, a pivotal moment of trust and devotion. These stories not only remind us of God's faithfulness but also challenge us to consider our own obedience to God and His purposes for our lives.

As a practicing Jew in the first century, Jesus would have observed Rosh Hashanah. It was a time for Him, as it is for all Jews, to reflect on God's faithfulness, pray for a fresh start, and seek reconciliation with God in preparation for Yom Kippur. Take some time to research Rosh Hashanah and discover how

Jesus might have celebrated this day. Explore the foods and customs associated with this holiday, such as the symbolic apples dipped in honey, and learn more about the Jewish traditions of reflection and repentance. You could even try cooking a traditional Rosh Hashanah meal to immerse yourself in the customs of the season, allowing it to deepen your understanding of Jesus's cultural and spiritual life.

Reflections ...

TODAY I AM GRATEFUL FOR ... _____

_____
_____
_____
_____
_____
_____
_____

JOYOUS FAITH

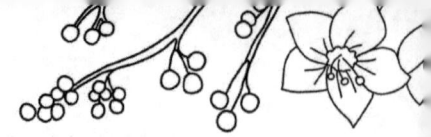

Yom Kippur

OLD TESTAMENT READING: LEVITICUS 16:29–34
NEW TESTAMENT READING: HEBREWS 9:11–14

Yom Kippur, the Day of Atonement, is all about seeking forgiveness for sins and being reconciled with God. In Leviticus 16, we see the Old Testament practice of atonement, where the high priest would offer sacrifices to cleanse the people from their sins. This ritual, though meaningful, was only temporary and had to be repeated year after year.

Hebrews 9:11–14 is a powerful New Testament reflection on Yom Kippur because it shows how the Day of Atonement in the Old Testament foreshadowed the ultimate and final atonement brought about by Christ. This connection brings deeper meaning to the celebration of Yom Kippur, pointing us to the work of Jesus as our true High Priest, who has made the ultimate sacrifice for our sins.

Explore your own need for atonement, and thank God for the sacrifice Jesus made on your behalf. You could even spend time journaling or praying, asking God to cleanse your heart, and receive His forgiveness in a fresh way. Maybe even set aside time to pray for others, remembering that through Jesus, reconciliation is available to all.

Reflections ...

TODAY I AM GRATEFUL FOR ... _____

_____

_____

_____

OTHER IMPORTANT DAYS

Sukkot

OLD TESTAMENT READING: LEVITICUS 23:33–43
NEW TESTAMENT READING: JOHN 7:37–39

I enjoy learning about the Jewish holidays, and I have so much to learn. In Leviticus 23:33–43, God gives His people specific instructions for celebrating Sukkot. This festival is a reminder to dwell in temporary shelters, called *sukkahs*, to remember how God provided for and protected the Israelites during their time in the wilderness. God wanted His people to celebrate by living in these shelters for seven days to commemorate His faithfulness, love, and provision.

Then, in John 7:37–39, we see how Jesus, during His time on earth, celebrates Sukkot with His followers. He uses this moment to reveal a deeper truth: while the Israelites looked back to God's provision in the wilderness, Jesus offers living water—a gift that satisfies our spiritual thirst forever. He is the ultimate fulfillment of what was celebrated during Sukkot, offering us not just temporary shelter, but eternal sustenance in Him.

Looking at these passages, we're invited to celebrate God's past faithfulness while also embracing the living water Jesus offers to us today, bringing both physical and spiritual refreshment. Use this time to research Sukkot, its rich history, and the traditional foods enjoyed during the festival.

Reflections ...

TODAY I AM GRATEFUL FOR ... _____

_____

_____

_____

Thanksgiving
(Canada or US)

Psalm 111

Psalm 111 centres on praise and gratitude, celebrating the works of the Lord and giving thanks for His faithfulness, greatness, and provision. The psalmist speaks of God's wonderful deeds and how they display His goodness, which perfectly aligns with the spirit of Thanksgiving—taking time to acknowledge and give thanks for God's blessings and goodness in our lives.

During Thanksgiving, I like to remember my grandmother and her beautiful lesson on prayer. She taught me the importance of dedicating a significant portion (70 per cent) of my prayer time to gratitude, a practice that has stayed with me throughout my life. This Thanksgiving, let's intentionally focus on gratitude in our prayers. Reflecting on the blessings in our lives not only deepens our relationship with God but also cultivates a spirit of joy and appreciation that we can share with those around us.

Reflections ...

Today I am grateful for ... _____

_____
_____
_____
_____
_____

Shemini Atzeret / Simchat Torah

LEVITICUS 23:36–44

Shemini Atzeret and Simchat Torah are joyful and meaningful holidays in the Jewish tradition. Shemini Atzeret, the eighth day after Sukkot, is a day of rest and reflection, where God's people draw near to Him in prayer and gratitude. The following day, Simchat Torah, celebrates the completion of the annual Torah reading cycle and marks the beginning of a new cycle with dancing, singing, and great joy. In Leviticus 23:36–44, God instructs His people to observe these days with joy and thanksgiving, offering sacrifices and celebrating His goodness.

Make time to discover the significance of the Torah and Shemini Atzeret and Simchat Torah by exploring the history and meaning behind these holidays. You can read books or watch videos about the Torah and how Jewish people celebrate these important occasions.

Reflections ...

TODAY I AM GRATEFUL FOR ... _____

_____
_____
_____
_____
_____

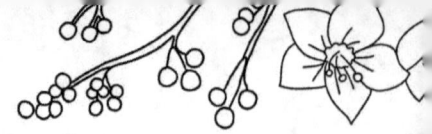

Hanukkah
(BEGINS AT SUNDOWN, LASTS FOR EIGHT DAYS)

John 10:22–23

In John 10:22–23, we see Jesus in Jerusalem during the Feast of Dedication, which is the celebration of Hanukkah. This moment ties Jesus to the theme of light, as Hanukkah celebrates the miracle of the menorah's light burning for eight days despite having only enough oil for one. Jesus, in the Gospels, refers to Himself as the "light of the world," and during this festival, He is in the very place where light is symbolically celebrated. For Christians, this connection reminds us that Jesus is the ultimate light, illuminating our paths and bringing hope, peace, and salvation.

As you consider the symbolism of light this Hanukkah season, consider creating a space for light in your home or life. You could light a candle, gather with loved ones for a simple meal, or take time for reflection and prayer. Just as the menorah's light represented God's provision and hope during the festival, allow this simple act to remind you of Jesus, the true light of the world.

Reflections ...

TODAY I AM GRATEFUL FOR ... _____

_____
_____
_____
_____

www.ingramcontent.com/pod-product-compliance
Lightning Source LLC
Chambersburg PA
CBHW052055230426
43662CB00037B/1787